Not Saussure

A Critique of Post-Saussurean Literary Theory

Raymond Tallis

Second Edition

MACMILLAN

First edition 1988
Second edition 1995

Published by
MACMILLAN PRESS LTD
Houndmills, Basingstoke, Hampshire RG21 6XS
and London
Companies and representatives
throughout the world

ISBN 0–333–63925–1 hardcover
ISBN 0–333–63926–X paperback

A catalogue record for this book is available
from the British Library.

10   9   8   7   6   5   4   3   2   1
04 03 02 01 00 99 98 97 96 95

Printed in Great Britain by
Ipswich Book Co Ltd
Ipswich, Suffolk

*This explanation of my absences is dedicated
to Terry, Ben and Lawrence with all my love*

Contents

PART TWO

Acknowledgements

The author and publisher would like to thank the following who have kindly given permission for the use of copyright material:

The Johns Hopkins University Press, for the extracts from Jacques Derrida, *Of Grammatology*, translated by Gayatri Chakravorty Spivak (1976);

Northwestern University Press, for the extracts from Jacques Derrida, *Speech and Phenomena and Other Essays on Husserl's Theory of Signs*, translated by David B. Allison (1973).

Note

I have usually referred to the reader (and the writer) as 'he'. This is not because I believe that only men read or write books or that the only books worth reading or the writers worth considering are male. I did experiment with 'he or she', 's/he' and 'he/she' but found the results clumsy. And for a male writer such as myself to refer to readers and writers consistently as 'she' would be hypocritical pretence. And so I conformed to what is still the normal usage, fully aware that behind linguistic use there is much extra-linguistic abuse. Increasingly, published literature and literary criticism is being written by females, to whom it will come naturally to refer to the reader and writer as 'she'. By this means, rather than a nervous linguistic tic, the assumption that the normal or canonical form of the human species is a male will be gradually eroded.

Preface to the Second Edition
Theorrhoea 1988–1995: The Band Plays On

Argumentum ad Hominem

The mood in which I wrote *Not Saussure* seems in retrospect to have been over-optimistic. When the book appeared in 1988 along with a companion volume *In Defence of Realism*,[1] I confidently expected that the purveyors of post-Saussurean 'theory' would be stopped in their tracks. After all I thought I had demonstrated the following things beyond doubt:

  i) the most important ideas in post-Saussurean theory are mistaken – in particular they are based upon a deep misunderstanding of the nature of language, arising out of a mis-reading of Saussure;
 ii) in the unlikely event of the crucial ideas of post-Saussurean theory being true, their promulgation would be pragmatically self-refuting;
iii) even if the ideas were true and their promulgation not pragmatically self-refuting, they would not have *any* implications for literary theory or criticism or indeed for any specific human activity other than the pursuit of tenure in humanities departments in institutes of higher education.

I expected a scandal to result and the post-Saussureans to die of shame or to apply for re-training as useful citizens. I was astonished when the arguments of both books were largely ignored and it was business as usual. *Not Saussure* received a handful of largely hostile or dismissive reviews, *In Defence of*

Realism went unreviewed and is out of print – though it, too, is shortly to be re-issued – and the deconstruction industry continued to boom.

I can see now that it was naive in the extreme to assume that the *arguments* of the books would be addressed. I blame this naivety on my training in science, where competing theories are usually evaluated on their basis of the relevant factual evidence, their internal consistency, their power at predicting new facts and the success or failure of their applications. This training left me ill-prepared for the standards and practices of the intellectual community whose views I criticised.

There are two reasons for prefacing the Second Edition of this book by discussing the reception of the first edition. Firstly, it should act as warning to anyone embarking on a critique of post-Saussurean thought: your views will be 'placed' or dismissed and you may even be abused but none of your arguments will be given serious consideration. Secondly, this reception explains why I have not attempted a radical revision of *Not Saussure*. My anxiety that there might be mistakes which the defenders of Derrida and Lacan – those scholars and disciples who devote their lives to their works – would pounce upon, proved also to be naive. None of my critics examined my exposition with sufficient care to identify any errors of fact or logic. This is a pity; for there may well be such errors and they will be printed unchanged in this Second Edition.

My hope that *Not Saussure* would be the beginning of a fruitful dialogue with the intellectual community I had challenged ended with the first review – a short piece by John Sturrock in *The Times Literary Supplement*.[2] He at least made some gesture towards engaging the arguments, though he did not appear to read the book itself with the care he devoted to examining the biographical details on the dust-jacket. Under the headline 'Laughing at the Anti-realists' he noted that I was a Liverpudlian and concluded that the book was about 'scouse common sense' being 'brought into play against the charismatic inanities of modern French thought'. The slightest acquaintance with discourse in Liverpool – discouse perhaps – would dispel that impression. Approximately 26,000 words devoted to a critique of Derrida alone, focusing on phonocentricity, logocentricity and the Husserlian origins of Derrida's ideas on 'presence' seemed to me an atypical form of scouse common sense and I wondered when he had last walked down Lime Street. The *arguments*, he claimed, 'do not ordinarily work'. The nearest he came to being specific about this failure was in relation to my critique of Lacan's theory of the Mirror Stage. This he conceded to be 'decisive' but it was set aside because a) the Mirror theory was a soft target (nobody takes it seriously) and b) I had not considered the use to which Lacan had put the theory as a 'founding myth' and as 'disruptive of Cartesian notions of the integrity of the self'. The denial of the importance of the Mirror Stage in post-Saussurean thought is disingenuous in the extreme – or would be were the denial itself not undermined by the immediate assertion of its centrality to the idea of the de-centred self. Reading Sturrock, I got the impression that it was less important that Lacan's theory was wrong than that it was important. Sturrock's other substantive point – the rest was crude biographism, relating my clinical interests to my supposed diagnosis of structuralists and post-structuralists as 'altogether gaga' – was that Derrida's *'il n'y a pas de hors-texte'* did not mean what it said. Derrida did not intend to deny the extratextual referentiality of language. This 'revisionist' interpretation of Derrida has been crucial to the continuing survival of post-Saussurean thought.

Several subsequent critics were content to explain *Not Saussure* by the personal defects of its author. The mildest suggested that Tallis' hostility to the writings of Derrida, Lacan and others was due to an unreflective, even panic-stricken clinging to unreformed common sense. It should hardly be necessary to point out that if one opposes the unfounded, inconsistent, poorly argued and explanatorily weak notions of a writer such as Lacan whose ideas also happen to outrage common sense, it does not follow that one believes that common sense has the last work on anything. As a scientist, I an aware that understanding advances by continually overturning common sense about everything from the movement of large objects to the position and velocity of small ones – as Wolpert[3] has pointed out.

The assumption that opposition to post-Saussurean thought

is driven by an unreflective attachment to common sense, an instinctive intellectual conservatism, by an unreasoning hostility to 'strange new ideas' – that the basis of any critique is not the observation that these ideas are wrong, or poorly argued or self-contradictory but that they are *novel* – is irritating. It is even more irritating to be diagnosed as follows, by a reviewer who, in the course of a fifteen-page review, cannot muster one counter-argument in defence of his post-Saussurean heroes:

> Your life will not go astray if you believe in [Tallis'] principles. Certain comfortable notions of what the human self is, of what language is, and of what reality is, have been placed in jeopardy and will need new champions. The threat – which is basically, I contend, a deep-seated aversion for French and German 'meta'-physics and a fear of revitalised Marxism – is apparently quite tormenting.[4]

It is not often that such diagnoses are checkable and can be shown to be wrong. The reader may find my 'comfortable notions of what the human self is' set out in my book on the philosophy of mind *The Explicit Animal*[5] (devoted exclusively to restoring our sense of the mystery of human consciousness) and may judge my 'deep-seated aversion for French and German 'meta'-physics' by the following passage from the same book:

> I have learnt enormously from [the continental phenomenologists] and owe to Sartre and Heidegger some of the few metaphysical moments that have been triggered by reading. This book, and my attitude to human consciousness, is in part a late response to reading the continental phenomenologists at a time when I was being trained in medicine and taught conventional neurophysiology. (Tallis, ibid p. 289)

The perils of diagnosing the author of a book rather than addressing his arguments should be self-evident but this does not discourage certain critics from doing this – even some who have pronounced the death of the author and are opposed to 'biographism'! After all, it is easier to dismiss someone as a

Marxo-phobe than to see whether his critique of Derrida's use of the term 'signifier' is sound or not. It is more fun as well. Anthony Easthope, responding to a piece in which I restated my critique of Lacan, probably enjoyed referring to my 'mode of discourse' as 'facetiously complacent, commonsensically uncritical, intimately traditional' and condemning it as

> part of the nightmare that weighs on the brain of those living in England now. In cultural terms, this is the equivalent of 'The English Disease' in the economic domain.[6]

The commonest charge advanced by those who defend post-Saussurean theory against its critics is that the latter suffer from *insularity*.[7] It is a potent accusation because it plays upon a deep fear, haunting the inhabitants of an island separated by salt water from the European mainland, that even in the post-Caxton era of printed books, satellite television, faxes etc., they may be intellectually out of touch and, of course, 'complacent' about it. The example of Mr Podsnap is disturbing:

> Mr Podsnap's world was not a very large world, morally; no, nor even geographically: seeing that although his business was sustained upon commerce with other countries, he considered other countries, with that important reservation, a mistake, and of their manners and customs would conclusively observe, 'Not English!' when PRESTO! with a flourish of the arm, and a flush of the face, they were swept away. Elsewise, the world got up at eight, shaved close at a quarter-past, breakfasted at nine, went to the City at ten, came home at half-past five, and dined at seven. Mr Podsnap's notion of the Arts in their integrity might have been stated thus. Literature; large print, respectively descriptive of getting up at eight, shaving close at quarter-past, breakfasting at nine, going to the City at ten, coming home at half-past five, and dining at seven. Painting and sculpture; models and portraits representing Professors of getting up at eight, shaving close at a quarter-past, breakfasting at nine, going to the City at ten, coming home at half-past five, and dining at seven. Music; a respectable per-

formance (without variations) on string and wind instruments, sedately expressive of getting up at eight, shaving
close at quarter-past, breakfasting at nine, going to the City at
ten, coming home at half-past five, and dining at seven.
Nothing else to be permitted to those same vagrants the Arts,
on pain of excommunication. Nothing else To Be – anywhere![8]

It is possible that British cultural life has been seriously
damaged by chronic self-denigration prompted by a fear of
Podsnappery. Mr Podsnap is not, of course, without his exem-
plars. Nor is he without his counterparts across the Channel: M.
Podsnap who dismisses anything alien as 'Not French!' and
Herr Podsnap who waves away the new as 'Not German!'.
Even so, his ludicrous example has made a particular impres-
sion on British intellectuals and the terror of insularity makes it
very difficult to acknowledge that some things that are 'Not
English' may be not as good as others; that while Husserl is a
great thinker, the equally Not-English Derrida is not; that being
'Not English' isn't enough.

Of course, I had anticipated the accusation of insularity:

Many of the ideas I shall discuss in this book originated,
directly or indirectly, from Paris. And so long as the panopticon of Paris is not part of Britain and the British Isles are not
part of mainland Europe, anyone who questions the outpourings of the Parisian *maîtres à penser* runs the risk not only
of being branded an aesthetic and political reactionary but of
being accused of exhibiting a characteristically insular suspicion of nasty foreign ideas. (p. 3)

This seems not to have deterred denigrators (who may not, of
course, have reached page three).

The accusation of insularity easily passes into the rather
graver slur of xenophobia. Anthony Easthope even went so far
as to accuse me of 'xenophobic Protestantism',[6] holding that the
'opposite of good old English Protestant common sense is
foreign Popery represented by a "Parisien intellectual"'. The
fact that I am an atheist has not, it seems, diminished my

religious bigotry. The threat of being charged with intellectual racism sometimes makes honest critical discussion of ideas emanating from beyond these shores almost impossible. Presumably one cannot publicly detest Gobineau's repulsive ideas without being accused of Francophobia. And to disagree with the notions advanced by the author of *Mein Kampf* is to exhibit anti-German sentiments. In my opinion, the true xenophobe is one who patronises writers from abroad by demanding lower standards of them than one would of English thinkers. For me, a lousy French writer remains a lousy writer despite being French. And a good French writer is not a good writer simply because he/she is French. Conversely, my admiration for Wittgenstein, Husserl, Merleau-Ponty, Kant, Schrodinger is not based upon my deluded belief that they are in some Pickwickian sense English, or that they are scousers at heart.

How can I be so confident that my critique of post-Saussurean thinkers is not motivated by *unconscious* hatred of foreigners? My background is in medical science and the latter is so effortlessly international that it does not even stop to applaud itself for its freedom from xenophobia.[9] A given issue of a medical journal such as the *Lancet* will rarely have contributors from less than a score of different countries. Consequently, I am accustomed to judging ideas by their merits (the greatest of which is that there is some evidence in their favour) and not by their provenance.

I have indicated that such a background is a poor preparation for 'disciplines' in which argument by slur is deemed an appropriate way of advancing the cause of truth. This was brought home to me with particular force in connection with the Derrida–Cambridge affair. *Not Saussure* was cited on the flysheet put out by the Department of Philosophy at Cambridge as one of the main prosecution witnesses in the case made by the *non placets* against Derrida's being awarded an honorary doctorate at the University of Cambridge. In her article on this affair, Marian Jeanneret, then a lecturer in French and a strong supporter of Derrida's nomination for the degree, made a scathing attack on *Not Saussure* and its author.[10] She criticised the signatories of the fly-sheet – especially the block of twenty-five members of the Local Examination Syndicate – for recommending a book marked by 'limitless vulgarity', 'vanity', and 'raucous complacency'. She even suggested that in making their recommendation the signatories may have been remiss in their pedagogic duties towards students and colleagues. Failing to stop just short of libel, Jeanneret informed her readers that the author of *Not Saussure* might not be entirely intellectually honest:

> Again, they [the examiners] might, if they applied the tools we use in examining Ph.D. dissertations, conclude . . . that Mr Tallis has, in all likelihood, no knowledge of the German philosopher Husserl not derived from Derrida's own writings, so that when he attacks these latter, the phrases which imply a separate and informed reading of Husserl are specious . . . They would make a mental note to use the Ph.D. viva to get at the truth.

When I read this, I braced myself for incontrovertible proof that I had actually misunderstood Husserl, that I had confused his ideas with those of Derrida, and that *Not Saussure* was pockmarked with philosophical blunders. *No such evidence was offered*. Indeed, the philosophical arguments were passed over *in absolute silence* and Professor Jeanneret went on to discuss other things. Abuse, yes; argument, no. Such are the perils of opposing a confederacy of dunces!

Jeanneret was not to know that 'Mr' Tallis is, as noted already, the author of a book on consciousness heavily influenced by Continental Phenomenology.[4] Even *argumentum ad hominem* is obliged to get *something* right; the facts about the *homo* in question. But to be drawn into this personal defence is perhaps to risk falling into the intellectually derelict territory from which those who have criticised *Not Saussure* have written. *Argumentum ab hominem* is perhaps, ultimately, no less demeaning than *argumentum ad hominem*. The main point is that Jeanneret, along with other critics of *Not Saussure*, made no attempt whatsoever to address the ideas and arguments of a book that is densely argued for most of its 270 or so pages.

Is it Worth it?

In retrospect, the knowledge of post-Saussurean theory necessary to write *Not Saussure* should have prepared me for the reception – or non-reception – of this book. One does not have to be excessively cynical to realise that scrupulous argument may be impotent against ignorance, dimness and the vested interests of those who are on the inside track. It may even be that those who live off post-Saussurean ideas are not equipped to follow difficult but non-glitzy thought. At the very least, their motivation to do so must be slight: to live in an intellectual realm where empirical tests of truth are despised and logical thought viewed with disdain must be intoxicating indeed. 'The light dove, cleaving the air in her free flight, and feeling its resistance, might imagine that its flight would be still easier in empty space'.[11] Our contemporary free-wheeling intellectual entrepreneurs have realised the dream of Kant's dove. I also had not taken into account the power of consensus (error, however egregious, and frequently repeated hardens into truth), the disinclination individuals have to re-think when they have only half-thought in the first place, and the pressure to fall in with the dominant paradigm. This third point is one that requires further addressing.

Before I started researching this book, I had always taken post-Saussurean theory on its own estimate as, at least in 'insular' England, a voice in the wilderness, a paraiah living on the margin, excluded from the high tables by provincial, timid, conservative and unreflective hostility. I soon saw that this was not the case. The actual dominant position of 'marginal' and 'marginalised' theory was confirmed by a substantial correspondence with readers of *Not Saussure*. I received letters from young academics utterly oppressed by a mode of thought with which they were entirely out of sympathy, but which had to be swallowed and regurgitated, for that way lay advancement in their chosen discipline. Several postgraduates wrote that they could not get anyone to supervise a thesis that was overtly hostile to, or that chose not to engage with, post-Saussurean thought. (The spread of post-Saussurean theory within departments of literature is extraordinary: there is now hardly a major university without its representative theorrhoeaist).

For this reason I did not regret the hours of spare time I had devoted to researching and refuting structuralism and post-structuralism. I was also heartened by the large numbers of letters I received from eminent scholars in many countries who took the trouble to write in support of the book – as well as, in some cases, to point out minor errors of fact that I have taken the opportunity of this Second Edition to correct. The generosity of the private responses of such busy individuals was as gratifying as the intellectual poverty of the public responses was dispiriting. It has certainly caused me to reflect on the place of literary studies in the world at large.

Since I am a physician and a medical scientist and teacher, and not a professional critic, about 90 per cent of the time it is very hard to feel that it matters if some literary critics want to abandon academic standards and travel the international gravy jet on the strength of self-regarding outpourings born of the marriage of incompetent philosophy and worse linguistics. It poses no threat to my family, my patients, my country, the education of my students, my practice of medicine or the scientific disciplines upon which it is founded. My patients in Salford were not awaiting the outcome of the debate between Derrida and Searle with baited breath; nor were they dismayed by the former's refusal of serious discussion. And the legislators and administrators and practitioners who determine the resources available for health care and how they should be spent are unlikely to have heard of Paul de Man, let alone be influenced one way or the other by his writings.[12] About 10 per cent of the time, however – when, say, Derrida is awarded an honorary degree by a university that in other fields has a reputation second to none – I feel differently. I am reminded that there is something not altogether harmless about academic discourse that vacillates between emptiness, mischievousness and error, beyond the fact that its loud noise of easy untruth drowns out the soft signals of hard-won truth.

For a start, post-structuralist theory consumes public resources that could be spent on other things. By this I do not mean, for example, better health care for the elderly, cancer research, aid for the Third World or shelter for the homeless.

The money squandered on theorrhoea is not taken from that pot. I am thinking of the shrinking budget for higher education. The relevant points were well made in the *non placet* fly-sheet.

> So far Derrida's bad influence has been felt more widely in the humanities than in the sciences. This is bad enough in itself, and in the credibility it gives an already widespread public and political prejudice against the humanities, namely that they lack both the practical utility and intellectual seriousness to justify public funding . . . Their endorsement by the award of an honorary degree to Jacques Derrida would, at a most difficult time for higher education, reflect adversely on the University as a whole.

Leaving aside the understandably exaggerated estimate that humanities departments in Cambridge have of their own place in British intellectual life, it is difficult to see how one could quarrel with this. The Derrida affair was not just a storm in a sherry glass. Resources consumed by charlatans frolicking to no purpose in the Groves of Hackademe, except to further their own advance-ment as they deny the validity of appeals to academic stan-dards, are lost to other, more useful ends: for example, teaching young people to think clearly, rationally and honestly. It is of course self-defeating to assert that clarity, rationality and honesty are nothing but a sham, as post-Saussureans often do in their own defence – although they will deny their denial when it no longer suits them. As the fly-sheet pointed out,

> By denying the distinctions between fact and fiction, observ-ation and imagination, evidence and prejudice, they make complete nonsense of science, technology and medicine. In politics, they deprive the mind of its defences against danger-ously irrational ideologies and regimes.

At the very least, they remove the rationale for most teaching and scholarship in the humanities. It cannot be unimportant if large numbers of students – who represent a privileged minority and a significant slice of the future intelligentsia of the country – are taught an all-encompassing view of the world-as-self-deconstructing-text, a view that is so difficult to grasp that they have only the choice of uncritically accepting or uncritically rejecting it. Such active dis-education will at best breed cynicism towards academe; at worst, it will lead to stupefaction of anxious students whose primary academic concern will be to learn how to replicate enough 'radical' theorrhoea to be able to pass their examinations. Their situation has been well described by Nicholas Tredell in his lively and perceptive *The Critical Decade* (Manchester: Carcanet, 1993):

> Literature is refracted through theory and then through commentary. Harassed students, who after all have their degrees to get as well as their teachers' revolution to make, will be forced to catch the sense of literary texts at two removes if at all.   (p. 24)

Post-Saussurean theology, at once opaque, all-encompassing and simplifying (every text is reduced to the same narrow circle of scholastic concerns), if it lives on in the consciousness of students after it has ceased to figure in examinations, will intervene between them and everything they read. Reading the classics will simply be a matter of catching authors out, as Eagleton recommends in a recent article addressed to sixth formers. We must, he says

> take from [this elitist culture] what we can, read it against the grain, expose the labour and oppression which went into its making, and thus turn it against the kind of society which gave birth to it. If we can find ways of reading and interpreting which allow is to do this, then the study of English literature might be just defensible, even important.[13]

This is ultimately a sterile exercise and, because it reduces variety, a dull one. The young reader will be in permanent state of superiority to literature (and other comparable texts such as the scripts of soap operas and car parking notices) and, insofar as she herself is a text, in a permanent state of inferiority towards the great *textualissimi*, the deconstructors and the unmaskers and the demystifiers, by whose unreadable text she, and her fellow students, are themselves read. It is one thing to approach the canonical works with a reflective and sometimes dissenting intelligence; quite another to approach them with a permanent sense of superiority that comes from having access to an all-purpose tool to place, deconstruct, unmask and demystify them. As an education for our future administrators, legislators and educators, this leaves much to be desired.

Beyond this matter for public concern, there is another reason for continuing to challenge post-Saussurean thought: it has expropriated many of the most interesting and profound philosophical questions. There is hardly a fundamental problem that it has not pre-empted with its know-it-all-know-nothing arrogant scepticism, its confident uncertainties. The problem of universals, the nature of the self, the relationship between language and extra-linguistic reality – all these questions and many more have been wrapped in its meta-textual fog. These philosophical questions require urgently rescuing.

It was this concern, perhaps, more than any other, that lay behind the present critique of post-Saussurean thought and my pleasure that the publishers have given *Not Saussure* a second chance to be read and its arguments judged.

Notes

1. Raymond Tallis, *In Defence of Realism* (London: Edward Arnold, 1988). This is to be re-issued by Ferrington in 1994.
2. John Sturrock, 'Laughing at the anti-realists' *The Times Literary Supplement*, 13–19 May 1988, p. 541.
3. Lewis Wolpert, *The Unnatural Nature of Science* (London: Faber, 1992).
4. Art Berman, 'Not So Fast: Raymond Tallis on post-Saussurean Theory', *Critical Review* 1989: 3(1): 45–55.
5. Raymond Tallis, *The Explicit Animal* (London: Macmillan, 1991).
6. Anthony Easthope – Letter to *PN Review* 1988; 14(6): 8–9.It seems to me that, if there *is* 'a nightmare weighing on the brain of those living in England now', it is that there are reasonably well-educated people who are so impressed by thinkers they are not able (perhaps through lack of philosophical training) to evaluate critically that they attribute any attempt to carry out such an evaluation as being due to personal problems.

7. Nicholas Denyer also makes this point in 'The Charms of Jacques Derrida', *The Cambridge Review*, October 1992, pp. 103–5.
8. Charles Dickens, *Our Mutual Friend*, Chapter 11, 'Podsnappery'. It is desolating to think that if the campaign against Dead White Males (not to speak of Dead White Females) achieves its aims, children will have an even smaller probability of being introduced to writing such as this.
9. I discuss the cosmopolitan nature of science – and the fact that it is one of the least ethnocentric of human cultural activities – in *Newton's Sleep* (London: Macmillan, 1995). My own current collaborators include individuals from Brazil, Hong Kong, Romania and the People's Republic of China.
10. Marian Jeanneret, 'Opinio Regina Mundi?', *The Cambridge Review*, October 1992, pp. 99–103.
11. Immanuel Kant, Introduction to *Critique of Pure Reason*, trans. Norman Kemp Smith (London: Macmillan, 1964), p. 47.
12. This thought is uncomfortable to some 'advanced critics', as Stanley Fish has pointed out in 'Why Literary Criticism is Like Virtue', *London Review of Books*, 10 June 1993, pp. 11–16:
   The conclusion, unhappy for many, is that the effects of one's actions will always be confined to the disciplinary settings even when those settings receive some grandiose new name like Cultural Studies.
13. Terry Eagleton, 'English in Crisis', *The English Review*, pp. 25–6:
   Most of the agreed major writers of the literature, for example, have been thoroughly imbued with the prejudices of their age, elitist, sexist, frequently reactionary in outlook, illiberal in opinion. Of the agreed major authors of twentieth-century English literature, two (Pounds and Yeats) fellow-travelled with fascism, while others (Eliot, Lawrence) displayed extreme right-wing, pseudo-fascistic sentiments. Wordsworth wrote in praise of capital punishment, Edmund Spenser advocated the oppression of the Irish people, Joseph Conrad detested popular democracy, George Eliot feared the radical working class, Alexander Pope sneered at women and Shakespeare is unlikely to have been over-enthusiastic about Jews.

Introduction

For over two decades, literary criticism has been dominated by theories originating from the structuralist and post-structuralist schools of thought. The baleful influence of these 'post-Saussurean' thinkers upon academic critics will be evident to anyone who has more than a passing interest in literature. Much more serious than the present unhappiness in the Groves of Hackademe, however, is the adverse effect of advanced critical scorn for realistic fiction upon the evaluation of serious novelists. Whereas we used to be told that the novel itself was dead, influential academics now inform us that it is only realistic fiction that has died while the non- or anti-realistic novel is appropriately alive and kicking. In consequence, talentless anti-realism is more likely to receive respectful academic critical attention than the most talented realistic fiction. Now some novelists may feel that 'academic critical attention' is something they could well do without. Even so, it cannot be a sign of health in the republic of letters if critics and creators are not talking to one another except where, as in the case of academic critics writing novels about the lives of academic critics, critic and creator are one and the same person.[1]

Of course, realistic novels continue to be written and read. But, we are given to understand, this evidence of life is illusory. According to Robert Scholes, those who still write in the realist tradition are like 'headless chickens unaware of the decapitating axe'. Michael Boyd asserts that, although

> hacks will no doubt continue to write soporific illusions just as some readers will continue to require such products for their easy consumption . . . the modern novel defines itself in terms of its rejection of the conventions of formal realism.[2]

In parallel with the denigration of realistic fiction, there is an almost grotesque overestimation of the importance and impact of anti-realism. For the present purposes, a single example will have to suffice – the famous and much-discussed opening paragraph of Alain Robbe-Grillet's *In the Labyrinth* in which one sentence announces that it is raining and the next that the sun is shining. This contradiction has been interpreted as a profound critique of

1

the mimetic contract implicit in realistic fiction. The initial assumption that the novel refers to an external reality is ruthlessly brushed aside and we are, according to one critic, 'forced to realise that the only reality in question is that of writing itself which uses the concept of the world in order to display its own laws'.[3] What power there is in anti-realism! To tear the mimetic contract to shreds and to subject the referential function of language to a searching interrogation, all I have to do is inscribe the following sentence:

THIS IS NOT A WRITTEN SENTENCE

To write, as one of Elizabeth Bowen's characters once said, is always to rave a little. And to write as a critic is not uncommonly to rave a lot. But the wild claims made on behalf of many modern anti-realistic writers who – to use Eagleton's delightfully silly phrase – 'explode our assurance',[4] are symptomatic of a widespread critical belief in the perniciousness of realism and its ripeness for destruction. Antipathy to realism is probably ultimately a matter of taste; but it has mobilised some apparently powerful arguments in its support. Now it happens that my own taste is for realistic fiction; I also believe that realism remains a great unfinished adventure and that the realistic novel is one of the most powerful literary instruments available to us for furthering human consciousness and self-consciousness. I therefore resent the implication of much current literary theory that my taste in fiction is symptomatic of an infantile disorder.

Not all the arguments against realism originate from the post-Saussurean theorists – only the most interesting and annoying ones – and that is why I shall be examining them in the pages to come. While a wish to defend realism is an important motive for writing *Not Saussure*, another, possibly stronger, motive is my anger at the way post-Saussurean 'thinkers' have collectively muddied the waters of philosophical discussion to a degree paralleled in the secular intellectual history of the West only by Marxist ideologues. Post-Saussurean fallacies about the nature of language, reality, meaning, truth, consciousness and self-consciousness and the various relations between them constitute a giant leap backwards in contemporary thought. These fallacies have often been arrived at by extraordinarily simple errors of reasoning and it is at first puzzling how they should have gained so wide an acceptance. The explanation is almost as simple: those who are used to handling philosophical ideas have for the most part ignored or dismissed post-Saussurean theory; while those who have been most impressed by the theories are, with only a few exceptions, unaccustomed to or uninterested in evaluating philosophical ideas.

Which is not to say that post-Saussurean notions – variously elaborated or watered down – have been unopposed in the literary-critical community. But the opposition they have met has been entirely of the wrong sort: few hostile writers appear either willing or able to address the underlying philosophical issues. On the whole critics seem either to accept the main tenets of post-Saussurean literary theory or to dismiss radical criticism out of hand, usually in the latter instance padding out feeble, or sometimes dishonest, counter-arguments with rhetoric (characteristically described as 'bleating') about the 'old, humane values' implicit in the study of literature. Even those critics who repeatedly refer to philosophical ideas seem unused to developing or assessing them and frequently resort to displays of scholarship rather than coherent argument: key arguments are often documented rather than confronted and philosophical discussion tends to peter out into lists of names as in, for example, Frank Lentricchia's *After the New Criticism.*[5]

Consequently, post-Saussurean arguments begin to seem incontrovertible. Hostility to them can be more readily dismissed as mere resistance to the radically new, symptomatic of the conservatism of the bourgeois intellectual. There is a further problem for anyone from the British Isles who wishes to disagree with the post-Saussurean masters. Many of the ideas I shall discuss in this book originated, directly or indirectly, from Paris. And so long as the panopticon of Paris is not part of Britain and the British Isles are not part of mainland Europe, anyone who questions the outpourings of the Parisian *maîtres à pensers* runs the risk not only of being branded an aesthetic and political reactionary but of being accused of exhibiting a characteristically insular suspicion of nasty foreign ideas.

It is essential not to be intimidated by the prestige of the Hautes Ecoles. Error remains error, however elevated its provenance. But there is another barrier to serious evaluation of post-Saussurean thought. Those who feel hostile towards much recent literary theory but are unwilling or unable to formulate their objections often lazily dismiss it as merely another Parisian fashion, citing the rapid displacement of structuralism by post-structuralism as evidence that the writings of Barthes, Derrida, Lacan and their American epigones constitute a craze rather than a serious intellectual movement. There may be some justification for the (insular) suspicion that when the Emperor is restocking his wardrobe he usually shops in Paris; but the fashionability of ideas does not of itself constitute an honest argument against them; indeed, to offer this as one's main response is to betray intellectual bankruptcy. It is less easy, but more interesting, to try to understand *why* ancient radical doubts about the ability of language to express a genuine extra-linguistic reality have been revived in recent decades to the point where they seem to have achieved an almost popular appeal.

It is possible to interpret the ideas to be discussed in this book as being, at the deepest level (one that few imaginations visit though many pens refer to), a remote consequence of the evaporation of religious belief and of the desacralisation of The Word. When language and the world it expressed shared the same divine origin, there could be no question of the one being only contingently related to the other. Word and world were the two links between God and man, the world being fully indexed in The Word. Reference was not problematic because word and object, language and world, were related not by mere accident, united through a merely human convention that arbitrarily connected the sign and the significate. Indeed, they were not, in the last analysis, *externally* related at all; rather their connection was internal, and hence necessary. The supreme expression of this faith in the necessary relationship between words and things was to be found in the writings of the Protestant mystic Jacobus Boehme for whom words and objects were but two dialects of the same language, two registers of The Voice of God. But this belief was also apparent in the concept of a Universal Grammar and the Leibnitzian dream of a *Characteristica Universalis*, an utterly transparent alphanumeric code that would permit unfettered communication between all men of all races throughout all ages.

The emergence of modern linguistics at the beginning of the nineteenth century and the transformation of language into an object of empirical study signalled and hastened the end of this religious or para-religious view of language. Although the development of modern linguistics was associated with the Romantic, and hence semi-religious, project of unpacking the evolving spirit of man through tracing the transformations of his language and so recovering the sense of the past by reviving knowledge of ancient forms of the language, the resultant corpus of scholarship could not be assimilated back into the vision that inspired its acquisition. Internal developments within linguistics and changes taking place outside of it – in the other human and physical sciences and in society at large – interacted with one another: the desacralisation of the word and what Weber has called 'the dis-enchantment of the world' proceeded in parallel. The word-mysticism that was so central to Symbolist poetics at the end of the nineteenth century was merely a resumption at the conscious level of beliefs that had ceased to enjoy collective and unconscious authority. What had once been belief became a manifesto; so that the Mallarmean claim that language was the true interior of the world and that words alone were the home of depth can be seen at once as a revival of the past and as a pointer to the future.

Any account of the origins of post-Saussurean literary theory must grant Mallarmé – or the idea of Mallarmé – a central position. Structuralists saw him as the intuitive forerunner of the interplay between literary and linguistic theory and as the first writer to direct attention away from the psychology, feelings and experiences of the writer to the structure of the system in which he is writing. Although the correspondence available from the years of his spiritual crisis indicates that literature was for him at first a flight into language from the emptiness left by the absence of God, the evidence suggests that he soon felt that words could not reconstitute the spiritual depths that God had once underwritten. Mallarmé had no doubt, however, that language was deeper than the poet who used it; that the utterance exceeded the speaker. A poem was not a repository for a poet's feelings and intuitions but an experiment with the system of language; or an attempt to discover the system. Poetry was made not with ideas but with words. As Barthes has written,

In France, Mallarmé was doubtless the first to see and to foresee in its full extent the necessity to substitute language itself for the person who until then had been supposed to be its owner. For him, for us too, it is language which speaks, not the author; to write is, through a prerequisite impersonality . . . to reach that point where only language acts, 'performs', and not 'me'.[6]

Mallarmé, who sought to hide from the absence of God in words, came to regard language as the only god-like thing there is; the system as the only 'sacred text'. Although in practice, this was not simply a matter of substituting the boundless system for the bounded interior of the writer, we can, nevertheless, see how his poetics represent a watershed: rooted in the old word mysticism, it still points to a future systematic linguistics, in which language is bottomless and autonomous not because it houses the accumulated spirit of man or (to take the earlier view) opens on to the consciousness of God; but because it operates in accordance with its own rules, rules that are too numerous, too ramifying and too complex to be knowable. This has been well expressed in Valéry's many essays on Mallarmé. For example:

He [Mallarmé] dreamed of a poetry that would be as it were deduced from the system of properties and characteristics of language. Each work of Beauty that had already been created represented for him some page of a supreme Book which would be arrived at by an ever greater consciousness, and purer utilisation of the functions of speech. To the poet's act he attributed a universal meaning and a kind of value that one would be tempted to call 'mystical', were this not a forbidden word.[7]

Surrealism – or at least the Surrealist project of subverting ordinary consciousness and the order of everyday life by yielding to the genius of language – was an important intermediate step between Mallarmean and structuralist poetics. The inspiration of Freud permitted the identification of the unknown depths of the self with the unknown depths of language. Language and dream converged in puns and the chance association of words; the abdication of conscious control allowed language to be the means by which the unconscious might be conducted from the depths to the surface. The spirit thus released was not the knowledge of a transcendental God but the spirit of chaos and mischief, of laughter and desire.

Surrealism was born – and subsequently died – in a series of manifestos. The identification of the depths of language with the unconsciousness, however, opened directly on to a central theme of structuralism: that the unconscious is structured like, or is deposited in, or is an effect of, a language which is used by speakers but structurally is not grasped by them. The sense that the system is greater than the speaker – who (falsely) imagines that *he* uses *it* – at first relocates depth outside of the individual and then undermines the spiritual conception of depth altogether. 'Depth' can no longer take refuge in a language romantically conceived as the treasure house of the human spirit. The displacement of diachronic by synchronic linguistics as a result of the posthumous influence of Saussure completed the process whereby scholarly interest in language had shifted from the private past of words and groups of words and individual languages to the depthless lattice of a system of phonetic, syntactic and semantic co-ordinates. The most explicit connection between the Surrealist preoccupation with the unconscious and systematic linguistics was in the work of Lacan who also revelled, like the Surrealists, in mischief and abuse.

The iconoclastic tendency of Surrealism – which even as it relocated depth from the individual into the collective, the common language, the universal unconscious, also debunked the ideal of spiritual depth – paved the way for trends in both novelistic practice and literary theory that came to prominence in France in the fifties and sixties. Barthes's championship of Robbe-Grillet who specifically announced the passing of 'the old myths of "depth" ', was an early manifestation of this convergence of literature and linguistics. Robbe-Grillet himself wrote,

> There is today a new element separating us, and radically this time, from Balzac, Gide, or Madame de La Fayette: this is the poverty of the old myths of 'depth' . . . While essentialist conceptions of man were facing their doom, and the idea of 'condition' henceforth replacing that of 'nature', the *surface* of things has stopped being the mask of their heart for us, a sentiment that serves as a prelude to all the 'beyonds' of metaphysics.[8]

At about the same time, Barthes was situating, and defending, Robbe-Grillet and the experiments of the *nouveau romanciers*. In

Writing Degree Zero[9] he observed that 'Literature [in Queneau] is openly reduced to the problematics of language; and indeed, that is all it can now be' (p. 88), and that 'it is now writing which absorbs the whole identity of a literary work' (p. 91). Within ten years, French literary theory was dominated by a desacralised linguistics. The goal of criticism was to dominate rather than to interpret literature and it denied literature's traditional claim to establish independent 'spiritual' values. Literary theory encompassed literature and the former was encompassed by linguistics or the more general science of signs.

That at least is one version of the origin of modern structuralist poetics and subsequent post-structuralist developments. Doubtless many others equally plausible, equally sketchy could be confected. My version overlooks the very important element of accident; for example the chance encounter between Lévi-Strauss and Jakobson in the United States during the Second World War. More seriously, it ignores the paramount influence of Sartre – the unmasker of bourgeois values, the scourge of essentialism – upon literary theorists such as Barthes and practitioners such as Robbe-Grillet. Most seriously of all, it does not sufficiently acknowledge the powerful example of Paul Valéry and his insistence that both critics and creators should be concerned less with particulars and more with the underlying general principles, methods and so on. And finally it does not take into account the fact that, in the case of some structuralists, notably Todorov, the wheel has come full circle with the restoration of Universal Grammar and an essential, rather than a contingent, relationship between language and extra-linguistic reality:

> universal grammar is the source of all universals and it gives definition even to man himself. Not only all languages but also all signifying systems obey the same grammar. It is universal not only because it informs all the languages of the universe, but because it coincides with the structure of the universe itself.[10]

This brief sketch of the aetiology of post-Saussurean literary theory is not intended, however, as a scholarly account of origins of the major intellectual movement of the present time but as a way of showing the inadequacy of any response – all too common in the English-speaking world – that would dismiss much contemporary post-Saussurean writing simply on the grounds that its underlying ideas are 'fashionable'. If the ideas *are* fashionable, the fashion has deep (and interesting) roots.

Not Saussure is intended as a critique rather than a survey: I have not attempted a comprehensive coverage of post-Saussurean thought. I make no apology for this. As I have already suggested, too much of what has been written about structuralism and post-structuralism has been merely descriptive at the expense of actually confronting the underlying ideas. This may be due to idleness: it is easier to discuss how *A* influenced *B* or to debate the extent to which *C*'s ideas are post-*D*-ian, than it is to think through and evaluate the ideas of any of *A*, *B*, *C* or *D*. I hope that enough has been said to make clear that anyone who wishes to express valid – as opposed to merely heartfelt – opposition to post-Saussurean literary theory must be willing to engage the underlying philosophical arguments – however difficult, however technical. Just as it is not sufficient to dismiss the ideas on the basis that they are (or were) fashionable, so they cannot be ignored because they are complex and obscure (they often are), because they are badly expressed (this is very often the case), or because they are an affront to common sense. Anyone who disagrees with post-Saussureans must be prepared to stand his ground when powerful counter-arguments are brushed aside as merely 'knockdown', derided as symptomatic of Western logocentricity or phallogocentricity or shrugged off, like the charge of pragmatic self-refutation, as being unworthy of response because it has been made many times before. One must seek out the basis of post-Saussurean thought and, in particular, expose the submerged arguments from which its basic principles derived their apparent authority. Where those principles seem to be factual theses, the empirical evidence must be carefully scrutinised. Where they are not subject to empirical testing, they must be examined for internal consistency. Where they owe their authority to the claim that they are the logical outcome of well-established theories, this claim must be examined. The (punning) title of this book (a rare resort to what is often – but inaccurately – called 'the free play of the signifier') points to an important theme: the falsity of the suggestion that many of the ideas of structuralist and post-structuralist literary theorists can be derived from the principles put forward by Saussure.

I have explained some of my reasons for writing this book, why I felt it was needed. Even so, one or two of my friends have asked me why, if I consider so much of structuralist and post-structuralist writing to be arrant nonsense, I have devoted nearly two years of my free time to refuting it. Quite simply this: the ideas, though mistaken, are immensely interesting. Post-Saussurean thought represents not merely any old wrong turning, but a big and important one. It is essential to see what went wrong, find a way back out of the mess, in order to make a fresh start in trying to understand the mysteries of language, literature and consciousness.

There is a strong case to be made against post-Saussurean theory. So long as it remains unstated, there is a serious gap in the republic of letters. *Not Saussure* is intended to fill that gap.

Part One

1

Literature, Language and Reality: An Introduction

1.1 THE FUNDAMENTAL IDEAS

Every general statement about language worth making invites a counter-statement or antithesis.[1]

There seem to be two complementary strategies for dissolving the connexion between literature and the real world. One . . . is to exorcise the other-than-literary presence of the real world by reducing everything to text. The other is to emphasise the nature of the literary text as a collocation of arbitrary linguistic signs that can be joined together only on the basis of internal principles of coherence even as they pretend to be determined by objects outside themselves to which they supposedly refer. In this view, reality, whatever it may be, is inaccessible to the literary text because of the text's very constitution.[2]

Much hostility towards realism in fiction is, consciously or unconsciously, rooted in fundamental doubts about the relationship between language and reality and the true status of apparently referential discourse. These doubts may crystallise into one of two theses: either that referential discourse is impossible because extra-linguistic reality lies beyond the reach of language; or that it seems possible only because apparently extra-linguistic realities are in fact the product of language, that is to say intra-linguistic. The two theses are, of course, complementary but different writers tend to highlight one or other of them in attacking realism.

The linguistic case against realism is central to both structuralist and post-structuralist literary theory. It depends upon the assumption that behind the commitment to realistic fiction is a

13

false belief in a 'straightforward' relationship between language
and reality such that:

(a) reality is constituted independently of, and pre-exists,
     language;
(b) but, nevertheless, language can reach out to reality, refer
     to it successfully and so express it as it really is.

Opponents of realism tend to direct their arguments against one
or other of these assumptions, it being correctly supposed that, if
either of these assumptions is invalid, so too is the realistic
enterprise.

It is sometimes suggested that to believe (a) and (b) is to
subscribe to the extraordinarily naïve view that language is a
'mirror of' or 'a window on' extra-linguistic reality. It is further
implied not only that most realists implicitly or explicitly subscribe
to such an implausible conception of language but also that
language has to be a mirror or window for realism to be possible
or valid. *These* assumptions – along with the idea that realism
requires an isomorphism or a one-to-one correspondence between
language and reality – are wholly mistaken as we shall discuss in
Chapter 4. For the present, let us consider the more radical
attempts to dissolve the connection between language and reality.

(a) Denying the Language-independence of Reality

The denial may take place at various levels:

(i)   Language, at the very least, *stabilises* the categories into
      which the objects we perceive fall; it fixes the ways in which
      they are grouped together. The stereotypes of discourse
      influence the manner in which we attend to the world. That
      which is customarily spoken of partly determines what
      counts as real now, and what in future will be acknowledged
      as being there.
(ii) Our perception of reality is permeated through and through
      by language. Language does not merely provide the *signs* of
      categories but is the source of those categories. Moreover,
      when we perceive objects as objects, they fall under
      concepts, and concepts are linguistic in origin. While there

are natural differences between the contents of extra-linguistic reality there are no natural *kinds*.
(iii) Reality is differentiated only in or through language. Meaning, intelligibility, order, division are effects of language. Not only, for example, do objects owe their significance, their meaning, to language, but also their status as distinct objects, their very edges.

(i) leads writers to emphasise 'the relativity of facts to language'; (ii) to a more radically nominalist denial of an extra-linguistic basis for the classification of the contents of the world; and (iii) to the even more extreme claim that extra-linguistic reality (in so far as it can be said to exist at all) contributes nothing to the differentiation of meaning or the ordering of the common world. Those who hold (iii) deny that meaning is first embodied outside of language and then captured or reflected in it, asserting that it is an effect of, or produced through, language. This last position is, most notoriously, that of Derrida. It also appears to be held by Lacan, an authority often invoked by critics of a radically nominalist persuasion: 'It is the world of words that creates the world of things – things originally confused in the *hic et nunc* of the all in the process of coming-into-being.'[3] In other words, any reality other than a postulated primordial flux of becoming is mediated through, and owes its structure to, language.

(b) Denying Linguistic Access to an Extra-linguistic Reality

The reason most commonly given for denying that words can reach out to extra-linguistic reality is that language is a system with its own laws and it is consequently sealed off from reality. Reality can be represented in language only at the cost of being distorted or denatured.

If language sometimes seems to express reality 'as it really' is, this is only because a second reality has been constructed within language. Language is windowless; or if it has windows, they open not on to reality but on to a second order, linguistic 'reality' that gives the impression of being the real thing. Reality itself, however, is a nameless residue, the inexpressible x of Lacan, that remains unspoken and unwritten when language has done its work.

Although it is helpful to distinguish the denial of the language-independence of reality from the denial that reality can gain access to language, it is important to appreciate that these views complement one another and touch at many points. For example, if the reality that human beings are aware of has always been contaminated by language, then we shall be denied access – linguistically or otherwise – to uncontaminated 'natural' extra-linguistic reality. Reality, in so far as we get to know it, is to a greater or lesser degree inside language. To think this way is to imply that language and consciousness – and not merely language and *communicable* or *publicly acknowledged* consciousness – are conterminous. The windowlessness of language then becomes a limitation of our consciousness of reality rather than merely of what we can express of it. Language and consciousness will both suffer from the same restriction of access to reality and the relationship between language and reality, or 'reality' and reality, becomes analogous to the Kantian one between the phenomenal and the noumenal realms.

The intimate connection between the denial that there is a reality independent of language and the denial that language can reach out to extra-linguistic reality is well illustrated by the use that is made of the concept of 'intertextuality' in literary theory. 'Intertextuality', like 'ideology' is a magic word whose scope can be altered dramatically to answer to the polemic needs of the moment. At their least radical, the arguments arising out of the appeal to the influence of textual forces are a mild version of the view that language does not give us access to an uncontaminated reality: how we write about the world will be influenced from within language by the way others have written about the world. We will not even notice our most completely assimilated influences because they will determine how we actually see the world we choose to write about. This observation opens the way to the claim that works of literature do not refer to the world but to other words of literature and this, in turn, creates a bridge between the view that reality is not independent of language and the view that language cannot reach outside of itself to a genuine extra-linguistic reality – the 'closed system' view of language. We move back to the original view, however, when it is further suggested that not only literary but *all* discourses refer merely to other discourses and that we may replace the concept of 'intersubjectivity' by that of intertextuality. 'Natural' reality is totally eclipsed by social reality; consciousness is intersubjective; and reality becomes 'the boundless text of society'. We arrive at a position, similar to that of Derrida, that:

> reading . . . cannot legitimately transcend the text toward something other than it, toward a referent (a reality that is metaphysical, historical, psychobiographical etc.) or toward a signified outside the text whose content . . . could have taken place outside of language . . . outside of writing-in-general. *There is nothing outside of the text* [there is no outside-text; il n'y a pas de hors-texte].[4]

The arguments from intertextuality permit simultaneous movement towards the assertion that reality cannot be extricated from language and the seemingly opposite but in fact connected assertion that language cannot reach out to reality. The two converge in the view that referential discourse is an illusion in so far as language cannot reach out to an *extra-linguistic* reality.

These ideas set the agenda for this book. In Chapter 2, I shall deal with the elusive concept of intertextuality. Chapter 3 will be addressed to the claims that reality and language are mutually implicated; that language is divorced from reality; and that language can reach out to reality only to the extent that it creates it. These counter-intuitive views are difficult to sustain even for those who believe them as I shall show in Section 3.4. In Chapter 4 I shall present a theory of language that is intended to avoid the absurdities of extreme linguistic relativism while taking account of the difficulties that have given the attacks on referential realism their credibility. This theory of language will, it is hoped, refute once and for all the belief that there are logico-linguistic grounds for denying the possibility of a valid realistic fiction. In Chapters 5 and 6, I shall deal with the specific arguments that Lacan and Derrida adduce for espousing the radical nominalism that has been taken for granted in post-Saussurean literary theory. The book will end with a defence of one version of the Correspondence Theory of Truth (Chapter 7).

Before proceeding to examine the particular arguments against realism that have arisen out of a consideration of the relationship, or lack of it, between language and reality, it will be useful to make some general observations about post-Saussurean critical practice and in particular the method by which the popular

paradoxes of structuralist and post-structuralist writing are usually
arrived at.

1.2   THE METHOD

The most efficient way of generating interesting and yet plausible
paradoxes is to begin from an obvious or even truistic statement
and then to move on from this towards its apparent implications
by means of one or more general principles that should preferably
remain unstated and should certainly be only partly visible. Let
us illustrate the method with an example: the derivation of the
paradox that language cannot be used to refer to anything other
than itself.

The starting truism is 'Language has its own rules'. This is
connected with the final paradox by means of two general
principles. The first is: 'Whatever obeys its own rules is an
autonomous system.' The second is: 'All autonomous systems are
closed systems, sealed off from whatever is outside of them.'
Neither of these general principles is true, as reference to the
nervous system, or indeed to any physical or biological
thermodynamic system will at once make clear. (We shall discuss
this in more detail in Chapter 3.2.) But the strength of these
general principles lies not in their truth but in their *invisibility*:
they are not in the foreground of our attention and are therefore
passed 'on the nod', as it were. They permit the intermediate
conclusion that language is an autonomous system and the final
paradox that it is therefore sealed off from reality, unable to refer
to anything other than itself. Realistic novels, which seem to refer
to the 'real world' are therefore a sham, because access to the real
world is denied to language. The steps from truism to paradox
may be presented as follows:

   (i) Initial Truism:
         'Language has its own rules'
  (ii) Invisible general principle:
         'Whatever has its own rules is an autonomous system'
 (iii) Intermediate conclusion
         'Therefore, language is an autonomous system'
  (iv) Second invisible general principle

'All autonomous systems are sealed off from whatever is outside of them'
(v) Final paradox
'Therefore, language is sealed off from extra-linguistic reality'.

Not infrequently, both the intermediate statement and the final paradox are literally unthinkable or unimaginable; so the reader has great difficulty in envisaging counter-arguments and even greater difficulty in thinking up counter-examples. The method can therefore be summarised as a passage from the obvious to the paradoxical via enthymeme and obscurity.

The role of enthymeme in the glide from truism to paradox is illustrated by this passage from Frank Lentricchia's *After the New Criticism*: '[Saussure's] view of language as "a play of differences" affirms that there are no isolate texts, no atomic cores that can be fenced off as untouchable private property . . . no poem in itself.'[5] In the twinkling of an eye we move from Saussure's well-known views that the linguistic signifier and the signified are 'opposing, relative and negative entities' and that 'in language there are only differences *without positive terms*' to the suggestion that 'there is no poem in itself'. The deleted steps are:

(i) if the values of the signifier and the signified are only differential, then the meaning of a stretch of language such as an utterance or a poem is only differential;
(ii) if the meaning of a stretch of language is differential, then no statement – utterance or poem – is isolated;
(iii) if no poem is isolated, then there is no poem in itself.

The speed of movement is so great that it is difficult, during the course of a long book, to spot the argument, never mind the flaws in it; the writer is always just ahead of the cracks in the thin ice he is skating across. As soon as the movement is arrested, however, it is possible to unpack a good deal of falsehood and absurdity. (i) is specifically denied by Saussure: there *is* a fundamental difference between the system of language and its particular use, between 'langue' and 'parole': 'Although both the signified and the signifier are purely differential and negative when considered separately, their combination is a positive fact . . .'[6] (ii) is either obviously true or obviously false, depending upon how one construes 'isolate'. If isolate means 'completely cut off from all other utterances', then of course it is true but it scarcely needs theoretical linguistics to prove this. But if 'isolate' means identifiably distinct from other utterances – in particular other poems – then of course the enthymeme is quite false. (iii) is either meaningless or false.

It is difficult to be sure how sympathetic Lentricchia is to the idea that there is no poem in itself: the passage occurs during a somewhat sceptical examination of critics who *do* believe that there are no poems, only inter-poems. If it *were* Lentricchia's intention only to show the rationale behind their opinions, then he has rather exceeded his intention; for the arguments he mobilises prove with equal certainty that there are no statements only inter-statements, no rude remarks, only inter-(rude remarks) and so on. We shall return to intertextuality in Chapter 2 and here note only that this example from Lentricchia demonstrates vividly how, by suppressing all the vital steps in the argument, by elision, telescoping and condensation – in short by writing as if in a dream – even a somewhat sceptical critic such as Lentricchia may find himself making it easy for a hypothesis he himself considers unlikely to be true to gain temporary plausibility. It is easy, in other words, to be seduced into fellow-travelling with the absurdities of post-Saussurean criticism.

Two supportive ploys are available to throw the doubters off the scent so that even the unpersuaded may feel inadequate before the paradoxes, often suspecting that it is not the ideas but their own ability to respond to the radically new that is at fault. These are The Body of Evidence Gambit (by which it is implied that either the final paradox or the intermediate general principles have been established as true elsewhere); and The Promissory Note Ploy (in which it is indicated that essential arguments or crucial evidence will be presented later in the text).

The Body of Evidence Gambit is a favourite with Roland Barthes: 'We now know . . .'[7] and 'Contemporary research has shown . . .'[8] are his characteristic ways of introducing ideas that would be unlikely to be accepted by the independently minded without an assurance that conclusive proof is available elsewhere. Under normal circumstances, statements beginning 'Contemporary research has shown . . .' would be heavily referenced, but many post-Saussurean critics disdain references altogether; or such references as are offered are chosen more by random association of ideas than by their relevance to the fundamental arguments. For some, this represents a desire to exhibit a post-structuralist stance of winsome Ariality and an ecstatic intellectual frolicking ('the free play of the signifier'). In others, it does represent a genuine honest-to-goodness intellectual dishonesty. Barthes is also a great writer of Promissory Notes: just around the corner, there is 'a general method', 'a science of . . .' and, of course, 'a demonstration of . . .'. He confesses as much himself: 'I passed through a euphoric dream of scientificity . . .'.[9] The writer's 'dream of scientificity' is the reader's nightmare of scientism.

There is an especially revealing passage in Jonathan Culler's *Structuralist Poetics*, where he speaks of 'confirmation of the axioms that modern research has established'.[10] Outside of post-Saussurean gnosticism, an axiom is 'A self-evident proposition requiring no formal demonstration to prove its truth, but received and assented as soon as mentioned' (*Oxford English Dictionary*). In other words, precisely the kind of belief that requires no research, modern or otherwise, to prove its truth. It is fortunate that research is *not* required because the kind of study that would demonstrate, for example, that language is a closed, non-referential system could not, for obvious reasons, be carried out.

Whatever lies behind these tactics, a very desirable result, from the post-Saussurean critic's point of view, is an indefinite postponement of the moment when the reader feels that he is in position to judge the validity of what he is reading. He does not know at any given time whether to expect proof of the major theses of the work he is reading or whether that proof has already been achieved; whether he is moving towards the establishment of a general principle, or whether in fact he is witnessing the working out of its consequences. The reader of Derrida's *Of Grammatology* will be familiar with this feeling of suspension: he doesn't know whether to break his silence and question what he is reading or to read on, leaving his doubts on ice, pending imminent proof and/or clarification. He is kept in a state of permanent uncertainty as to when the writer has been given 'a fair hearing' and has had an adequate opportunity to make his points. This uncertainty is even more acute when one tackles the vast secondary literature that has gathered around the major texts.

The 'suspension tactic' goes some way towards explaining why it is that, although post-Saussurean criticism has many sympathisers, the majority of them, correctly surmising that most of the fundamental arguments are beyond them (they are beyond anyone who insists on imagining ideas before trading in them), seem content to be mere fellow-travellers. Even those few who have grappled with the underlying philosophy – Frank Lentricchia, Jonathan Culler, Christopher Norris – appear unwilling to ask questions that would enable them to assess the truth or otherwise of some of the major principles within which, or on the far side of which, such criticism operates.

Culler's position is neatly captured in the grammatical construction that John Searle so justly condemned in his review of *On Deconstruction*.[11] Culler's entire *oeuvre* – which incidentally has done more to make post-Saussurean critical theory available to and even accessible to Anglo-Saxon readers than that of any other commentator – could be summarised as saying: 'If it is true that [X], then [Y]'. Between the first pair of brackets, will be found a claim that the average reader might object to only with moderate vigour; and between the second pair of brackets will be the view that Culler is expounding and which normally the reader would reject totally. Now, it is very difficult to object to something that is presented only tentatively, as a recipe for a possible thought experiment. To challenge the protasis of a conditional seems to invite the retort: 'I only said *if* . . .'. The trouble for the reader who approaches such writing in the spirit of humility is that the conditionals multiply and the moment of assessment and possible challenge is postponed for so long that objections, rather than being voiced and met, are blocked until they wither away *in situ*. The reader then either acquiesces through weariness or turns to think of other things. And it is round about here that the 'ifs' disappear. If their disappearance passes unnoticed it may also be because the ideas have by then achieved the kind of acceptance that comes from familiarity. In this way a fellow-travelling critic such as Jonathan Culler is able to run with the hares of radical critical theory without losing touch with the hounds of common sense. Those who are totally unconvinced will have lost the thread of the argument and may find themselves muttering empty rhetoric about the 'humane values' implicit in pre-structuralist criticism.

Some post-structuralist writing consists solely of knowing allusions to what has been 'established elsewhere'. The worst examples are to be found amongst the Yale deconstructors – those who 'deconstruct on the wild side'. Amongst these, the supreme master of an intellectually derelict mode of writing that hangs its arguments almost entirely upon enthymemes is Geoffrey Hartman. His *Saving the Text* is a kind of allusion paste, a thick tar of erudition, an almost inpenetrable fog of knowingness:

> At the beginning of *Glas*, the similarity in the sound of *Sa* (acronym for 'savoir absolu') and Sa ('signifiant') is such a knot with a positive philosophic yield. Yet because of the equivocal, echo-nature of language, even identities or homophonies sound on: the sound of Sa is knotted with that of ça, as if the text were signalling its intention to bring Hegel, Saussure and Freud together. Ça corresponds to the Freudian Id ('Es'); and it may be that our only 'savoir absolu' is that of a ça structured like the Sa-signifiant: a bacchic or Lacanian 'primal process' where only signifier-signifying-signifiers exist.[12]

The style is almost a parody of post-structuralist discourse: *'as if* the text were signalling its intention to bring Hegel, Saussure and Freud together . . . it *may* be that our only . . .'. Nothing is clearly stated though many contentious ideas are hinted at, implied, suggested or assumed. The reader is not invited to apply his own critical faculties to what is asserted; he is scarcely in a position to protest at its untestability. He is there only to marvel at the ingenuity of the idea of a text 'signalling its own intention to bring Hegel, Saussure and Freud together' in the homophony of 'ça' and 'sa'. Whether as a sophisticate who 'knows already' what is being alluded to or as a gape-mouthed yokel who is somewhat lost in the cultural centrifuge of Hartman's brain, the reader is a mere spectator whose judgement is *not* appealed to. Stunned, he will permit the nonsensical phrase 'a bacchic or Lacanian primal process' to pass. He will half-recognise 'the Lacanian primal process' as the primal process that Lacan wrote about; so he won't be misled into thinking that it refers to some Bacchanalian event Lacan himself presided over. But what then of 'the bacchic primal process'? Won't the uninstructed reader be liable to think that this is something that *Bacchus* wrote about? He may then demand to know which journals published Bacchus' writings. (Quite a scoop for the journals in question.) This distracting question will, however, prevent him from querying the rather insubstantial nature of the primal process: a site 'where only signifier-signifying-

signifiers exist'. This suggests a lot of noise and no action, or a lot
of sound and no meaning. Or even less: for it is a fundamental
axiom of Saussurean theory that signifiers can no more exist in
the absence of their signifieds than one side of a sheet of paper can
exist without the other.

This last point would be dismissed without difficulty by the
experienced post-Saussurean critic. To object to Hartman's writing
on the grounds that it is inconsistent with the basic premises
from which it takes its rise is to invite the pleased response that it
therefore confirms the even more fundamental premiss of post-
structuralist criticism that all writing contradicts itself. To argue
against it by the conventional appeal to logic, common sense,
factual truth and so on would be as misconceived as trying to
clear a fog by stabbing it to death.

Parody remains the only weapon of any value here; and it may
still remain effective when the target has tried to defend itself pre-
emptively by self-parody. I therefore offer the reader the following
analysis of a sentence extracted from my unwritten book on
Geoffrey Hartman.

'Piss off, Hartman'. Nothing could at first sight seem more
straightforward. But in the echoland of language, clarity is a
sham and plain speaking a rhetorical figure. It is Hartman's
absence that is so ardently desired but absence and presence
are not so easily extricated from one another. As if in
confirmation of this, the absence itself is made excessively
present, at the level of the signifier, in the onomatopoeia
implicit in the idea of a voice charged with venom saying 'piss'
(piss/hiss). Moreover, 'piss', by virtue of its second, unvoiced
's', proleptically embodies the very absence the speaker would
wish to bring about. The second, silent 'f' in 'off' also *enacts* the
disappearance corresponding to the perlocutionary force of the
command. The statement thus deconstructs itself by *presenting*
absence.

This has the additional effect of putting into question the
implicit temporal co-ordinates of the reported utterance. The
command ('Piss off . . .') refers to a future state which the
speaker desires to bring about. But that state has been achieved
already at the level of the signifier as soon as the unvoiced 's' of
'piss' and the unvoiced 'f' of 'off' have been silently sounded.
The sentence, *written down* as *something uttered* becomes in

consequence the scene of a conflict between the deictic time frame – a real-time clock – implicit in the *utterance-act* and the timeless, authorless text-sentence that represents it. In the silence of the visible but inaudible characters, Hartman's absence is a *fait accompli*; in the sound of the uttered sentence it is a *future* state of affairs.

This future state of affairs exists only in so far as it is picked out by desire. All desire originates from and reaches into a primordial difference that may present itself under the aspect of nothingness. Accordingly, the text-sentence ends with a final (?) absence: the more usual spelling of 'Hartman' is 'Hartmann' and we are therefore conscious of a missing 'n' and so, too, of a missing end: the end is un-enned.

Nevertheless, the sentence affords us a kind of closure: in telling *Hart*man (i.e. heart man) to 'piss' off, the speech act brings together the cardiac and genital seats of desire and so reconstructs the whole 'man'. Presence pitches its tents in the very eye of the storm of absence, and plenitude is created out of emptiness.

The allusion to emptiness almost permits this text (or metatext) to end on an unvoiced 's', opening up a vertiginous prospect of displacement and regression, however . . .

The unconvinced reader unable to find a *point d'appui* for his dissent may find an uneasiness, even a bad conscience, left at the heart of his common sense by post-Saussurean, and in particular post-structuralist, writing. The above parody may help him to overcome that unease and to dispel any guilt that he may feel at squarely insisting on exercising his usual critical faculties.

There are many reasons for being sceptical of the framework of common sense that supports everyday consciousness; but post-Saussurean literary theory is not amongst them. To say this is not, however, to invite the reader to dismiss recent literary theory as merely 'fashionable'.[13] Of course the ideas that we will examine in this chapter *are* fashionable – and may shortly become unfashionable – but it does not follow from this that they are superficial. As I have argued in the Introduction, the fashion has deep roots: structuralism and post-structuralism reflect profound changes in our attitude to a mystery – that of language – second only to that of consciousness itself. Some day we may be able to return to those roots; but there is a good deal to be cleared away first. We may eventually reach a position from which it is possible to see what went wrong; how so many insights came to be squandered in dazzling but cheap paradox.

The first step is to examine the philosophical and linguistic arguments behind much post-Saussurean theory. These arguments are all the more powerful for being more often assumed than proved; more often alluded to than stated plainly.

2

Literature as Textual Intercourse

2.1 INTRODUCTION

a text . . . is a multidimensional space in which a variety of writings, none of them original, blend and clash. The text is a tissue of quotations drawn from innumerable centres of culture.[1]

influence as I conceive it means that there are no texts but only relationships between texts.[2]

The meaning of a work lies in its telling itself, its speaking of its own existence.[3]

Like many of the more startling ideas developed by literary theorists, the thesis that a work owes its origin to, and primarily refers to, other works has its roots in common sense.

No one, I think, would wish to claim that writers are entirely original; that a novelist, say, is the 'absolute origin' of his novels. After all, he creates neither the genre within which he writes nor the language he uses. Much is, inevitably, owed to predecessors who, at the very least, shape his literary responses to the world around him. Indeed, they make it possible for the writer to have *literary* responses: the production of literature is, after all, a socially mediated form of behaviour rather than a personal, or an impersonal instinctive, reaction to the world. Moreover, many, perhaps most, writers have to work their way through an apprenticeship in which they consciously or unconsciously imitate or borrow from predecessors whose work they admire, though of course a real writer does not stop there.

We tend to underrate the role of influence in shaping a new work and to overrate the originality of the individual artist. We pay disproportionate attention to what is new in a new work. In consequence, we imagine that a genre is undergoing rapid change when in reality the underlying tradition and the basic assumptions are changing only very slowly. Even revolutionary literature has more similarities to than differences from the orthodox or traditional writing that precedes it. The pathbreaking new work puts out only a little from the mainland of the already said, the already written. Real change is inevitably rather gradual because of the 'boxed in' situation of literature. Its production and consumption belong to a rather specific form of human behaviour: literature is a sub-genre within the wider genre of 'prepared communication'; this in turn is a sub-species of verbal communication; and the latter is itself only one mode of human interaction. The very process by which a work is perceived as literary – makes literary sense – depends upon its being more or less explicitly located within a comparatively narrow universe of discourse whose co-ordinates have been established by previous works of literature. The new work owes part of its intelligibility to being situated with respect to, or within, a tradition it for the most part continues even while repudiating aspects of it. 'Literary meaning depends on codes produced by the prior discourses of a culture'[4] – and many of these codes will be specifically literary traditions, habits and principles. In so far as tradition shapes the form of a work, earlier writing is the latter's implicit framework; or (to use the fashionable terminology) the context of individual texts is, to this extent, more text.

It is easy to see how these observations apply to form – how at the level of form, literary works imitate, hark back to and hence implicitly refer to, one another. But they are equally applicable to content. For previous writing will in some degree determine what is worthy of *literary* notice, even what is noticeable – and hence writable – not only at the level at which 'suitable' themes are identified for literary treatment but also further down, in the manner in which they are handled and even in the selection of empirical detail. The poet's choice of 'daffodils' as a theme will be fully intelligible only in the context of a tradition of 'simple pastoral' verse, even though such a tradition may have been renewed by the poet's personal dissent from, say, a more consciously sophisticated urban verse devoted to social, satirical or abstract philosophical themes. The sub-genre of 'lyric poetry' will be a major influence in determining that there shall be a literary result of the encounter between the poet and the flower – that the latter should count as the theme of a poem. Moreover, the selection of detail, once the theme has been established, is never governed purely by an unmediated openness to the topics and objects that form the overt subject of a piece of writing. What is included in the poem about daffodils will not be fixed solely by the poet's personal experiences and private memories of daffodils. He is talking about daffodils, yes; but in a way that no mere daffodil sensation or daffodil feeling could have triggered or organised. And other things besides the structure and properties of daffodils and the poet's personal experiences of them will influence what is excluded from as well as what is included in the poem. The contemporary idea of 'a poem' – the current rules of the game – will make it unlikely, if he is, say, Wordsworth writing in the first decade of the nineteenth century, that his poem will make reference to recent modifications of the position of daffodils in the Linnaean classification or to the primitive biochemical observations of his botanist contemporaries. And the rules of the game will also ensure that when he writes he will forget much of what he has himself seen – for example the blackbird droppings on the specimen he looked at yesterday.

The example comes from poetry; but other literary discourses, though less deliberately offset from the wider realm of everyday communication, are also written to or against – at any rate in relation to – a generic prescription. Just as no one's memories or feelings fall naturally into iambic pentameters, so the soul does not spontaneously secrete its hoarded experiences as novels. To adapt what La Rochefoucauld said of falling in love: no one would write novels unless he had read about them first. The sense of genre within or against which he is writing exerts both conscious and unconscious constraints upon the writer. But it also establishes the space into which he can write. If genre is a prison-house, it is one that the writer can escape only at the price of abandoning literature altogether.

Tradition is as potent an influence upon how we read as it is in determining what is written. What seems to be offered to us when we confront a particular work is at least partly determined by the silent presence of other works belonging to the genre to which we assign the one we are actually reading. The wrong 'mental generic set' will prevent us from being able to assimilate or even make sense of it. Anyone who reads, say, *Philosophical*

Investigations under the impression that it is a detective story or *The Red and the Black* in the hope of learning the rules of snooker will simply read past what is essential in these works or find them incomprehensible. Likewise, it is the 'generic mental set' of the reader that makes, say, William Carlos Williams's jottings count as more than banal diary entries unaccountably chopped up into lengths. The verse-like form of his fragments means that they can command, or commandeer, a readerly attention, an intensity of noticing, that they would not otherwise receive and certainly do not warrant. (The freedom of much 'free verse' is bought at the cost of the enslavement of the reader to the ideas of genre and the different forms of attention owing to different genres.) As E. D. Hirsch has written (with an exaggeration that is only too typical of literary theorists): 'an interpreter's preliminary generic conception of the text is constitutive of everything that he subsequently understands, and . . . this remains the case until the generic conception is altered.'[5] The consumption, as well as the production of literature, then, is an activity that takes place within internal traditions of form, content and genre. Extra-literary reality, the manifest theme of the work, is by no means the exclusive determinant of its shape or content; its extra-linguistic referents are not its only referents.

So much would be accepted by anyone not under the spell of semi-mystical ideas about the feelings, perceptions and inspirations of authors. But this is a far cry from some of the claims that have been advanced under the banner of 'intertextuality'. It will shortly become apparent that the term 'intertextuality' is sufficiently ill-defined for it to mean all things to all critics. Its infinite elasticity makes possible the conjuring tricks whereby the rabbits of paradox ('texts refer only to other texts', 'there are no poems only inter-poems', 'literature is about itself') are pulled out of the hat of common sense ('no one writes in isolation', 'the poet is influenced by other poets, as well as by his own experiences'). The reader, acquiescing in a fairly unexceptionable claim about the nature of literature, takes 'intertextuality' on board. Once safely installed, 'intertextuality' undergoes spectacular metamorphoses. Its scope expands enormously until it can license almost any conclusion about the nature of literature, of language or even, as we shall see, human consciousness itself.

2.2   THE INTERTEXTUALITY OF LITERATURE

At its least ambitious, the 'intertextuality' thesis is about literature. Non-contentiously, it takes its rise from the obvious fact that many literary works are explicitly or implicitly allusive. Scholarly references, quotations, echoes, reworkings of traditional themes, deliberate employment of established styles and retelling of classic or archetypal 'literary' stories, the deliberate contrivance of ironic effects by the juxtaposition of disparate and incompatible styles – these intertextual features have been the very stuff of literature since ancient times. Some writers – David Jones and T. S. Eliot are typical instances – create much of their *oeuvre* out of echoes and the ironies of cultural dissonance. Successful literary composition has often involved the conscious recovery of formal archetypes; while, at a lower level, second-order and second-rate writers have created an *oeuvre* out of a largely unconscious reiteration of stereotypes.

The contemporary obsession with 'intertextuality', however, goes much further than acknowledging those aspects of literature that make it necessary to read one text in the light of or context of another. A pre-structuralist critic would read even David Jones's great poem 'In Parenthesis' as being primarily about the catastrophe of the First World War and subsume its densely allusive style under the poet's attempt to render that bottomless event thinkable. But intertexuality for many critics is a concept used to undermine both the idea that the author is the source of 'his' works – or even that he personally intends them – and the belief that they refer to an extra-literary reality. The author-creator and external reference are to be classed along with the 'true voice of (unmediated) feeling', and 'direct transcription of empirical, sensory reality' (by a pen seen as a neutral, handheld camera) as simply parts of a now-discredited mythology of literature. In other words, contemporary concern with intertextuality takes the argument beyond the obvious fact that literature is in conversation with other literature to the conclusion that a work of literature is *only* about literature – either about itself or other works. We are asked to believe that the relations between one work and others eclipses the relations between any work and an extra-literary world; and to infer from the fact that, say, poems refer to one another that other poetry is the only reference (or occasion) of all poems. To accept, in short, that literary writing is shaped entirely by literary, textual forces and that it reflects neither extra-literary reality nor the experiences, feelings and conscious intentions of their authors; that literature is 'contextualised' from within rather than being governed at least in part by non-literary or even non-discursive influences.

Theories about the nature of poetry provided one of the more important roads to both the French and American acceptance of the more contentious ideas about the scope of intertextuality. In fact it is probably neither a simplification nor an exaggeration to say that 'intertextualism' began life as a specific thesis about poetry, though it did not rejoice under that name. More precisely, it was about the proper function of verse and about defining the poetry that certain critics – and, indeed, practitioners – approved of. It arose, that is to say, out of normative principles.

The history of Symbolism – Mallarmé's famous remark about poetry being 'made with words rather than ideas', Valéry's claim that poetry stands to prose as dancing does to walking, and so on – is too well known to require potted rehearsal here. It is sufficient for our present purposes to note Jakobson and Sartre as important intermediaries between Symbolism and modern French 'intertextual' poetics. Both cordoned off poetry from other discourses by asserting that poetry was non-referential. For Sartre, a poem was an opaque object without external reference that invited the reader to look at, rather than through, it. Opaque poetry stood to transparent prose as a jewel to a window.[6] Jakobson's views on language, 'literariness', poetry and referentiality will not be discussed in detail here. Suffice it to say that his pronouncements were influential in popularising the idea that poetry, or the poetic parts of literature, or language in its essential poeticalness, were non-referential.

As for the American critical scene, Lentricchia convincingly argues that there is a continuity between the present popularity of post-Saussurean ideas about literature and the theoretical notions associated with the New Criticism that flourished in the middle decades of this century.[7] A brief glance at the New Criticism will show how it prepared the ground for the massive extension of the critical conception of literary influence, imitation and tradition that subsequently took place under the cover of the term 'intertextuality'.

Lentricchia makes only passing reference to I. A. Richards, though he is generally acknowledged as one of the founding fathers of the New Criticism. His early belief that poetry was distinguished from other modes of discourse by being essentially emotive rather than informative[8] was crucial both for the development of the New Criticism and for its eventual displacement by post-Saussurean theory. If, Richards maintained, poetry sometimes seemed to convey information, this was either illusory (apparently factual statements were 'pseudo-propositions') or incidental to its central purpose. Poetry is not about 'extra-literary' reality. Its meanings are non-referential and as such they are a more suitable subject for psychological measurement – by a kind of 'affective calculus' – than for empirical verification or logical investigation. A poem is not empirically true or untrue – it is not in that sense open to the world – rather it is powerful or weak, affecting and effective or feeble and inert.

Richard's ideas about the true nature of poetry imperceptibly became a prescription for true poetry; they changed from a theory about what poetry was to a theory about what poetry should be. At about the same time, Archibald MacLeish was declaring (in a poem) that a poem should be 'palpable and mute/As a globed fruit':

> A poem should be equal to:
> Not true
>
> A poem should not mean
> But be.[9]

A poem should be an object in itself; for objects, unlike factual statements, are not hollowed out by reference; nor do they live or die by their truth values; they simply are. Such ideas are similar to those Sartre was advancing twenty years later in *What Is Literature?*

Cleanth Brooks was one of many critics who accepted the essential non-referentiality of verse and he elaborated the more specific thesis that a poem should *be* what it asserts. It would achieve the required non-referentiality by referring only to itself. Donne's 'The Canonization' is satisfying as a poem because it *is* itself the 'well wrought urne' that it invokes at its climactic moment. 'We'll build in sonnets pretty roomes' the poet writes, as he builds his pretty sonnet-room.[10] In so far as 'The Canonization' has a reference, it *is* that to which it refers and, as such, is exemplary. Contemporary poets should follow Donne's example and refuse to write poems that are about anything other than themselves. Poems that attempt to be other than self-referential are defective, contaminated; in short, non-poems. To use verse as a medium for talking about one's feelings, one's beliefs, one's sufferings or about any aspect of the world outside of the poem, is to show that one has misunderstood the name and nature of true poetry. It betrays one's insufficient sophistication. The ideal poem is 'above the battle' and the true poet is a disinterested virtuoso playing with (rather than asserting) ideas, assuming voices, creating in the space of the poem unique harmonies out of phonetic, tonal and stylistic dissonances. (The poem as a 'space' is another metaphor favoured by the New Critics.) Since true verse is not about anything other than itself, any attempt to explicate its meaning, to say what it is 'about' is to traduce it, to commit 'the heresy of paraphrase'. The critic should instead pay close attention to verbal and formal features of poetry and ignore as far as possible its biographical, historical and philosophical contexts. (It is not, of course, possible to do this, as was discovered at a more fundamental level by those linguists who tried to develop a comprehensive semantics-free grammar.) And so it came about that, as Gerard Graff has noted, 'the key principle of the New Criticism [became] its hostile (or at best equivocal) view of the referential powers of literature'.[11]

From the idea that real *poetry* is non- or self-referential it is but a step to the position that real *literature* should have no external reference; that literature in its essential 'literariness' does not stoop to the representation of external reality but rather aims to be a fragment of a second, perfected, reality where all is 'luxe, calme et volupté', to realise that Utopia of language where feelings, ideas and images are subordinated to the creation of a linguistic site composed explicitly of none of them. Such literature has no external, non-literary origin: like the ideal poem, it is a series of little closed universes that have no other occasion than themselves or each other. By these standards most of fiction and prose non-fiction could be safely disregarded as sub-art, unworthy of serious critical attention.

It is interesting to speculate how the lack of an external refer-ent changed from a New Critical criterion of good literature to the inescapable condition of literature itself. Lentricchia makes a convincing case for the major influence of Northrop Frye's

Anatomy of Criticism in this regard. For Frye, literature is a closed universe of order, outside of which there is only chaos. Literature does not emerge out of, nor does it reflect, extra-literary reality: 'poems can only be made out of other poems'. Being without external origin or external reference are not only necessary features of good verse but the inescapable condition of all literature, which is uniquely intelligible and ordered in an unintelligible and chaotic world. The sheer inclusiveness of Frye's scheme, which brought all literature within a single system – so that any given work could claim to have been foreseen, occupying a pre-determined position in a closed literary universe – must certainly have been influential in carrying his larger quasi-metaphysical claim that the individual work is not about the real world – which is chaotic and formless – but is merely a figure, a position in a map that has already been drawn. The artist will struggle in vain against the curse by which literature is cut off from the world: the price of making a work that has an intelligible order is conformity to a genre and the inturning of reference. The primary relation of the poem or novel is to the genre to which it stands as token to type and not to a world which it expresses or reflects. And the fundamental critical task is not to mediate between literature and extra-literary reality – adjudicating the extent to which the one is true of the other – but to develop a sensibility and a critical apparatus which permits an ever more refined and precise allocation of works to genres discriminated within a system that is at once rigorous and all-inclusive.

The stage is set for the full acceptance of a critical approach that treats the work as an intertextual construct. It will be evident from what has been said so far that this is a position that will prove difficult to evaluate. Defining a counter-position will require that one should be able to draw the boundaries that separate internal from external reference in literature. Few people can command the necessary erudition to determine the extent to which *all* writers are consciously or unconsciously influenced by other writers. Besides, it is not merely a matter of (encyclopaedic) knowledge but also one of interpretation. It is possible, for example, to argue that all literature is characterised by such a degree of inturned intertextuality as to be really about the difficulties that lie in the way of its being written. Todorov, in a much-noticed passage tells us that

Every work, every novel, tells through the fabric of its events the story of its own creation, its own history. . . . The meaning of a work lies in its telling itself, its speaking of its own existence.[12]

So every novel is guaranteed to be, if not 'a well wrought urne', at least 'a well cooped hoggesheadde'. Several critics have claimed that inturned, indeed ingrown, intertextuality, is a feature of even the most apparently naïve and outgoing of realistic novels. We shall discuss this (self-defeating) position elsewhere; for the present, it is sufficient to observe that, if it can be argued that the *central* theme of the novels of Dickens, Conrad and Thackeray is a meditation on the art of fiction,[13] then no one is so placed as to be able to assess the extent of the presence of intertextuality in literature.

One method of counter-argument would be to look at actual cases. Supposing we compare two artists operating under roughly the same generic constraints and find that they have apparently two quite different attitudes, topics, themes and referents – would this not then undermine the argument that all works have, say, their genre as their primary, or even sole, referent? For identical genre should mean identical reference. Or, even more tellingly, suppose we compare several pieces by the same writer, again operating under the same generic constraints – let us say Shakespeare writing sonnets. A thoroughgoing textual analysis could dissolve much of the content of these sonnets into a play of allusions, and read them as highly formalised exercises typical of the style of the Renaissance sonnet. But how well does this stand up when we look at the verses themselves? Compare this:

> What is your substance, whereof are you made,
> That millions of strange shadows on you tend? . . .
> (no. 53)

with

> Farewell! thou art too dear for my possessing,
> And like enough thou know'st thy estimate . . .
> (no. 87)

and

Th'expense of spirit in a waste of shame
Is lust in action; and, till action, lust
Is perjured, murd'rous, bloody, full of blame . . .

(no. 129)

No one reading these three sonnets could surely doubt that within the very closely circumscribed limits of the Renaissance love sonnet totally different messages may be transmitted and different referents discriminated. The enawed sense of mystery experienced by the lover contemplating his beloved in Sonnet 40, his resigned grief in Sonnet 87 and his anger – directed at his lust and, by implication at his lust's object in Sonnet 129 – are all, of course, stylised; but they are nevertheless also highly differentiated and make sense in relation to the widely divergent experiences, attitudes and postures they invoke and thus refer to. Although it would be absurd to deny the formal elements that run through the sonnets, it would be perverse to see them as being solely designed to draw attention to themselves, to earlier sonnets or to the sonnet form itself. This is emphasised even by those scholars who consider that the formal element of the sonnets has been underestimated. 'Attentiveness to Shakespeare's handling of form' generates

> the discovery that the greater the immediate effect of the sonnet, the more surely does it prove, upon examination, that the effects rest no less surely upon form than upon the appeal of the sentiments or of the imagery. . . . A close study of the language of *The Sonnets* makes it clear that, great as was Shakespeare's ability to use imagery not only for its beauty but also for its integrating power, he possessed in even greater measure the power to make the formal elements of language express the nature of the experience with which the language deals.[14]

There are some who would remain unimpressed by the fact that, although the genre exerts constraints upon both form and content, it does not determine the referent of a work of art because the latter can vary enormously even within the tightest of generic constraints. They would be unmoved by being reminded that assigning the work to its correct pigeon-hole is consequently not the same as making sense of it and identifying its reference;

so that even if every work could be assigned a place within such a schema, and an individual novel or poem were an instance of a pre-established type, it would not follow that the type was the only or even the primary reference of the work. For there is nothing to prevent the committed intertextualist from claiming that, notwithstanding the variety of referents available to a writer working within even the most narrowly defined genre, the range of referents is still internal to literature; and that apparently different, apparently extra-literary, referents merely represent different positions within a closed universe of literary discourse.

Such a claim will again render radical intertextualist theses immune from testing against external evidence. Or perhaps not entirely immune. And it is appropriate at this juncture to mention Barthes's famous attempt to construct a 'rhetoric' of love, in which the experiences and adventures and reflections and strategies of the lover were read as figures, tropes, as scenes of language, nodes in a network of amorous discourse.[15] Apart from certain isolated insights, the project was not a success. This is admitted as much in the sub-title of *A Lover's Discourse:* 'Fragments'. The reason for Barthes's inevitable failure to transcribe all the lover's experiences from content to form – to make of 'being in love' a matter of differences without positive terms – can be stated very simply. It overlooks the element of accident, of particularity, and ultimately the irreducible *haecceitas* of being there, that constitutes *all* experiences, not just amorous ones.

But we hardly need to turn to empirical evidence to test the ideas of extreme intertextualists. We can usually rely upon advanced critics to provide us with internal or self-refutation. In the case of certain prominent intertextualists, our expectations are generously fulfilled. In some instances, the theory contradicts itself; in others, the theory is contradicted by the critic's own interpretive practice. A few critics – amongst them Harold Bloom – manage to pull off both forms of self-contradiction, showing how the business of adhering consistently to dubious ideas requires constant vigilance.

For Bloom, intertextuality is the key to the artist's inner struggle and creative power.[16] A poet is concerned not so much to write about the world, or about the things that happen to him, but to write poems that are different from other poems – more specifically from the poems written by those whom he has identified as his precursors: 'poems . . . are neither about 'subjects' nor about 'themselves'. They are necessarily about *other poems*; a poem is a response to a poem, as a poet is a response to a poet.'[17]

Becoming a poet consists essentially of falling in love with and being engulfed by a precursor; falling out of love with him; and then fighting against his influence. The 'strong' poet is one who successfully overthrows those who, by virtue of being his forerunners, count as father figures. The motor of the poet's creativity is not excitement about the world, anger or astonishment at the way things are, delight at the discovery of a talent not possessed by others or even a desire to save a bit of reality, but the 'anxiety of influence' which causes him to launch a parricidal attack upon his unsuspecting precursor. This, rather than any personal angle on things or the happy accident of being gifted, is what generates his poems. It is perhaps fortunate for the luckless ephebe that his precursors are few in number and that the influence that preoccupies him emanates only from one or two forebears rather than the whole of preceding literature. It is not clear why he should alight upon those few rather than experiencing the whole of literature weighing down on him as incubus. I suspect, to judge from some of the examples Bloom has given, it is because they are usually found together in the college syllabus. Yeats cannot abide Shelley, nor Whitman Emerson because they have spent too much time together in Subsidiary 289. (This is not entirely just. Some of the lines of influence that he traces seem convincing and illuminating: Spenser as Milton's 'massive precursor', for example.)

The first thing that strikes one about Bloom's thesis is that it is an astonishingly candid example of the common critical vice of attributing one's own preoccupations to the writer one is studying. Critics have been most typically concerned with the provenance of works and establishing who influenced whom in the history of literature; and so, according to Bloom, influence is the central concern of artists. In order to render this more plausible, Bloom develops the thesis that the artist *is* a critic and, of course, vice versa: 'As literary history lengthens, all poetry necessarily becomes verse-criticism, just as all criticism becomes prose-poetry.'[18] The conflation of the artist–critic and the critic–artist is inevitable in an age of latecomers when all but the strongest artists feel an insuperable sense of belatedness. (Latecoming began after Homer.) Both artist and critic, poet and teacher of poetry are present at the Primal Scene of Instruction, at first as ephebes or pupils and later as precursors or teachers. This Primal Scene of Teaching is anterior even to the Primal Scene of Writing: intertextuality antedates textuality; or the text is born of intertextuality.[19] No wonder, then, that artists are, like critics, more interested in the influences upon works than the works themselves; for there *are* no works: 'influence as I conceive it means that there are no texts but only relationships between texts' (see note 2). The meaning of a poem is another poem or, perhaps, another poet. There are no poems, only inter-poems.

This is, of course, a comparatively restricted version of the intertextuality thesis. In Bloom's scheme of things, the work does not refer to the outside world, true; but at least it does not dissolve into an infinite nexus of other works, into a comprehensive schema corresponding to the closed universe of literary discourse or into the great mass of literature itself. The text refers to other texts – but to a finite number of texts: it is possible to identify the corpus upon which the artist is committing his necrophobic revenge. And there in part lies its vulnerability. For the evidence Bloom adduces for his lines of influence is sketchy indeed; and at times almost laughable. It is necessary to read the original texts to appreciate the full weakness of Bloom's argument but the reader may deduce the irresponsibility of his scholarship from his claim – without further evidence – that Shelley's reference to

> a deep, autumnal tone,
> Sweet though in sadness

alludes both to Wordsworth's 'sober colouring' in 'Intimations of Immortality' and to the 'still, sad music' of 'Tintern Abbey'. It is upon this kind of evidence that ephebe–precursor relations are established and the key to the inmost penetralium of the great poet's soul found. At this level, everything alludes to everything else and any reference to autumn or its colours could be seen to be an inter-reference to any other reference to autumn and its colours. Bloom, however, is not anyway too worried by the quality of his evidence.

> Poetic influence, in the sense I give to it, has almost nothing to do with the verbal resemblances between one poet and another. Hardy, on the surface, scarcely resembles Shelley, his prime precursor, but then Browning, who resembles Shelley even

less, was yet more fully Shelley's ephebe than even Hardy was.[20]

No, true resemblance lies in the identity of spiritual forms – 'at once the aboriginal poetic self and the True Subject'; and here we have to take Bloom's word since spotting this kind of thing lies beyond ordinary critics. And, indeed, beyond poets themselves: 'The theory . . . has encountered considerable resistance . . . I take the resistance shown to the theory by many poets, in particular, to be likely evidence for its validity.'[21] Even making allowances for the rueful irony of one who may have received a bruise or two on the podium and the endemic Freudianism of Bloom's world, this is unconvincing.

The most obviously implausible aspect of Bloom's vision of the vengeful artist–son (the ephebe) murdering the father figure (precursor) is that it overlooks the process whereby someone becomes a poet in the first place (rather than, say, a doctor or a race-track owner) and the long personal evolution that antecedes the identification of themes and hence of rivals and forerunners. A lengthy chapter of accidents, decisions, self-interpretations, encounters with canonical texts and so on will predate the moment when an individual decides to dedicate himself to verse and then emulates those who become his precursors. Bloom's defence that he is fully aware that 'even the strongest poets are subject to influences not poetical' but that he is concerned only with the poet as a poet, 'the aboriginal poet', is weak. It leads one to suspect that, for Bloom, the essence of a poet is that part of him that confirms Bloom's theories.[22]

The sincerity with which Bloom holds his views may be judged from his practice when he deals with particular poets. Take Hardy, a writer whom he reveres above all the moderns:

> In Hardy's best poems, the central meter-making argument is what might be called a sceptical lament for the hopeless incongruity of ends and means in all human acts. Love and the means of love cannot be brought together, and the truest name for the human condition is simply that it is loss.[23]

This sounds very much like a vision of the world, rather than a vision of a poetic precursor, an anxiety about life rather than an anxiety of influence. So what happened to the central criticism-making argument advanced by Bloom earlier, that poems are not 'about subjects', that they are necessarily about *other poems*? It seems to have been put to one side: 'but whether the theory is correct or not may be irrelevant to its usefulness for practical criticism, which I think can be demonstrated.'[24]

What Bloom in fact demonstrates is that his theory can be usefully – and quietly – laid to one side when he settles down to practical criticism and becomes one of the most moving and exciting critics writing today. Which shows, perhaps, that one can go a long way as a literary critic even when one is in the grip of foolish notions. Perhaps the sign of the true critic is that he can find his way into the interstices between his own – and anyone else's – ideas. He has (to parody what T. S. Eliot said of Henry James) a mind so fine that even when it has been thoroughly violated by the least plausible of ideas, he can still talk excitingly and even sensitively about literature.

Bloom is his own straw man; he lacks the guile of other intertextualists. He is foolish enough to allow his assertions to be testable – at the least against his own practice. But if we are to avoid the charge of merely tilting at windbags, we must confront the more diffuse and slippery intertextualists. For reasons given earlier, however, the intertextualist position as a thesis, or group of theses, about literature as a whole is quite simply beyond evaluation. It is only when it is seen to imply larger claims about *all* writing, *all* language or *all* consciousness, that it can be evaluated, though even then it is not available to formal verification or refutation. Many critics already subscribe to the view that intertextuality is not merely a literary affair; so that it might seem that the job has already in part been done for us. But we shall have to re-do this work in order to bring out the fact that the essential invulnerability of the appeal to intertextuality – and the claim that the context of a literary text is only more text – lies in its infinitely extendable scope. But in this extendability resides its downfall. For once the theory is extended to the limit, it is seen to have all but lost specific content.

2.3 THE INTERTEXTUALITY OF CONSCIOUSNESS

There is no unmediated experience of the world; knowledge is possible only through the categories and laws of the symbolic

> order. Far from expressing a unique perception of the world, authors produce meaning out of the available system of differences, and texts are intelligible only insofar as they participate in it.[25]

> Some scholars glibly mistake the intertext for sources and seem to think that intertextuality is just a newfangled name for influence or imitation. We must be clear that intertext does not signify a collection of literary works that may explain the text or its influence on readers, nor one that may be used as a basis of comparison to point out the author's originality. An intertext is a corpus of texts, textual fragments, or textlike segments of the sociolect that shares a lexicon, a syntax with the text we are reading (directly or indirectly) in the form of synonyms or, even conversely, in the form of antonyms.[26]

Those who are not convinced of the special or unique intertextuality of literature will point out that there are many 'intertextual' features in everyday discourse. Much of what we say is consciously allusive; indeed, there are certain people – especially in adolescence – whose conversational output consists almost entirely of jokey references, quotations, assumed voices, deliberate collisions of dissonant linguistic registers and so on. But even such people are able to maintain this only when the engine is idling: camp evaporates in a crisis, when life, livelihood or comfort is threatened. The argument against the unique intertextuality of literature could be pressed further, however, by correctly observing that even 'serious' or 'straight' conversation is shaped by a framework of expectation as to what is appropriate in the oral sub-genre that is being engaged in. A unique situation is always seen under a general aspect. This is implicit in the very fact that it is *intelligible* to its dramatis personae: *particulare sentitur; universale intelligitur.* Thus apprehended, it makes a finite range of conversational choices available: a certain 'user area' (to use the computer terminology) within the thesaurus of catch phrases is opened up; the transitional probabilities between themes, between phrases and between individual words within phrases are set and are, in theory at least, calculable by social linguists or discourse analysts. Between the stereotyped aperture and the stereotyped closure, the conversation will take a familiar course across citations, clichés, platitudes and other conversational ready-to-wears. The entire discourse is pervaded by oral intertextuality. Does it, however, follow from this that its only, or even the primary, reference is other discourse rather than the outside world? I think not. Consider this example. During the course of a conversation, I tell you that my child is sick. My account of the situation utilises words that have high intrinsic and transitional probabilities. I employ no nonce words or *hapax legomena* and the content and course of my report could have been at least in part predicted by a computer and, as the conversation proceeded, Bayesian logic could be employed to this end with increasing precision. Your sympathetic response is equally stereotyped. Even so, after we have met, you make a *particular* journey to the shops and buy a particular toy that you know that my child has had his eye on for some time. Endemic oral intertextuality has not prevented our conversation from having specific reference to extra-discursive reality and being governed by, and projected upon, non-discursive grounds. Despite its intelligibility, it has (to invoke the terms of Duns Scotus's dissent from Aquinas) *haecceitas* as well as *quidditas.*[27]

The splendid scorn that Joseph Weizenbaum poured upon the artificial intelligentsia for their naïve response to his ELIZA program[28] is relevant to the naïve believers in the omnipotence of textual forces. The limitations of computer predictions and simulations – obvious to all but the besotted – apply equally to the belief that the course of a discourse can be predicted/explained by reference to textual forces. No 'dialogue programs' could take into account the fact that the interlocutors in any normal conversation are open to a world not defined or circumscribed by the theme of the discussion. As you are expressing a stereotyped sympathy, a dog runs across the road. A calculus of probabilities will not have predicted the transition from ' I am sorry to hear that he is unwell. It must be a terrible worry for you' to 'Just look at that stupid animal!' But then neither computers nor discourses as viewed by certain literary critics are open to the exigencies of the moment. Nor do they contain deictic reference to spatial and temporal co-ordinates. In short, they are not *there* in the way that real people or real discourses are.

Let me take the counter-argument further by considering this more dramatic example.[29] I am on call for emergencies in the hospital. The phone rings and I receive this terse, prefabricated message: 'Cardiac arrest, Ward 6A'. My acting upon this message will depend upon my interpreting it within the context of my situation as an on-call medical practitioner. Moreover, it is a piece of discourse that belongs to a highly specialised genre of utterances, to a discursive formation that will have been governed by the history of technology, of our conception of the human body, of duty and salaried labour, as well as by the development of certain institutions such as a National Health Service and by various other discourses that influence, and guarantee, the meaning of statements made within the context of professional medical discourse. It is, in other words, contextualised by more text. None of this will prevent the message from referring to an extra-textual reality – in this instance a dying man in a hospital ward – and from carrying a truth value that may be ascertained by empirical observation. It is governed by non-discursive grounds. The textual context of 'Cardiac arrest, Ward 6A' does not prevent it from being true and (on this occasion) 'No cardiac arrest, Ward 6A' or 'Cardiac arrest, Ward 2A' from being (disastrously) untrue. Textual forces are *always* at work; but they are not omnipotent and they never act in isolation.

The intertextuality of the oral text does not cut it off from the world, from society, from the suffering, living human being. From which it follows that intertextuality *per se* does not itself close the text off from external reality, bending reference in exclusively upon itself. So the intertextuality of literature does not enclose the individual work within a sealed universe of literature. Or at least it does not unless one takes the further step of claiming that *all* texts, even the oral texts of everyday conversation, are somehow sealed off in a closed textual universe. In order to sustain that claim, it is necessary to take the final step of asserting that the real referents of ordinary conversation are themselves textual.

There are many prominent critics prepared to do this and to maintain that the world, the society, the suffering human beings to which discourses – ordinary conversation as much as allusive or highly stylised literature – refer and in which they are operative, are themselves huge and boundless texts. The relation between the conversational text and the apparently extra-linguistic reality to which it refers is simply another mode of textual intercourse – between a small text and a big one. The world outside of the text is itself a text, as are the consumers and producers of the texts. If the literary text reaches outside of itself, by virtue of which it appears to have verisimilitude, this is because it is grafted on 'to another general and diffuse text which might be called "public opinion" '.[30] Public opinion is something held by texts about texts. According to Barthes, for example,

> This 'I' which approaches the text is already itself a plurality of other texts, of codes which are infinite or, more precisely, lost (whose origin is lost). . . . Subjectivity is a plenary image, with which I may be thought to encumber the text, but whose deceptive plenitude is merely the wake of all the codes which constitute me, so that my subjectivity has ultimately the generality of stereotypes.[31]

As for the codes

> The code is a perspective of quotations, a mirage of structures . . . they are so many fragments of something that has always been *already* read, seen, done, experienced; the code is the wake of that *already*. Referring to what has been written, i.e. to the Book (of culture, of life, of life as culture), it makes the text into a prospectus of this Book. Or again: each code is one of the forces that can take over the text (of which the text is the network), one of the voices out of which the text is woven . . . these voices (whose origin is 'lost' in the vast perspective of the *already-written*) de-originate the utterance: the convergence of the voices (of the codes) becomes *writing*, a stereographic space where the five codes, the five voices, intersect.[32]

Julia Kristeva speaks of 'the notion of intertextuality' coming 'to have the place of the notion of intersubjectivity'.[33] The intersubjective world becomes an inter-text and each text is contextualised by the boundless text (or inter-text) of a culture or society.

This at first appears to be a more radical position, that will save the less radical one. It goes far beyond the valid claim that much of the outside world is mediated to us via stories to the suggestion that outside world itself *dissolves into* those stories. Nevertheless, the wider intertextuality claim de-radicalises the intertextuality thesis as a specific thesis about literature. Literature again seems to be open to the world at large. Or rather, literature has no less access to extra-literary reality than our daily conversations have. As Riffaterre expresses it

> An intertext is a corpus of texts, textual fragments or textlike segments of the sociolect . . . .

> 'Sociolect' . . . is language viewed not just as grammar and lexicon but as the repository of society's myths, commonplace phrases and descriptive systems (stereotyped networks of metonyms around any given lexical nucleus) [see note 26, p. 43]

The context of literary, as of non-literary, discourse is apparently boundless. Meaning is context-bound but the context in question is boundless – it is the boundless text of society. This much is conceded even by Derrida;[34] and Culler, drawing out the implications of intertextualism, tells us that 'To understand the language of a text is to recognise the world to which it refers'[35] – which represents a considerable retreat even from the position of some New Critics.

2.4 TOWARDS NON-REFERENTIALITY

We have seen how the scope of 'intertextuality' is extremely variable: it may be interpreted as a property of certain highly abnormal literary texts that seem to refer primarily to themselves, to the genre to which they belong or to other literary texts; or it can balloon to encompass the whole of reality. We begin with the claim that literature is closed off from the world outside of it, is non-referential in the ordinary sense, because individual works are shaped by and/or refer to other works or to themselves. When it is pointed out that non-literary texts – such as conversations – can refer to one another without apparently becoming non-referential, the response is to widen the scope of intertextuality enormously. Ordinary statements in fact, we are told, refer primarily to other statements and if they seem to be contextualised by the real world and by real people it is because that world and those people are themselves texts. The outside world to which all statements refer is simply a boundless intertextual construct. There is an outside of texts but that outside is composed solely of text. The thesis that literature is a closed system thus expands until it changes imperceptibly into the thesis that language is a closed system – so that it does not refer even in ordinary daily life to an extra-linguistic reality. This in turn shades into the position that there is no extra-linguistic reality. Consciousness, reality and society become conterminous with language. The constraints of genre reflect the prison-house of language which in turn constrains consciousness. Consciousness, the world, reality, society become a single closed system. At its limit, where there is nothing but language – 'wall-to-wall text' in Edward Said's striking phrase – intertextualism becomes a linguistic version of neo-Kantian idealism. At this limit, it is scarcely surprising that 'Il n'y pas de hors-texte' because, as *texte* is defined, it is coextensive with all that there is. But before that position can be earned, the advocates of extreme intertextuality must demonstrate that reality is intra-linguistic.

3

The Illusion of Reference

Criticism has taken the very idea of 'aboutness' away from us. It has taught us that language is tautological, if it is not nonsense, and to the extent that it is about anything it is about itself.[1]

3.1 THE ARTICULATION OF REALITY

There is no unmediated experience of the world; knowledge is possible only through the categories and the laws of the symbolic order.[2]

We dissect nature along lines laid down by our native languages.[3]

No one, I think, would wish to challenge the obvious truth that language is implicated in the construction of reality. The question that I wish to address in this section, however, is the *extent* to which reality is intra-linguistic and language is the agent or medium in virtue of which reality is structured or constituted. More particularly, I shall question the radically nominalist assumption, common to many post-Saussurean critics, that the traffic is all one way: that language structures reality but reality does not influence the structure, the system of differences, that is language. And, more specifically still, the claim that such radical nominalism is licensed by the ideas put forward by Saussure.

There is a sense in which it is true to say that reality consists of what gets talked about: to be is to be the subject of an assertion. Many writers have emphasised the extent to which this is true of social reality and acknowledged that the transformation of an infant into a fully developed human being consists at least in part

49

of a process of induction into a set of discourses about the world. Becoming a person and entering language are intimately connected processes: becoming situated in the world is in part the acquisition of a verbally mediated world picture. An age – an historically generated and historically unfolding universe – transmits itself through time and enters its newest inhabitants largely through words. The concept of the 'world'[4] and many of the higher-level abstractions through which we comprehend or even apprehend the world – 'country', 'duties', 'culture' – do not have an aseity or unity outside of the words that denote and describe them. There is a plane of conception, that is to say, above which most of our dealings with external reality are intra-linguistic. Our knowledge of the world – as well as our sense of there being a boundless but continuous thing called 'the world' – is 'by description' rather than 'by [direct or personal] acquaintance'. We learn the world through being told about it rather than by experiencing it for ourselves. This is true not only of abstract 'observations' such as 'The economic trends are unfavourable' but also of apparently concrete ones such as 'Africa is a hot country'. No life is long enough, no consciousness is large enough to house the empirical experiences corresponding to a statement about a whole continent, a whole country, a whole city or even a whole street. The individual, therefore, encounters much of 'his' world in a linguistically packaged form. The realm of knowledge is verbally organised and access to it is verbally mediated. The reality that any individual inhabits is a vast inverted pyramid of discourse poised on a tiny apex of experience.

What of this apex? Is this free of language? Apparently not. Language is not only a means of transmitting knowledge but also of categorising, and so of making sense of, experience. We make sense of what we experience through our senses by subsuming it under linguistic categories. Though *sensations* may be of particulars, *perception* involves classifying experiences under universal categories, the majority of which will be derived from or enshrined in language. Perception totally divorced from language is severely defective;[5] in extreme cases scarcely able to rise above brute intentional awareness to extensional consciousness of a meaning-ful object out there.[6] In so far as an object is perceived, it enters knowledge and is at least nascently verbalised. Language, then, not only structures higher-order, more general, abstract and explicit, sentential knowledge of the world but also permeates our experience of particulars. The way we perceive the world, the manner in which reality seems to be ordered, the reality that counts as being there – all of these, therefore, will be influenced by 'our native languages'.

So much is incontrovertible. But does it force the conclusion that reality is intra-linguistic and that 'realistic' novels, novels that seem to be 'about' an extra-linguistic reality, are a kind of fraud? Only if one takes the observations made so far to imply that (to use Lacan's famous phrase) 'the world of words creates the world of things'; or that meaning is entirely the product of, or an effect of, language rather than being only expressed or signified in it.

The more radical hypotheses go beyond nominalism – where words and things are only contingently related and there is consequently no extra-linguistic basis for the verbal classification of things – to a curious kind of essentialism: an intra-linguistic or inverted essentialism where it is language rather than reality that is, as it were, calling the shots. We shall come to this shortly. Let us for the present see how the claim that factual reality is relative to language stands up to closer examination.[7]

This relativity thesis was an early post-Saussurean fallacy (we shall discuss why it does not follow from Saussure's ideas presently) and the first generation of structural linguists sought evidence to support Saussure's assertions about the intra-linguistic nature of the signified in the manner in which notional fields were divided up in different languages. Since the thirties, the example most often invoked in support of the structuralist claim that factual reality reflects language rather than vice versa is the vocabulary of colour terms. The spectrum of colours is a continuum but this continuum, it is pointed out, is invariably spoken of and, indeed often experienced, as if it consisted of distinct and discontinuous segments. The segmentation of the visible spectrum varies from language to language: English, for example, has a range of eleven primary terms whereas the Philippine language of Hanunóo makes do with four.[8] This has been taken to imply that the perception and discrimination of even such basic sensory experience as those of colour are determined by one's native language and used to support the more general hypothesis that reality is experienced in accordance with the manner in which it is linguistically structured. We see, or at least discriminate, the spectrum – or the world – 'along lines laid down by our native languages' (see the Sapir–Whorf hypothesis).

More recent comparative linguistic studies[9] have cast doubt on this relativism by suggesting that there is a universal set of eleven colour categories from which individual languages take different sub-sets. This evidence, though it may undermine the Sapir–Whorf hypothesis, is an unnecessary weapon in the attack on structuralism since the linguistic relativity argument collapses under the weight of its own contradictions. The suspiciously well-worn example of colour terms, far from being a decisive case for structuralism, is a conspicuous own goal.

If it *is* a universal property of the human mind or brain to segment reality (or to impose its own segmentation upon reality) and to stabilise that segmentation through language, how could it be possible that (to use Culler's words) 'everyone knows that the spectrum of colours is a continuum'?[10] What do they know it with? Not the brain, nor the mind. Can it be with ESP? And how, furthermore, are they able to *say* (as Culler does) that it is a spectrum? It seems as if the linguistic straitjacket can be taken off at will so that we can inspect it and talk about it and can compare reality as it really is (the continuum of colours) with reality as it is said to be or is conventionally perceived (the segmented spectrum). If we do dissect nature along the lines laid down by our native languages, it would appear that we are not always obliged to do so. There is a core of directly experienced sensation which would seem to be able to bypass – or be the basis for reforming – linguistically mediated knowledge. Moreover, the classification of an object is always provisional. Every particular is available for indefinite reclassification. This is connected with the fact that no real object can be classified, or described, without remainder. That which can be literally seen, felt, bumped into, transcends any classification applied to it: its *haecceitas* transcends its *quidditas*.

One of the key arguments for extreme linguistic relativism would seem, therefore, to be self-defeating: it depends upon our performing what, *ex hypothesi* should be impossible, namely seeing the difference between the world as presented through language and the world as it actually is in itself. Once this distinction has been admitted and, indeed, invoked in favour of linguistic relativism, it must be inconsistent to go on to assert that what counts as reality is, inescapably, determined by the way in which nature is linguistically segmented. The observation that different races of people dissect the same bit of nature differently according to their different native languages presupposes that the same bit of nature can be repeatedly identified *as* the same bit of nature which is being differently dissected. Unless we could identify that 'same bit' independently of language, we would not be in a position to observe how it is articulated in different ways and the evidence crucial to the relativity hypothesis would be simply unavailable. The very fact that there is evidence for the relativity hypothesis constitutes evidence *against* the hypothesis. Moreover, Leech has pointed out that 'even though there is no corresponding concept in one's own language for a concept in another language, one can nevertheless provide a description (if necessary, a very detailed description) of its referents.'[11] We often *say* what it is that 'they' or 'we' do not have a word for.

I do not wish to deny that facts are to some extent relative to language or that the way things are usually spoken of in the linguistic community in which we find ourselves influences even the way we 'directly' perceive things. I am opposed only to the idea that this influence is insuperable, that our native language constitutes a tight mental straitjacket binding us to see reality in a manner that has little relation to the way it really is; that language, rather than non-verbal experience, is paramount in determining the manner in which we perceive what surrounds us. My argument, in short, is against the suggestion that linguistic relativity is absolute and binding and that the structure of reality passively reflects the (autonomous) structure of our language. Culler is able to talk about the continuity of the spectrum and contrast it with the discontinuous, segmented spectrum of discourse, only because reality is experienced directly as well as via language. The sensory colour spectrum is both the basis of and a potential critique of the linguistically segmented one, permitting new cuts to be made. While it may be true that we

> cut up nature, organise it into concepts, and ascribe significance as we do, largely because we are party to an agreement to organise it in this way – an agreement that holds throughout our speech community and is codified in the patterns of our language.[12]

it is *not* true that the terms of the agreement

are ABSOLUTELY OBLIGATORY; we cannot talk at all except

by subscribing to the organisation and classification of data which the agreement decrees.[13]

If it *were* true, this fact could not be noticed – the evidence for it would be simply unavailable – and even less could it be *said*. The linguistic organisation of a piece of reality such as the colour spectrum is not binding – because we have language-independent or perceptual access to it. And the best evidence for this is (to quote Culler) that everybody 'knows that the spectrum of colours is a continuum' – everybody, that is, can appreciate the difference between the sensory and verbal dimensions of reality.

Even in its least radical form, the hypothesis that apparently extra-linguistic reality is so deeply penetrated by language as to be effectively intra-linguistic does not withstand scrutiny in the light of the very facts that are invoked when it is put forward. If the hypothesis were true, the relevant facts could not be noticed and the theory could not be illustrated by example. It might be objected, however, that I have not touched upon the more powerful evidence that comes from a consideration of the nature of language itself. In particular, that I have so far said nothing about Saussure. This is because much of what Saussure has to say bears more closely upon the thesis that language does not reach out to reality (or that discourses create their own second-order realities) than upon the claim that reality itself is intra-linguistic. For this reason, I am postponing discussion of some of his ideas to the section 3.2. There is, however, one place where Saussure may be thought of as advocating the more radical view that reality itself is intra-linguistic; or that it is ordered and differentiated only through the mediation of language.

In the course of the arguments by which he attempts to establish that 'language is only a system of pure values', Saussure asserts in his *Course in General Linguistics*[14] that

> Psychologically our thought – apart from its expression in words – is only a shapeless and indistinct mass . . . without the help of signs we would be unable to make a clear-cut, consistent distinction between two ideas. Without language, thought is a vague, uncharted nebula. There are no pre-existing ideas before the appearance of language. (*Course*, pp. 111–12)

Moreover,

Phonic substance is neither more fixed nor more rigid than thought. It is not a mold into which thought must of necessity fit but a plastic substance divided in turn into distinct parts to furnish the signifiers needed by thought. The linguistic fact can therefore be pictured in its totality – i.e. language – as a series of contiguous subdivisions marked off on both the indefinite plane of jumbled ideas . . . and the equally vague plane of sounds . . . (*Course*, p. 112)

He concludes that

the characteristic role of language with respect to thought is not to create a material phonic means for expressing ideas but to serve as a link between thought and sound, under conditions that of necessity bring about the reciprocal delimination of units. Thought, chaotic by nature, has to become ordered in the process of its decomposition. Neither are thoughts given material form nor are sounds transformed into mental entities; the somewhat mysterious fact is rather that 'thought-sound' implies division, and that language works out its units while taking shape between two shapeless masses. . . .

To consider a term as simply the union of a certain sound with a certain concept is grossly misleading. To define it in this way would isolate the term from its system; it would mean assuming that one can start from the terms and construct the system by adding them together when, on the contrary, it is from the interdependent whole that one must start and through analysis obtain its elements. (*Course*, pp. 112–13)

I have quoted at length because these famous passages have been widely misunderstood and have inspired much erroneous thought about the nature of the relationship between language and reality. The question we must ask ourselves is this: even if everything Saussure here asserts about the intra-linguistic nature of the signifier and the signified were true, would we be obliged to conclude that reality is intra-linguistic?

Consider first what he says about the signified or thought: 'Without language, thought is a vague, uncharted nebula. There are no pre-existing ideas, and nothing is distinct before the appearance of language.' Does this really mean anything more than that outside of language consciousness is not propositional or sentential? If that is what is meant, it hardly amounts to a startling claim; indeed it is self-evident and certainly does not imply an enormous extension of the influence of language in our apprehension of reality. For what are the criteria by which thoughts are judged to be vague or otherwise? They must be linguistic, since assessment of vagueness requires that thoughts shall have been yielded up for public inspection, in other words communicated, and this implies embodiment in language. The same applies to the distinctions between ideas: ideas, perhaps, have distinct boundaries only when they are expressed in distinct sentences; they do not come with their own edges. Moreover, their 'distinctness', like vagueness, can be assessed only when they are made public; that is to say communicated; that is to say uttered or written.

There is an interesting, and revealing, juxtaposition, in the quotation, of 'vague' and 'uncharted'. 'Uncharted' does not of course, imply 'vague': large sections of the universe are uncharted; but this does not mean that they are (in themselves) vague. No; it is our *idea* of them that is vague. In the case of material objects, it is easy to separate the entity from our idea of it; this separation, however, is less readily understood in the case of thoughts, where the degree of vagueness of precision with which they are apprehended is one of the determinants of what the thought actually is. We may not be permitted to imagine thought as being pre-linguistically 'vague' because it is 'uncharted'. In so far as thought exists to the point at which it can be assessed as vague or otherwise, it must be 'charted'. What Saussure probably means is that prior to language consciousness is uncharted experience; and one could legitimately distinguish between the vagueness of consciousness as unarticulated experience and the 'sharpness' of consciousness as explicit and articulated thought.

Be that as it may, the intimate relation between thought and language is not something that would cause even a naïve realist any anxiety. No one, I think, is committed to the position that thoughts and ideas are asemic or that they exist fully developed in an asemic form prior to linguistic expression. The very *criteria* for a completed thought or a formed idea are plausibly linguistic, even grammatical. Prior to language, then, *thought* is indeed uncharted and as for ideas they are not even 'vague'. But it does not follow from this that *consciousness* has no specific objects or that the reality it experiences is undifferentiated. Nor does it follow that pre-linguistic consciousness is 'an indefinite plane of jumbled ideas' or that the reality of extra-linguistic consciousness is a 'shapeless mass' of the ideas that will acquire specificity in language. A child playing football is not, even though he is unaware of the laws of motion, acting in a mental theatre composed of jumbled ideas and vague thoughts that physicists have differentiated and clarified.

The non-revolutionary implications of Saussure's observations about 'the phonic substance' are even more striking. It is perfectly correct that the sounds of language are not intrinsically differentiated to correlate with the concepts. They are not independently derived and then welded on to pre-differentiated concepts. A phoneme is a value within the system and that value, like that of a unit of currency, depends upon its being differentially related to other sound-values. Speech sounds are not noises but bundles of contrasting features and it is the contrast rather than the individual acoustic elements that matter. This is well-illustrated by the fact that if I talk with a hot potato in my mouth, the material elements that go up to make the individual tokens are changed enormously; but the contrasts are retained – all tokens being deformed in the same way – and my speech remains comprehensible.

A vast amount of research into speech production and comprehension carried out in the seventy or so years since the publication of the *Course in General Linguistics* has only confirmed the accuracy of Saussure's assertion that sound operates in language to instantiate a form rather than to be a substance. Phonemes are not, from the purely acoustic point of view, invariants. Indeed, there may be more difference between the frequency spectrograms of two successive realisations of a given phoneme than between the realisations of two different phonemes. Furthermore, not all acoustic parameters are relevant to speech perception nor is what we perceive determined entirely by physical properties of speech sounds. The elegant experiments of Lieberman and his co-workers, conducted over many years, have shown how the perception of speech sounds is crucially bound up with expectations derived from their syntactic and semantic structures.[15] Sound is differentiated within language in a way that is quite different from the manner in which it is differentiated outside of language in the perception of natural sounds.

This – one of the central structuralist points – in fact works against any radically nominalist conclusions. For it implies that we can *see* – and indeed define and measure – this difference. The fact that we cannot map the manner in which sounds are naturally differentiated on to the manner in which they are correlated with meaning and in which they operate within the system of language is itself an indirect reminder that there is an extra-linguistic reality and that it is independent of language – so much so that it can be compared with language. The very contrast between the shapeless mass of sound outside of and the reciprocal delimitation of units within language is itself a reminder of the existence of a language-independent acoustic reality. As for the supposed 'shapelessness', this is only a relative affair; relative, that is to say, to the needs and functions of speech – of an arbitrary mode of signification. Extra-linguistic acoustic reality has of course plenty of non-linguistic shape: it is highly differentiated. We classify sounds according to many features: volume, pitch, sweetness, source, significance, and so on. The non-linguistic universe of sound is exceeded in richness and variety of differential meaning only by that of sight.

There is nothing, then, in Saussure's theories to oblige us to subscribe to the idea that reality is differentiated only through the medium of language. Even so, it is not easy to formulate convincing arguments against extreme claims such as Lacan's assertion that 'It is the world of words that creates the world of things'.[16] It is necessary to do so, however, since his influence upon literary theory, even twenty years after the publication of his opaque *Ecrits*, remains considerable. Catherine Belsey's assertions that 'it is language which offers the possibility of constructing a world of individuals and things, and of differentiating between them',[17] and that words seem to be symbols for things because things are inconceivable outside the system of differences which constitutes the language'[18] are typical of post-Saussurean criticism and reflect the Lacanian perspective in which mangled Saussurean linguistics is fused with ill-founded extensions of Freud's ill-founded theories. Those who are interested in the more detailed arguments against Lacan's psychoanalytic–linguistic structuralism will find a critical examination of the theory of the mirror stage in Chapter 5. Here, I wish only to examine the self-contradictory implications of an extreme and radical nominalism.

The first point to be made is that if Belsey's Lacanian claims
were true, then they should be inexpressible. It is difficult to see
how her world-picture could allow for the existence of the very
meta-language in which she describes the relationship between
language and reality. If there is no outside-of-language, then
there can be no position from which the role of language in
'constructing a world of individuals and things' can be viewed
and described. Lacanian literary theory, that is to say, involves
the speaker in pragmatic self-refutation. Pragmatic self-refutation
seems to be an occupational hazard of post-Saussurean thinkers.
'Pragmatic self-refutation' refers to a situation where the very act
of asserting something provides the best possible counter-example
to what is being asserted.[19] The classic example is the speaker
who says that he cannot speak or that he cannot say a particular
word which he specifies by saying. We shall not dwell on this
here as it has been widely remarked upon by many other writers.
(Though a valid point remains valid even if a hundred pens affirm
it. Some post-Saussureans feel that the charge of pragmatic self-
refutation can be shrugged off *because* it has been made so often.)

The second consideration argues even against nominalism that
falls short of the Lacanian extreme. Lacan, of course, is not
content merely with claiming that the way in which we apply
words to the world is arbitrary, that extra-linguistic reality does
not call the shots when it comes to choosing what to call things
and how to classify things. He goes further and asserts that
language is not only independent of non-linguistic reality but is in
control of it: language is not merely its own master but actually
gives reality its shape, its divisions, its differentiated meanings.
The main objection to nominalism, however, still applies – indeed
applies with increased force – to his super-extreme version. If
there is no basis outside of language for the classification and
division and organisation of the objects it apparently refers to, if
anything can in principle be called anything, why call anything by
any general term in the first place? Why have general terms;
indeed, why have *terms* at all? If there are no extra-linguistic
constraints upon the linguistic groupings of objects, why is it
necessary to have tokens – 'dog', 'church', 'book' – instantiating
different types? Is it merely an inexplicable linguistic habit that
make it impossible for me to hear a belch as meaning, in rapid
succession a kind of lamp-post, the smell of freschias and 'fall-out
shelter'? Manifestly not. Any *individual* object or event can be

made to carry any meaning, to signify any other *individual* meaning or event; but *groupings* and *classifications* are not so arbitrary.

Although, as we shall discuss in Chapter 4, there is considerable latitude in the way we classify and reclassify objects, events and experiences, there are limits and these limits cannot be put down to the linguistic habits and conventions of a particular community. While it would be foolishly essentialist to pretend that every noun, for example, denoted a 'natural kind' – if only because there are many nouns ('day', 'economy', 'bourgeois', and so on) that do not correspond to naturally divided kinds – it would be even more foolish to suggest that language has the sole authority to legislate over the division and articulation of reality. If the world of words really did produce the world of things and if differentiated meanings did not pre-exist language, it would be difficult to see what possible function could be served by a language that discriminated meanings. Surely it is because there is an inescapable differentiation of meaning in the universe – food signifying differently from rocks and both having a different significance from fire or predators – that we have language, and linguistic behaviour has such a powerful influence on the one species that has managed to develop independently of biological evolution and become an historically unfolding as well as an organically evolving creature. If there were no differentiated significances prior to the emergence of language and other modes of signification, if reality were undivided before linguistic segmentation, there would be no purpose in communication. Not only would language be redundant, it would of itself be unable to produce meaning: for how should the production of signs bring (differentiated) meaning into a homogeneous universe?

The case against radical nominalism is, in brief, that unless language is rooted in extra-linguistic reality and has been shaped by it, it is a totally superfluous emission of sound (or ink) and its existence is entirely unexplained. To say this, however, does not imply a commitment to the belief that language passively reflects pre-linguistic, or even physical, reality. The concept of 'starvation' is, in a sense, an abstract category whose boundaries are in part determined by other, surrounding and contrasting, abstract categories. But the difference between starving and being well-fed is not a purely intra-linguistic affair. The suggestion that it *is* owes much to the confusion between: (i) the means by which different meanings are linguistically picked out and those different meanings themselves; and (ii) meaning and reference. We shall return to this in section 3.2.

One obvious way in which reality is cut up extra-linguistically is the spatio-temporal delimitation of individual material things and material events. The visual–tactile world is populated by spatially bounded objects. Their edges are not illusory; nor are they the shadows of semantic edges. The cup from which I have just drunk does not owe its boundaries to its being referred to by a single, temporally delimited, token that happens to be a noun. In addition, there are temporally edged non-linguistic events – such as, for example, non-linguistic sounds. Spatial and temporal edges are not amenable to being changed linguistically by reclassification, even though the unity of certain 'complex' objects may have been linguistically inspired in the first place. It may be, for example, that by calling this object a 'cup' I have picked it out from the background into which it was integrated when it was part of an unfocused sensory field. And the single, temporally delimited verbal token I have used to signify it confers unity upon it. But there is a clear-cut difference between picking out a particular like a cup and picking out 'Liverpool' or picking out 'justice'. In the last case, there is an inescapable coincidence between the borders of the 'object' and the semantic catchment area of a particular word. In the case of the cup, however, spatial boundaries have priority and the object can be dissected out extra-linguistically. Justice, on the other hand, cannot be grasped in the hand and it cannot be thrown across a particular room. Not only can the cup be accessed non-linguistically, but it can be reclassified linguistically in an indefinite number of ways: as part of a set; as 'a nasty cheap import'; as a 'medium-sized object'; as part of someone's estate; and so on. Through all these classifications, it still retains its spatio-temporal identity. Language merely offers a multiplicity of access routes to what remains one and the same referent. The cup retains its difference from a loaf of bread or a brick – even though all three may be classified together as 'contents' (of a house) – as a hungry man could testify.

In practice, even Lacan's wildly speculative (the term is used advisedly) nominalism admits – indeed presupposes – the pre-linguistic reality of spatially edged objects. According to his most widely discussed theory, the infant between the ages of six and eighteen months passes through what he calls 'the mirror stage' which is essential to the formation of the I. Crucial to this phase is the experience of being held up in front of a mirror by its parent – usually the mother. The child sees its own body – and sees it as an integrated whole. Out of this experience arises the intuition of the unity of the self and also of the unity and persistent identity of objects: the subjective reality of the unified self and an external world of permanent objects are born out of the same glance. (No wonder the infant is delighted to catch sight of himself in the mirror!)

> This jubilant assumption of his own specular image by the child at the *infans* stage, still sunk in his motor incapacity and nursling dependence, would seem to exhibit in an exemplary situation the symbolic matrix in which the *I* is precipitated in a primordial form.[20]

One of the crucial features of the mirror stage is the fact that the child is in a state of nursling dependency – is a helpless, indeed shapeless *hommelette* – and yet the image of himself that he receives from the mirror is fixed and stable, anticipating future maturation towards a stable, self-controlled body and ego. If, moreover, the infant's eye is fixed, fixated objects seem stable. It is from this fixity, we are told, and 'the images that are thus produced, that the subject is able to postulate objects of permanence and identity in the world'.[21] The gaze is not quite enough. Language is required to stabilise both the subject and its objects. But it can do so only in an infant who has already received the primordial pre-linguistic intuitions of subjectivity and objectivity in the mirror phase.

Lacan's ideas are discussed in greater detail in Chapter 5. Here we need only notice that Lacan's genetic epistemology requires that the child held up before the mirror should receive a unified image of himself. But this will be guaranteed only if the body he occupies is already objectively unified. Lacan's theory, therefore, presupposes a unified body distinct from the mirror (and from the body of the parent that is holding it up). It also assumes what Husserl would call the 'natural standpoint', an optics, in which object and image are distinct from one another and the fixation of gaze will lead to a corresponding stability of the image of one's own body. In other words, Lacan's claim that 'the world of words creates the world of things' seems to depend upon the presupposition of at least three *things* (infant, mother and mirror) as well as an 'objective' optics, pre-existing any encounter with words. In particular, the unity of the self in the mirror stage, explained as being the result of the introjection of the visual image of an already unified body, antedates any sense of self that may arise from the unification of the self implicit in its universalisation as 'I' – the subject of its own, and others', discourse. The world of things, even in Lacan's scheme, quite clearly pre-exists the world of words.

That there is a pre-linguistic body is accepted by many critics who are prepared to swallow most of Lacan's ideas. Barthes for example writes in *The Pleasure of the Text*, his most Lacanian book: 'Wherever I attempt to "analyse" a text, it is not my "subjectivity" that I encounter but my "individuality", the given which makes my body separate from other bodies and appropriates its suffering or pleasure: it is my body of bliss I encounter.'[22] The reader's response to the text apparently has as its site a pre-linguistically individuated physical body. This body has ideas of its own: 'The pleasure of the text is that moment when my body pursues its own ideas – for my body does not have the same ideas as I do.'[23] Lest Barthes be accused of anhistoric materialism, he adds, however, that the body of bliss 'is also my historical subject'. This is totally incomprehensible but it has the right historicist ring to it.

Once it is conceded that there is a pre-linguistic body, a pre- or extra-linguistic mirror outside of it and a (pre-linguistic) relation of that body to itself mediated by light behaving in accordance with the usual rules of optics, it is difficult to see what grounds there can be for denying the pre-linguistic reality of the rest of the world of material object particulars. What, ultimately, we learn from the mirror stage is that infants infer that there is a world of things because there are things in the world.

Conclusion: Putting Linguistic Relativism in its Place

It is obvious that there are interactions between language and our perception of reality. Through language, the experiences and life-situations of vast numbers of divers individuals can dovetail in a relatively stable intersubjective world. An infinitely complex public reality is made possible. Language is the instrument through which that reality is transformed through history and it is central to the transmission of what *counts* as 'there' from one age to another. These observations do not, however, license the view that factual reality is entirely relative to language or the more radical claim that reality is intra-linguistic.

Language is one of the elements that contribute towards the constitution of reality. It is not, however, the only one; and there is no incontrovertible evidence that it is the most fundamental one. Although the manner in which we perceive the world is strongly influenced by the way it is usually spoken of in our linguistic community, it seems likely that the latter in turn reflects the needs of that community. These, for the most part, will have an extra-linguistic basis. If (to use another suspiciously well-worn example) the Lapps have fifteen different words designating different types of snow, and no general word for snow, whereas Kalahari bushmen have neither, this is not merely an internal fact of the two languages. Nor is it a tribute to the degree to which language shapes our perceptual grids. Rather it indicates the influence of extra-linguistic – in this case climatic – experience and need over the development of language. Their rich snow vocabulary reflects the practical need that Lapland Eskimo have to make certain distinctions in the world in which they find themselves. If it were not for the pre-linguistic climatic realities, and the importance of being able to read and respond appropriately to those realities, the Lapps would have no more words for snow than do Kalahari bushmen. The local richness of the lexicon is a consequence of the physical conditions in which the native speakers live.

Language, to draw the more general point, is rooted in human experience and, ultimately, in the interaction between the needing material organism and the variegated world of material things. It is not, of course, confined to its roots; but the fundamental reality, the reality from which all human lives begin and which no human life ever fully escapes, is the intercourse of one body (the human body) with other human and non-human bodies. Language may mediate in many different ways between consciousness and 'reality' – if only because that which is talked about is that which is collectively acknowledged and so (in one sense of the word) 'objectively' there. But that does not mean that reality is intra-linguistic or that reality has been displaced by language. Language drifts away from reference to concrete objects; it develops its own depths and secondary self-referring realities; but reference to material realities that pre-exist or are independent of language remains the framework of its intelligibility. Whatever internal developments take place within the institution of language, this much remains unchanged. It is the world of things that underwrites the world of words.

3.2 THE CLOSED SYSTEM

for if, as Saussure had argued, the relation between sign and referent was an arbitrary one, how could any 'correspondence' theory of knowledge stand?[24]

If discourses articulate concepts through a system of signs which signify by means of their relationship to each other rather than to entities in the world, and if literature is a signifying practice, all it can reflect is the order inscribed in particular discourses, not the nature of the world.[25]

A language does not construct its formations of words by reference to the patterns of 'reality', but on the basis of its own internal and self-sufficient rules.[26]

All modes of writing have in common the fact of being 'closed' and thus different from spoken language. Writing is in no way an instrument for communication; it is not an open route through which there passes the intention to speak.[27]

No one disputes the principle of the arbitrary nature of the sign but it is often easier to discover a truth than to assign to it its proper place.[28]

(a) Misreading Saussure

We have examined the claim that reality is differentiated only in and through language so that what we experience as the 'extra-linguistic world' is in fact intra-linguistic. An alternative, but complementary, view held by some advanced critics is that, instead of reality being language-enclosed, language is closed off from reality. As we have already indicated, these views converge in the idea that language is cut off from 'nature' but that it does have access to a second-order, intra-linguistic, pseudo-reality.

The most powerful arguments in favour of the idea that natural languages are closed systems – so that they can only apparently be used to make true (or false) referential statements about extra-linguistic reality – originate from popular misreadings of Saussure. The very popularity of these misreadings has added the authority that comes from repetition to the authority these ideas owe to Saussure's justified prestige as a profound thinker about language. In consequence, they are almost unassailable. It is important to appreciate that much of what Saussure says in his *Course in General Linguistics is* hypothetical rather than empirically proven. Although much subsequent research has testified to the soundness of his intuitions and the fruitfulness of the framework provided by his ideas, a good deal remains conjectural. It is still, for example, a *claim* or a *hypothesis* that language is a (unified) system. The system has not yet been described and attempts to uncover a general syntax or a non-fragmentary semantics have been, despite an enormous expenditure of effort, unsuccessful, in some cases spectacularly so. Even so, certain key passages in his *Course* have acquired axiomatic status and they have been deemed to have implications that it is unlikely that Saussure would have himself have accepted.[29]

The essential arguments are too well known to require more than a brief résumé here.[30] Words, Saussure reminds us, are arbitrary signs. 'Cat' does not owe its meaning to a spatio-temporal association between the sounds of its token instances and actual cats. Nor is the connection between the sound and meaning of a word the result of a mutual resemblance: the uttered token 'cat' does not sound like, nor does the written token 'cat' look like, a generalised cat. Linguistic signs do not owe their meanings to a 'natural association' – either of recurrent contiguity or of resemblance – with the relevant portions or types of extra-linguistic reality. More specifically, linguistic signification does not operate through a natural association between a sound-type and a pre-existent natural entity or type: 'The linguistic sign unites, not a thing and a name, but a concept and a sound-image' (*Course*, p. 66). Although they are not linked by an inner relationship, both concept and sound-image are intra-linguistic in that they have distinct existence only within the linguistic *system*. A word is the union of a 'signifier' – defined as a set of contrasting features realised in sound opposed to other contrasting features realised in other sounds – with a 'signified' – defined as a concept whose boundaries are determined by its opposition to other concepts. The signifier and the signified are not *things* but *values*; and they are valorised only within the *system* where they coexist with other opposing or different values.

The most revolutionary aspect of Saussure's theory – and the one that has generated the most misinterpretation – is the denial of the pre-linguistic reality of the signified. The signified is not a 'thing' 'out there'; nor is it a pre-linguistic psychological entity, a concept correlated with a sound. The signified is a purely relational entity:

> The conceptual side of value is made up solely of relations and differences with respect to the other terms of language . . . differences carry signification . . . a segment of language can never in the final analysis be based on anything except its non-coincidence with the rest. *Arbitrary* and *differential* are two correlative qualities.   (*Course*, pp. 117–18)

All of this is true also of the material side of language: a signifier is not a particular kind of sound so much as the realisation of a bundle of features contrasted with other features, a set of phonic differences from other sounds.

Verbal meaning is therefore carried not by a relationship between a particular physical sound and a thing but by the relations between one word and all the others. It is the *differences* between the linguistic units that carry meanings; and the units, defined by such differences, can be grasped only through the network of other such units. At the heart of language is not an external relationship between a particular physical sound and a material thing but an internal relationship between oppositions at the phonetic level and oppositions at the semantic level.

Saussure is credited with putting paid to a naïve labelling theory of language, according to which sounds 'christen' pre-existing referents that somehow manage to be things and meanings at the same time. Language is not (to use Hughlings Jackson's witty phrase) 'a word heap', created piecemeal to label an external 'thing heap'. The insights recorded by his pupils in the *Course* mark a decisive and apparently irreversible shift from what Fries has called an 'item-centred' view of language to a system-centred one and created a linguistics concerned less with the relations between individual words and their seemingly autonomous referents than with the systematic relations between words.

So far so good. Few people would dispute that language is more of a system than a word heap and that its component signs are arbitrary. Words are not, and for the most part could not be, motivated. And it is perfectly obvious that the semantic catchment area of individual forms corresponds neither to patches of space–time nor to 'natural kinds' (or 'types of patches of space–time') but to locations in a multi-dimensional matrix of rival terms. Most people would be prepared to accept that linguistic *value* – either at the level of the signifier or at the level of the signified – is purely negative or differential. The trouble begins when these insights are wildly elaborated without heed even for the distinctions that Saussure himself introduced into theoretical linguistics. A good deal of carelessness is needed in order to secure the transition from Saussure's recognition of the systematic nature of language to the conclusion that language is a *closed* system; from the observation of the arbitrary nature of the linguistic sign to the claim that true reference is not possible; or from the idea that linguistic meaning is carried through values that are essentially differential or negative to the now popular belief that meaning is an *effect* of language or that the meanings carried by language are internal to the linguistic system. We shall spend much of the remainder of this section and Section 3.3 examining this carelessness.

In sketching some of Saussure's ideas, I may have given the impression that the purely negative or differential nature of the signifier and the signified is also shared by words – understood as audible or visible tokens. If I have done so, I shall have misled the reader. Many eminent interpreters of Saussure, however, appear to have been misled in this fashion. Literary theorists tend to use 'sign', 'linguistic sign' and 'word' as if they were synonymous with either the signified or the signifier or both; as if the negative and differential properties of the latter two could be ascribed to all five. This, the essential step in many 'post-Saussurean' misreadings of Saussure, is especially unforgivable since Saussure himself goes to great pains to distinguish them (*Course*, p. 121). Moreover, he develops a further, much reported, distinction in the *Course* between 'langue' and 'parole' which makes it clear that signifiers and signifieds belong to the former – to the system – while actual verbal tokens belong to the latter. It is language that is a pure form without substance; while speech includes at the very least a particular phonic substance. The conclusion that the differential and negative nature of the signifier and the signified implies that discourses have no external reference, that they are non-referential, depends upon a connected, and also elementary, mistake: the identification of signifier and signified with, respectively, sign and referent (see, for example, note 24). Saussure himself *contrasts* the negativity of the signifier and the signified with the *positivity* that results from their fusion in the realised linguistic sign – the actual verbal token as it appears in discourse: 'the statement that everything in language is negative is true only if the signifier and the signified are considered separately; when we consider the sign in its totality, we have something that is positive in its own class' (*Course*, p. 120). The signifier and the signified may be purely relational – indeed, as they can no more exist independently of one another than the recto and verso of a sheet of paper (*Course*, p. 113), they are purely notional – but the sign as a whole, realised and put to use, is none of these things. The intra-linguistic nature of the signified does not compel the characteristic post-Saussurean conclusion that the significate of the sign is intra-linguistic or that the extra-linguistic referent of the sign is illusory. An accurate reading of the *Course* would not authorise the radical nominalism embraced by so many self-styled 'post-Saussurean' critics. Catherine Belsey's claim that 'it is language which offers the possibility of constructing a world of individuals and things and of differentiating between them',[31] is chronologically '*post*-Saussure' but is certainly not *propter* him.

Supposing, however, we allow Saussure to be misread to the extent that the signifier and the signified are identified with sign and significate or (to follow Eagleton's misreading, see note 24) sign and referent, would we then be able to infer that, as a sign apparently owes its meaning to its place in a structured system, extra-linguistic reference is not possible? The answer is no, unless three further assumptions are made:

(i) that all structures or systems are closed;
(ii) that meaning is identical with that in virtue of which it can be specified;
(iii) that meaning is the same as reference.

All of these assumptions are mistaken.

(b)   Are All Structured Systems Closed?

Terence Hawkes begins his influential and much-quoted introduction to structuralist literary theory – *Structuralism and Semiotics* (see note 26) – with a Piagetian analysis of the concept of 'structure'. A structure, he says, is distinguished by 'wholeness' or 'internal coherence'; by having 'transformational procedures whereby it processes the material passing through it'; and by being 'self-regulating', in the sense that 'it makes no appeal beyond itself to validate its transformational procedures'. According to Hawkes, the transformations of a structure

> act to maintain and underwrite the intrinsic laws which bring them about, and to 'seal off' the system from reference to other systems.[32]

A language is, apparently, just such a structure. It

> does not construct its formations of words by reference to the patterns of 'reality', but on the basis of its own internal and self-sufficient rules. The word 'dog' exists, and functions within the structure of the English language, without reference to any four-legged barking creature's real existence. The word's behaviour derives from its inherent structural status as a noun rather than its referent's actual status as an animal. Structures are characteristically 'closed' in this way.[33]

Now it is unclear whether the discussion refers to tokens or types. This fundamental, and elementary, distinction is, however, crucial and Hawkes's failure to observe it makes his 'argument' very difficult to evaluate. If by 'word' he means the type, then he is making an obvious but banal point: of course the *type* cannot refer to a *particular* 'four-legged creature's real existence'. If, however, he intends 'word' to mean tokens or individuals, then his argument seems to depend on a confusion between the system, to which verbal types could be plausibly said to belong, and the use of the system on a particular occasion, when types are instantiated as tokens, which is not itself part of the system. If he hadn't confused the type and the token, the system and its use on particular occasions, it is unlikely that he would wish us to believe that words 'function within the *structure* [my emphasis] of the English language'.

When he talks about 'the word's behaviour', it is not at all certain what he means by 'behaviour'. Of course, the word 'dog' does not behave like a real dog. It doesn't, for example, defecate on the pavement. But this merely rules out of court a crude mimetic theory of language and the equally crude idea that words deputise for objects. Such a theory has not been held seriously outside of Laputa. (We shall return to this point presently.) Outruling this theory, however, has a kind of carry-over effect: it seems to suggest that the word's behaviour in another sense is also unrelated to what is happening in the outside world; in particular to the behaviour of dogs.

The earlier reference to the construction of 'formations of words' certainly hints that 'behaviour' refers to the word's occurrences and to the verbal company it keeps. Does Hawkes then expect us to believe that the occurrences of *tokens* are determined by the 'inherent structural status' of the types? How could any *system* anticipate or dictate the uses to which it is put, the occasions upon which its elements are to be instantiated? How could my use of the word 'dog' now (when our neighbour's dog has been making its usual racket) have been anticipated by the system?

Let us consider three 'formations of words':

The dog is barking.
The dog is quacking.
The dog is reading *Of Grammatology* with pleasure and profit.

The first is very common, the second very rare and the third has probably not appeared in print before. How very like the corresponding situations in life! Are we to imagine that the very frequent co-occurrence of the noun 'dog' and the verb 'to bark' and the relatively infrequent co-occurrence of 'dog' and the verb 'to quack' have nothing to with the former's use to refer to something that has 'the status of an animal'? If we do accept Hawkes's claim that language (and by this one presumes he means language in operation – i.e. 'parole' rather than 'langue') 'does not construct its formations of words by reference to patterns of "reality"', we must surely be at a loss to explain why the transition from 'dog' to '— is barking' has a high frequency in observed speech while those from 'dog' to '— is quacking' or from 'dog' to '— is reading *Of Grammatology* with pleasure and profit' have much lower, or even negligible, frequencies? For if these patterns of co-occurrence have nothing to do with 'patterns of reality', then there should be no reason why we should not encounter the third sentence as frequently as the first. Which is the more likely explanation: that it is a miraculous coincidence that the relative frequencies of these two verbal 'patterns' seem to match the relative frequencies of the corresponding forms of canine behaviour; or that formations of words *are*, after all, constructed (not by language of course but by language users) by reference to patterns of reality?

Of course, we do encounter word patterns that have little correspondence to reality – as in jokes, philosophical arguments about category errors or in grammars or lexicons (where grandmothers, postillions and lightning hobnob in ways that they would not choose to in extra-linguistic reality). But in such cases, the words are not in use: they are being 'mentioned'. The failure to observe the elementary distinction between 'use' and 'mention' – which is almost programmatic for Derrida – is very useful to anyone wishing to claim that there is no connection between words and co-occurrent reality.[34] This is reminiscent of the error of conceiving language as a purely syntactic system, or at least of imagining that it can be treated as if it had a grammar but no semantics.

This error reached epidemic proportions when syntax was given a central, indeed primordial, place in theoretical linguistics by Chomsky. After twenty years of trying to do without semantics, however, linguists are now on the whole agreed that not even syntax can be studied as if it were a set of rules governing the combination of meaningless tokens into strings: a speaker's knowledge of the grammar of his native language can be understood only by taking into account his knowledge of the world in which he uses it. The distinction between well-formed and ill-formed strings or even between one part of speech and another cannot be made on the basis of 'internal' rules of combination. Grammatical rules cannot be specified without explicit or implicit reference to meaning. The 'system' such as it is cannot even begin to be described without reference to its particular operations on specific occasions in the real world. It is my knowledge of extra-linguistic reality, rather than of the internal rules of grammar, that enables me to recognise that 'Golf plays John' is ill-formed. Such observations, along with the acceptance of the fact that there is no purely syntactic method of disambiguating many sentences occurring in ordinary discourse, have made it apparent that Chomsky's methodological tactic of treating language as primarily a syntactic structure has led linguistics to an impasse. It at first created a false sense of progress but has stimulated research programmes that have mainly ended in stalemate. The slow appreciation of the fact that no amount of multiplication of *ad hoc* grammatical rules can guarantee satisfactory disambiguation of all ambiguous sentences (accelerated perhaps by the attempt to implement computer models of language in the development of natural language computers and systems for automated translation) has prompted the realisation that meaning cannot be entirely controlled from within by syntax and that a context-based intuition of the speaker's intentions is necessary not only to determine the meaning but also the grammatical structure of what has been said. There is no syntax without semantics: without interpretation, without meaning, structure cannot be *seen*.

And the same observations apply to structuralist linguistics as a whole. It is ultimately on the basis of referential meaning that the oppositions that make up the field of a particular term are perceived. *The structure cannot be seen, the contrasts cannot be observed, without the referents of the elements being known, without interpretation.* The structuralist principle that 'where there is meaning there is also structure' could just as well be inverted: there is no structure without meaning.

We have touched upon what, in my opinion, is the fundamental flaw of structuralist thought – the incorrect assumption that the 'system' can be defined in isolation from its actual use in specific situations and without reference to extra-linguistic reality. This methodological assumption is responsible for most of the great 'discoveries' of structuralist thought – indeed the 'discoveries' are implicit in it. The manner in which structuralism reduces everything to structure – so that there is no content outside of structure and structure has priority over event – is well shown in the structuralist habit of regarding all experience as experience of binarily opposed signs.

Consider Hawkes's claim that '"Dark" is defined principally by our sense of its opposition to "light", "up" by our sense of its opposition to "down"'.[35] There is a kind of confusing half-truth in this: of course 'dark' and 'light' refer to opposing experiences and to this extent are in part defined by their opposition to one another. This is especially so as they are relative terms – 'dark' meaning 'comparatively dark' and 'light' meaning 'comparatively light'. Nevertheless, dark and light are not themselves defined exclusively or even principally in terms of this relation. The experience of degrees of illumination is not confined to an experience of a pair of symmetrical binary oppositions: the experience of light has a content over and above its formal opposition to the experience of dark. Indeed without the two kinds of experience there would be no basis for the opposition – and there would be no more grounds for seeing 'light' and 'dark' as an opposed pair than there would be for seeing 'light' and 'custard' or 'prime number' and 'Roland Barthes' as opposed pairs. And we would not recognise 'black' and 'white' as opposed without interpreting the two terms. It is experience, rather than language, that underwrites the opposition between the two terms. The meaning of even such obviously opposed terms as 'light' and 'dark' is only in part determined by their linguistic opposition. They may divide the semantic patch between them through having a common border (so that whatever is taken from the one is donated to the other) and give each other semantic shape through their mutual pressure. But this must not be taken to imply that *meanings*, even less *referents* are those borders, are that pressure. It is only (notional) values, not meanings or referents, that are pure edges or borders, without content. For the opposition between light and dark is based on previously intuited meanings in turn rooted in actual extra-linguistic experience. It is referential content and extra-linguistic experience that account for the intuitive appeal of most of the examples used to support the structuralist case for denying content and replacing reference and experience with form and contrast.

It is a structuralist commonplace that the *system* allocates meanings to words because 'there is no meaning without structure'. But I would say that precisely the opposite is at least as true: there is no perceptible structure without intuitions of meaning. Similarly, one can invert the other structuralist principle that 'where there is meaning there is also difference' and suggest that the nature of those differences is not clearly distinguishable from differences of meaning, in turn related to actual or possible differences of experience. At any rate, meaning does not reside solely in the differences (structure, contrast, and so on). Although 'green' is different from 'blue', these terms refer to experiences that go beyond the mere contrast between them. The experience of green is not merely experience of not-blue – or of everything that is not-not-green. And the same applies to the terms that refer to those experiences: they, too, have content as well as form, content as well as boundaries.

Structuralism aims ultimately to reduce everything – at the level of both signifier and signified – to contrast and, in the end, to reduce the entirety of language to the correlate of a single mental operation. It seems to achieve this aim by concentrating upon, and misreading, terms such as 'light' and 'dark' which have a relative meaning and also by making much of secondary developments – codes such as the Highway Code and that of the colours in traffic lights – and ignoring the fact that they are predicated upon more fundamental primary experiences. By paying disproportionate attention to contrasting terms, it gives the impression that the meaning of all terms may be reduced to contrasts. By focusing excessively on terms such as 'light' and 'dark', it gives the claim that most contrasts are 'binary oppositions' a temporary plausibility – though even favourite examples such as the elements of 'the colour system' could hardly be described as 'binary' – and then proceeds to suggest that, as all sign systems reduce the continuum of reality to sets of binary oppositions, this is a fundamental property of the human mind. It is no such thing. If it were, it would not be thinkable by or evident to the mind. No, it is only the fundamental fiddle of structuralist 'thought'.

We could summarise structuralism as the endeavour to see the whole of discourse – and since it denies its independence of discourse – the entirety of reality, to one kind of relation between entities. Experience is incorporated into discourse and discourse is reduced to system-values; values in turn are differences, or differences from difference; the whole of signifying and signified reality becomes a kind of double negation or absence. This – the reduction of reality to differing difference and of structuralism to absurdity – is the road taken by Derrida. This should have spelt the end of structuralism when, instead, all it has done is to inaugurate post-structuralism and to encourage even deeper misreadings of Saussure.

Let us now return to Hawkes's more specific claim that

'language' constructs its 'formations of words' without reference
to 'patterns of reality'. In practice, language does not construct
anything. In so far as *speakers* construct 'formations of words' they
do so by reference to 'patterns of reality'. At the very least, this is
because discourse is inescapably rooted in such reality – in the *hic
et nunc* context of the utterance. Thus much is implied by Hawkes
later in his book: 'What "shifters" indicate, of course, is the extent
to which *all* meaning is context-sensitive and the limited access to
so-called General Meaning that any communication can have.'[36]
What shifters – 'I', 'you' and so on – indicate is that the system
operates in a real world and that its referents are finally clinched
by the mobilisation of implicit or explicit deictic co-ordinates. Meaning
arises out of the interaction between system and context. These matters
are of immense significance and they have been universally overlooked or misunderstood by structuralist and post-structuralist writers.

Such considerations are perhaps too abstract and they distract
from the fact – obvious when the elementary distinction between
token and type is observed – that 'formations of words' produced
on particular occasions – and all words are produced on particular
occasions – *are* 'constructed by reference to patterns of reality'. Or
is it an extraordinary coincidence that when my neighbour
overhears a dog barking in the street he says 'There's that dog
barking in the street again'? Of course it is not; and the truth of
the relationship is so obvious that there must be more to Hawkes's
mistake than a failure to distinguish between token and type (at
the level of the individual word) and 'langue' and 'parole' (at the
level of discourse).

The word 'behaviour' may provide the diagnostic clue: 'the
word's behaviour derives from its inherent structural status as a
noun rather than its referent's actual status as an animal'. Would
we expect a word to behave like its referents? Clearly not. Does
anyone claim that the word 'dog' barks, pees on the floor or gets
under my feet? Not even the mythical straw men of the anti-
realist case – those sad creatures who are reputed to believe that
words are proxies or deputies for things and that reference takes
place by replication of the referent in miniature so that discourse
is a kind of Lilliput[37] – expect or claim this. But the difference
between the word's behaviour and that of its referents – the type
'dog' is instantiated, while actual dogs bark; 'dog' tokens associate
with other tokens while dogs prefer the company of dogs – hardly
counts as a case against the referential nature of language. Even

pre-linguistic modes of signification do not operate by mimicry. In pointing, neither the pointer nor the act of pointing behaves or looks like the pointee but no one would conclude that pointing was a closed system, sealed off from its 'referents'. The failure of the word 'dog' to pee or bark like real dogs and its preference for the company of words over that of dogs is an argument not against the referential nature of verbal discourse but against a mimetic or 'deputy' theory of language that perhaps only the Laputans, and the early Wittgenstein before he converted to nominalism, have ever held.[38]

The most interesting of Hawkes's erroneous assumptions is that an ordered, structured or self-regulating system is necessarily sealed off from reference to other systems, from whatever is outside of itself. This is best assessed by considering non-linguistic systems. One highly ordered, highly structured, self-regulating system is the nervous system. This is of course a sub-system within a co-ordinated set of such systems constituting the human body. The nervous system has wholeness – its function culminates in the moment of consciousness; it has rules of internal transformation, which have been described in great detail, at synapses, sense endings, in the cerebellum and in the cerebral cortex; and it is the supreme instance of a self-regulating system, subserving the almost miraculous self-regulation or homeostasis of the body as whole. These features are in fact more incontrovertibly present in the nervous system than they are in language.[39] Is the brain therefore 'sealed off' from extra-cerebral reality? Of course not. Precisely the opposite is the case: the brain is that by virtue of which the body is open to an outside world – is explicitly 'worlded'. And it is the *structure* of the brain, perhaps the supreme instance of a structure that preserves itself, which gives the nerve impulses (which are otherwise merely the passage of sodium ions through leaky membranes) their value as *signals*. It is no exaggeration to say that it is the very structure of the nervous system that creates the condition for there being *explicit* outsideness, a consciousness of extra-cerebral reality. Instead of blocking access to or genuine openness to the environment, the structure permits the events provoked in the brain by the environment to become the basis of the body's being explicitly environed.

This is not to imply that the brain simply reflects or in some way replicates reality. How could it? Electro-chemical activity could scarcely mirror smells, touches, and so on. Two handfuls of porridge – a not inaccurate description of the cerebral hemispheres – could hardly be expected to reflect a landscape. But no one is going to suggest that the events that take place in the brain are uninfluenced by external reality or that our brains do not give access to a common or public reality. For if there were no such reality, it would be strange that I should somehow get to know of and be able to quote from Hawkes's book. The suggestion that *Structuralism and Semiotics* is a coinage of my brain is not merely mildly insulting but also one that leads directly into solipsism and for that reason not worthy of discussion. For the suggestion itself would, if true, also be a coinage of my brain and there would seem to be little point in involving the general public in a metaphysically private, internal debate between one part of my left hemisphere and another.

Behind the idea that language is somehow closed off from reality so that it refers to nothing other than itself is a confusion between structure and event, between the system or institution and its use in discourse. The structure of the brain determines that patterns of nerve impulses shall have significance – that they shall refer to or have as their intentional object the things and events that occasioned them. But those patterns of impulses are not themselves determined by the structure of the brain; they are not endogenously generated without regard to the world impinging on the brain. Or, rather, they are only atypically so, as in epilepsy or other abnormal brain states. In the usual course of events, the structure of certain parts of the brain transforms nerve impulses into perceptions of the objects that have triggered off those impulses.[40] Structure, in other words (and to reiterate what we have said already), is a *condition* of the openness of the brain; it does not seal it off from reality but rather enables its response to extra-cerebral events, its place in the chain of happenings, to become an openness to a reality. *How* this happens is totally mysterious; but it must not on this account be denied. Analogously, the structure of language, which permits verbal sounds to become meanings does not close speech off from extra-linguistic reality. Of course, the structure of language is not altered by moment-to-moment changes in reality; but the choice of and the combination of words is. My choice of words will be influenced by what I want to refer to. Hawkes is quite right to say that *language* does not construct its formations by reference to patterns of reality. The institution does not change with every changing circumstance any more than the brain's wiring is altered radically by every event that impinges on it. Moreover, it is language users who put together specific formations of words. Language itself (an abstract construction if ever there was one) is not a language user; it is not an agent; it has neither the capacity nor the need to refer to anything. Hawkes's conclusion that language is sealed off from reality because it is structured is due ultimately to a confusion between the institution, the system, the structure called language, and the use of that system by individual speakers and writers in particular discourses that take place at a particular time.[41]

To summarise, if the systematic nature of language implies that it must be cut off from extra-linguistic reality, then the systematic nature of nervous activity should also imply that it bears no relation to extra-neuronal reality. To maintain the latter is to fall straight into solipsism. And with the advent of solipsism, all discussion, structuralism and Terence Hawkes himself become mere figments of my imagination.

(c) Is Meaning Identical with that by Virtue of which Meaning Can be Specified?

Some literary theorists tend, as we have seen, to confuse 'langue' and 'parole', the type and the token, the institution of language with specific discourses. An especially common and serious consequence of this confusion is the conflation of the idea of a word as a value or set of values within the system with the meaning of a word used on a particular occasion, that by virtue of which verbal meaning is specified with verbal meaning itself or, indeed, meaning *per se*. While there may be some validity, for example, in Trier's conception of the semantic field and his assertion that 'the meaning of lexical elements is specified only by their relatedness to and their difference from other relevant elements',[42] to progress from this to the claim that meaning is therefore entirely a matter of the relationship between terms is to confuse that by virtue of which words signify with that which they signify. This is well illustrated in the following quotation from Belsey:

> If discourses articulate concepts through a system of signs
> which signify by means of their relationship to each other

rather than to entities in the world, and if literature is a signifying practice, all it can reflect is the order inscribed in particular discourses, not the nature of the world.[43]

If this is *how* signs signify, then this is *what* they signify: thus the fallacy.

Some writers – notably Barthes – consciously embrace this fallacy as a principle. According to Barthes, 'language is the domain of *articulations*, and the meaning is above all a cutting-out of shapes'.[44] The generation of linguistic meaning, and indeed what is meant linguistically, is identified with the definition or specification of meanings. Meaning resides in the edges between rival meanings: it is all form and no content. Derrida takes this even further[45] and states that since meaning gets specified through difference, and there is no specific meaning without difference, meaning *is* difference. This is of course untrue, as consideration of a couple of examples will make plain.

Let us again consider colours and colour terms. The notational system that isolates colours and places them in opposition to one another or makes their oppositions explicit by stabilising them and separating them from coloured objects does not account for or generate all that is different between the colours, does not subsume all of their content. Colour words can be placed in any order and they can be paired off in any way to produce similar seeming oppositions: black is opposed to white, green is opposed to blue, and so on. In addition to their opposition, which is negative, there is the positive experience of these colours. Now this experience dictates that certain colour pairs share a common boundary and others do not. Blue is next to green, as is evident from the fact that there is no definite point at which the one begins and the other ends. We may be uncertain as to whether an object is blue or green – whether it is bluish-green or whether it is greenish-blue – and assigning it to one or the other may be regarded as a linguistic decision. Blue is not next to orange in the way that green is: there is no shared border between the two. This is not, however, a matter of linguistic but of experiential content corresponding to the term. Meaning, in the case of colour terms, reaches beyond negativity and oppositions to positive content. That is why, if I invented a new colour term 'reen', you would not know what its meaning was unless there were a colour experience corresponding to it. Its opposition to all other colour terms would be ensured independently of any experience but its position in the spectrum would remain undecided until the corresponding experience had been granted.

Consider another pair of opposed terms: 'edible' and 'poisonous'. These oppositions are clearly not conterminous with the boundaries of naturally occurring kinds; or not, at least, to types of spatio-temporal individuals. The classification is a higher-order one, involving a considerable degree of abstraction, and it is difficult to imagine the terms emerging except as parts of a semantic field that included both of them. Their meaning, however, does not end with the differences between them: they have positive *content* as well as differential *form*. 'Poisonous' embodies an oppositional value; but when it is used on a particular occasion, it signifies more than its opposition to edible. If the difference between edible and poisonous were simply a matter of opposing linguistic values, then it could be eliminated by proscribing certain sections of the language.[46]

What is the general conclusion to be drawn from these two examples? It is that value must not be confused with significance and that neither alone is sufficient to establish meaning. Curiously, this was fully acknowledged by Barthes at about the time when he was most taken with structuralist concepts. In *The Elements of Semiology*, he expounds Hjelmslev's schema for the analysis of the linguistic sign with approval. The schema recognises, on the plane of the signified, not only a *form* of content ('the formal organisation of the signifieds among themselves through the absence or presence of a semantic mark') but also a *substance* of content ('this includes, for instance, the emotional, ideological, or simply notional aspects of the signified, its "positive" meaning').[47] This represents a striking retrenchment from the classical structuralist identification of meaning with difference and the belief that meaning is entirely negative, that it resides in oppositions and contrasts, that it is purely a matter of form rather than of content. Elsewhere in this short book he is able to maintain both that 'the words in the field derive their *meaning* only from their opposition to one another (usually in pairs)'[48] and that 'meaning is truly fixed only at the end of this double determination: signification and value [my italics]'.[49] The latter view seems to make intuitive sense. To take the analogy of the currency, value refers to the relationship between different denominations while signification refers to that for which money can be exchanged. Signification partakes of the substance of the content while value partakes of its form. While the units in the lexical field derive their *value* from their opposition to another, their *meaning* is completely determined only in relation to a particular act of signification.

That differences or the system of differences transform sounds into values permitting the verbal expression of meaning does not imply that the differences or the system are what is meant, any more than it implies that the (in themselves meaningless) sounds are what is meant. The system apportions potential meanings or the capacity for carrying meaning between signs but does not fully determine the meaning a sign may have on a particular occasion. Even if we were to accept Saussure's view that the status of the signifiers as values makes them pure forms whose content is immaterial, this would not oblige us to believe the same of *the sign considered as a totality*.

If this distinction had been kept in mind by many structuralists, then it would not have been possible for them to confuse that by virtue of which a sign signifies (its value plus, as we shall discuss presently, its textual and non-linguistic context) with that which it signifies (its meaning or its reference). The system may be one of the things that makes value-mediated verbal meaning possible but it is not that which is meant. Language, or discourses, are not therefore non- or self-referential. More specifically, Saussurean linguistics does not license the view that the meaning of a discourse – literary or otherwise – is the sum of its differences from other discourses, or Belsey's view that all that literature 'can reflect is the order inscribed in particular discourses, not the nature of the world', that verbal communication is closed off from extra-linguistic reality. Even less does it entitle us to conclude that literary or other discourses are non-referential.

(d)   Is Meaning the Same as Reference?

The most discussed aspect of post-Saussurean literary theory, and the one most pertinent to the attack on realism, is the denial of extra-linguistic reference. Reference, it is claimed, is internal to language; if language is about anything, it is about itself: 'Criticism has taken the very idea of "aboutness" away from us. It has taught us that language is tautological, if it is not nonsense, and to the extent that it is about anything it is about itself.'[50] We have seen how the belief that meaning is internal to language depends upon muddling *value* and *meaning* (or the system and its use, 'langue' and 'parole', type and token). The idea that reference is internal to language depends upon treating *meaning* and *reference* as if they were the same. But meaning and reference are not identical; so that even if meaning were internal to language, it would not follow that reference was. An expression may secure a reference through its meaning but the two must be kept distinct. Ultimately, reference is to particulars; whereas meaning is inevitably general. At least the linguistic contribution to meaning must of necessity be so, otherwise meaning could not be conveyed.

The separation of meaning from reference and the delineation of the inter-relationships between them has been a major theme in modern philosophy of language since Frege's seminal paper.[51] Overlooking this distinction has been an equally major theme in modern Continental philosophy. (Chapter 6 of Derrida's book on Husserl[52] shows this great Continental tradition in its purest form.) In *On Sense and Reference*, Frege discussed the implications of the fact that two or more expressions with different meanings may have the same referent. 'The Morning Star' and 'The Evening Star' are two such expressions: they clearly have different meanings (or, to use Frege's term, 'senses') though the star in question is the same in both cases. There is an indefinite number of different descriptive terms that we may use to refer to a particular object or event. Referring expressions with different meanings may be thought of as alternative routes to the same destination.[53] Conversely, an unlimited number of referents may answer to a referring expression with a certain meaning. No description, however elaborate, will be sufficient of itself to secure unique reference to a particular. In so far as an expression is meaningful, it will be general – there will be some determinables left incompletely determined – and there will always be the possibility that more than one object may answer to it.

Ultimately, the transition from the (general) meaning of a referring expression to the particular, unique referent will involve utilising the context of the utterance in which the expression occurs. A significant part of this context will be the deictic or spatio-temporal co-ordinates of the act of utterance. Without the existential situations of speakers and hearers to provide an extra-linguistic point of reference, inescapably general meaning could not be used to pin down reference to unique particulars. Without the 'thisness' implicit in the fact that the utterance is originating

from a particular body, a particular mouth, and that it is being
emitted into a particular shared world whose co-ordinates could
be at least in part specifiable in spatio-temporal terms, reference
would remain indeterminate – or, more precisely, would not take
place.

Reference is, therefore, two steps away from value and the
'system'. A referent is not a position in the feature-grid. Words
have first to be combined to form sentences[54] and, although there
are both structural (or syntactical) and statistical constraints upon
the manner in which words are combined, not all permissible
word combinations could be anticipated, even less defined, by the
system, as the failure of the Chomskian programme (referred to
earlier) eloquently demonstrates. Moreover, word and sentence
combinations are used in particular situations. As Wittgenstein
says (admittedly exaggerating and simplifying on this occasion),
'an expression has reference only in the stream of life'.[55] In the
stream of life, deictic co-ordinates that have *nothing* to do with the
system are mobilised. Without the implicit or explicit deixis of the
utterer's or writer's situation, and his existential particularity, the
truth or falsity conditions of his utterance would remain
unsaturated and meaning would be determined only down to a
level above that at which it passes over into reference.

The difference between reference and meaning is brought out
by the fact that the possession of meaning by a referring
expression is not dependent upon the existence of a corresponding
referent. 'The Golden Mountain' is not meaningless simply
because there never have been any golden mountains.[56] Moreover,
there are many words that influence or contribute to meaning
which clearly do not have referents – for example, logical
connectives such as 'or', 'and' and so on. Other terms may have
reference but no corresponding spatio-temporally bounded
particular referents. One such term is a deictic shifter such as
'today'. Inasmuch as it is part of a system of opposed terms –
today versus tomorrow versus yesterday – it is a pure meaning,
or even a pure value, without reference. But when it is used in
conditions that would mobilise the implicit deictic co-ordinates of
the speaker and/or listener, it will have a specific referent. Yet
other terms have reference but only incidental or epiphenomenal
meanings that certainly would not fit into a system of binarily
opposed values. Proper names, for example, have meanings that
accrue independently of any system of paradigms: their denotative

meanings are such as even the most optimistic binarist could not hope to assimilate to any system; and any other meanings they have are connotative – encyclopaedic rather than lexicographic – and do not influence the term's status as a value.

Proper names, whose referential function is achieved with the minimum of, or no, meaning,[57] not only demonstrate most clearly the distinction between meaning and reference but also underline how the arbitrariness of a sign – and what could be more arbitrary than a proper name ('Bertha' could be made to label a woman, a gun, a ship, a dog, a hurricane, a particle accelerator . . .)? – does not prevent it from having extra-linguistic reference. (On the contrary, arbitrariness is one of the conditions for the full emergence of reference. Natural signs are too closely implicated in the processes they signify to remove to the distance from which reference is possible.) This is not to imply that language is a heap of terms that operate like proper names, but only that 'reference' and 'the system' are not as inextricably intertwined as most structuralist critics seem to assume. Barthes's claim that 'where there is meaning there is also system'[58] would not, even if it were true, license the conclusion that where there is reference there is also system. Where there are values in the Saussurean sense, there must also be system; but reference is not always mediated through value; and, as we have shown, reference cannot be realised solely through the system. *The system* has no referents; reference, if it utilises the system at all (rather than bypassing it by using ostensively defined proper names), must also involve the extra-linguistic reality within which the system is operating at the time; the deictic co-ordinates that are implicit in the spatio-temporal context of the utterance.

Barthes's assertion that 'where there is meaning there is also system' is, of course, *not* true. Natural signs have meaning but it would be difficult to sustain the claim that they belonged to or formed a system. It is not through belonging to or instantiating a set of differential markers that clouds mean rain. To suggest that natural signs *are* systematised in the way that a language is would be to go against the whole trend of Saussurean thought and to ignore Saussure's fundamental distinction between arbitrary, conventional signs and natural, motivated ones – between the way in which clouds mean rain and 'clouds' means clouds.

Experiences do not owe their meaning to their place in a closed or identifiable system. The difference between the experience of being kissed and being struck on the head with a crow-bar is not solely the result of their oppositional relationship to one another, even though these experiences may owe their different significances partly to semiotic conventions and the different descriptions they attract in system-based languages.

(e) Conclusion

The popular idea that language is somehow sealed off from extra-linguistic reality and that true reference is not possible is dependent upon at least three incorrect assumptions. The first is that all structured systems are in some sense closed, so that if, as Saussure showed, language is a system, then language is closed. The example of the nervous system was sufficient to dispose of the claim that structure seals a system off from whatever is external to it. The second is that if the instruments by which meaning gets specified are internal to the system, then meaning is itself internal to the system. More specifically, if meaning is carried by values (differences from other differences), and these are internal to the system, then meanings are also internal to, or a product of, the system. This assumption – that the vehicle by which meaning is carried is the meaning – is recognised to be incorrect as soon as it is made visible. It depends upon a conflation of the idea of the system itself and that of the use of the system on particular occasions and a rejection of one of the very distinctions that is fundamental to structuralist linguistics – between 'langue' and 'parole'. Finally, in order to pass from the observation that language is a system to the post-Saussurean critique of referential realism, a third assumption is necessary: that meaning is the same as reference, so that if meaning is intra-linguistic, then so also is reference. We have, I think, given adequate reasons for asserting that meaning and reference are distinct.

It might be appropriate to end this section, which began with a disagreement with Hawkes, by showing how, within the compass of his very small book, he profoundly disagrees with himself. It will be recalled that, in the early pages of *Structuralism and Semiotics*, the reader was informed that 'a language does not construct its formations of words by reference to patterns of "reality" but on the basis of internal and self-sufficient rules'. Elsewhere in the book, however, he tells us that: 'A poem consists, less of a series of referential and verifiable statements about the "real" world beyond it, than of the presentation and sophisticated organisation of a set of complex experiences in a verbal form' (p. 152). Reference to 'experiences' (albeit 'complex' – but then what experience is not complex?) hints at a retreat from the idea that words in the text have nothing to do with anything outside of the text. For experiences must be experiences of something and if they *are* of anything – rather than of nothing – it is surely likely that they are rooted in extra-linguistic reality. And if what is being presented 'in verbal form' *is* so rooted then surely the latter must influence the words that appear in the poem. This being the case . . . but the reader can guess the rest.

This half-way position prepares us for a startling volte-face when, in his seemingly sympathetic account of Jakobson's pronouncements, Hawkes informs us with the insistent authority typical of all his sweeping statements that 'all languages contain grammatical elements which have no precise meaning *per se*, and which are wholly sensitive to the *context*' (p. 83). Amongst these elements are 'shifters' which, apparently, 'indicate the extent to which *all* meaning is context-sensitive' (p. 84). He goes on to say that

if the communication is orientated towards *context*, then the *referential* function dominates, and this determines the general character of a message . . . which aims to refer to a context beyond itself, and to convey concrete, objective information about that. This seems to be the leading task of most messages. (p. 85)

which is really what most of us had thought all along.[59]

3.3 THE ENDLESS CHAIN OF SIGNIFIERS

Of course, since writers use words . . . their art must in the end be composed of signifiers without signifieds.[60]

With the second property of the signifier, that of combining according to the laws of a closed order, is affirmed the necessity of the topical substratum of which the term which I ordinarily use,

*namely, the signifying chain, gives an approximate idea: rings of
a necklace that is a ring in another necklace made of rings.*[61]

*From the moment there is meaning, there are nothing but signs.
We think only in signs. Which amounts to ruining the notion of
the sign at the very moment when, as in Nietzsche, its exigency
is recognised in the absoluteness of its right. One could call play
the absence of the transcendental signified as the limitlessness of
play, that is to say as the destruction of ontotheology and the
metaphysics of presence.*[62]

*Japan is a country full of rich and intriguing signifiers whose
charm is that they have no signifieds.*[63]

*Literary studies, in other words, are a question of the signifier,
not of the signified.*[64]

The [signifier] is purely a relatum, *whose definition cannot be
separated from that of the signified.*[65]

*in language one can neither divide sound [signifier] from thought
[signified] nor thought from sound.*[66]

Saussure made it plain that the signifier could not be separated
from the signified. Signifier and signified are like the recto and
verso of a sheet of paper: they are cut out at the same time and
the act that differentiates the one necessarily differentiates the
other. As Sturrock has expressed it: 'Signifiers and signifieds can
be separated only by theorists of language; in practice they are
inseparable. A truly meaningless sound is not a signifier because
it does not signify – there can be no signifier without a signified
. . . there can be no signified without a signifier.'[67] Or, as Saussure
said 'one can neither divide sound from thought nor thought from
sound; the division could be accomplished only abstractedly, and
the result would be pure psychology or pure phonology' (*Course*,
p. 113). In view of such clear statements, it is rather surprising that
there should be a prominent strain of thought – especially evident in
Barthes, Lacan and Derrida – claiming to be 'post-Saussurean',
which begins from the assumption that the linguistic sign is
essentially a signifier and one that is so enfeebled that it cannot even
reach out to its own signified, never mind to a proper extra-linguistic

referent. Indeed, Barthes severely disapproves of those who think otherwise, condemning the belief that a text is anything more than a galaxy of signifiers as a sympton of the 'bourgeois' mentality. 'The bourgeois sign is a metonymic confusion.'[68]

This anti-Saussurean use of Saussure's concepts has been a potent force in shaping contemporary literary theory. The case against realism rests, as we have seen, at least in part on the belief that linguistic signs cannot reach out to extra-linguistic reality. This case must be greatly strengthened if linguistic signs are not even able to cross the distance from signifiers to signified; for then any novel that suggests that it is more than black marks on a white page must be an illusionist fraud. An authentic work of literature should show the truth about language – that its signifiers are cut off from its signifieds. Such a work would be a 'free play of signifiers'; at the very least, so riddled with *verfremdungeffekts* as virtually to dismantle itself before the reader's eyes. Brecht's works are considered to be exemplary in this respect. They postulate 'that today at least drama has not to express the real so much as to signify it. It is therefore necessary that there be a certain distance between signifier and signified'.[69] As a prescription, this is not only self-contradictory (the first sentence contradicts the second), and faintly absurd, but also one that would render drama superfluous. For if the failure of the signifier to reach the signified were the *norm* of language, no particular use of language could demonstrate it. Nothing would distinguish one text from another: every sequence of verbal sounds on silence, every chain of black marks on white paper would mean the same nothing. And the illusion that it meant something would be unbreakable; for no specific set of linguistic signs could be made specifically to *mean* the fact that such signs have meaning only as the result of an illusion.

The confusion that has led from Saussure's observations on the arbitrariness of linguistic signs to the belief that signifiers cannot reach out even as far as signifieds, so that discourse is an endless chain of signifiers, is most painstakingly elaborated in Derrida.[70] The underlying mistake is one we touched upon in the previous section – that of merging linguistic value (and signifiers and signifieds are values) with meaning and, more seriously, with reference. We have already shown how the latter cannot be assimilated to the former but it is interesting to see how Derrida persuades himself that they can.

In his famous essay *Differance*, he argues that 'as the condition for signification, this principle of difference affects the whole sign, that is, both the signified and the signifying aspects'.[71] And he infers that the sign as a whole evaporates to pure differences: 'the play of differences . . . prevents there from being any moment or in any way a simple element that is present in and of itself'. Language is riddled with absence; and meaning – as it is carried by a particular discourse – being also a matter of difference is therefore an *effect* of language rather than pre-existing it and being expressed in it.

The argument is of course seriously flawed. It is not true that if the signifer and the signified are *separately* purely negative or differential, that the sign as a whole is; and even less that its meaning in use or its reference is. Nevertheless the arguments proceeds from there: if the sign as a whole is negative, then that which is referred to is also negative, differential; it is, that is to say, like a signifier. Hence discourse never reaches outside of itself, but is an 'endless chain of signifiers'. This argument is put especially clearly – and so especially vulnerably – by Jonathan Culler[72] who asserts that 'it follows from the purely differential, non-substantial nature of the sign that the difference between signifier and signified cannot be one of substance and that what we may at one point identify as a signified is also a signifier'. Since signifier and signified are purely negative, then the sign also is purely differential and its reference is purely differential too. Since being 'purely differential' is a feature of both signifier and signified, these are not 'substantially' different and so the signified is really a signifier.

Thus the argument. It is difficult to imagine how Saussure could be more completely traduced. And almost as difficult to see how the argument could have carried conviction, never mind been the foundation stone of a major strain in contemporary thought. In order that the conclusions drawn from this muddle should carry conviction, a smokescreen is necessary; this is created by a marvellously ambiguous term: 'the transcendental signified'.

'The transcendental signified' is used, variously, to mean: the signified; the meaning of a sign; the referent of a chain of signs in use; or the ultimate termination of the chain of signs – in plenitude or closure of meaning, in absolute presence or in God. Anyone who believes in the reality of the signified is thereby committed to taking on board 'onto-theology and the metaphysics of presence'.[73]

To believe in the signified is to believe in the transcendental signified and to believe in the transcendental signified is to believe that the chain of signs comes to an end, that a final meaning can be reached and that the place where the latter is reached or achieved is identical to that in which signs give way to absolute presence – to believe, in other words, in God, Who is both absolute presence and final meaning. Since most contemporary readers are liable to be atheists and since, too, Husserlian 'absolute presence' is so elusive,[74] merging the idea of the signified with that of the *transcendental* signified is certain to discredit the former and to give plausibility to the idea that discourse is an endless chain of signified-less signifiers. The concept of the 'transcendental signified' enables Derrida to move almost imperceptibly from the position that no sign opens directly on to a plenitude of meaning/presence, i.e. is underwritten by God, to the claim that there is no signified at all, or none, anyway, that the linguistic signifier can reach out to.

The transition takes place so quickly in *Of Grammatology* that the reader is liable to miss the steps by which it is effected and, as so many appear to have done, to take the result on trust. Derrida sets out from Peirce's definition of a sign as 'Anything which determines something else (its interpretant) to refer to an object to which itself refers (its object) in the same way, this interpretant becoming in turn a sign, and so on ad infinitum. . . . If the series of successive interpretants comes to an end, the sign is thereby rendered imperfect, at least' (quoted in *OG*, p. 50). Signs are interpreted and interpretation generates other signs: one sign leads to another. The chain of signs is endless; or, rather, it terminates only where it breaks down, where interpretation generates something that resists interpretation – that is, in other words, unintelligible. The paw marks on the ground mean the lion; the lion means danger; danger means, and so on.

The chain of signs is not only endless but also beginningless, since signs tend to originate out of signs. Peirce again: 'If a man makes a new symbol, it is by thoughts involving concepts. So it is only out of symbols that a new symbol can grow. Omne symbolum de symbolo' (quoted in *OG*, p. 48).

All well and good: the beginningless and endless chain of signs is but the coherence of the world made explicit; its partial intelligibility unfolding through time without end; the openness of consciousness to a future. It should cause us no concern. For the chain of signs could be broken only by the emergence of an uninterpretable – that is to say meaningless – object or event. Derrida, however, sees different implications in Peirce's sign theory. Since one sign means another, signs mean only signs: 'There is thus no phenomenality reducing the sign . . . so that the thing signified may be allowed to glow finally in the luminosity of its presence. . . . The self-identity of the signified conceals itself unceasingly and is always on the move. . . . The *represented* is always already a *representamen*. . . . From the moment there is meaning, there are nothing but signs. *We think only in signs*. Which amounts to ruining the notion of the sign at the very moment when, as in Nietzsche, its exigency is recognised in the absoluteness of its right' (*OG*, pp. 49–50). Presence is reduced to signs of itself – to traces. We never touch presence unmediated by signs – immediate presence, presence itself. Mediation is primary; immediacy but an impossible, elusive dream. Thus Derrida.

It is, of course, untrue that 'meaning' results in the evaporation of presence to traces of traces. To continue with the example given above, the paw marks are a sign to me of a lion. But, over and above their character as signs of a *general* meaning, they have particular existence as depressions in the dust. Yes, they are that which means 'lion', they carry the meaning 'lion' on this occasion; but that is not all that they are. They continue to exist when they are not meaning and they have features that are quite independent of their meaning, or that are not involved in the specification of the meaning 'lion'. Their location two inches rather than two feet from a particular bush, their being dampened by rain, their being seven in number rather than six, and so on, are not features relevant to the determination of their general meaning 'lion'. Like any actual existent, they are over-saturated, from the point of view of signification, with determinate determinables. It is even more clear that the lion signified by the paw marks is not merely a cluster of meanings. 'Objects' Robbe-Grillet emphasised 'exist before they signify'. Whether or not there can be truly non-signifying events is debatable; but it is at least true to say that they exist as well as signify. The lion's existence does not dissolve into a chain of signs that signify only other signs: signification is predicated upon actual individual existence. A paw mark, or a lion, unlike a signifier or a signified, is an entity, not a bundle of different values, a space or a system of differences. Only if it is thought of *exclusively* as a sign can a lion be regarded as having been generated by signs and as giving birth only to signs. 'Omne symbolum de symbolo' holds true only in so far as signs are thought of exclusively as signs and not primarily as events or objects. A sign is not only the sign of another object or event but also an object or event in its own right. So presence doesn't slip away into representation, into absence.

Now it is of course acceptable to think of linguistic signs as being *purely* signs: their shape has been determined, and their very existence occasioned, by the exigencies of signification; they exist in order to signify and, indeed, the component signifiers and signifieds exist only in so far as the signs signify. But we cannot extend this special status to non-linguistic signs; and it is interesting to see how the Derridan argument traduces Saussure in this further way – by eradicating the difference between linguistic and natural signs. The conclusion that all signs, not merely linguistic ones, lack signifieds is the inescapable reduction to absurdity – or the self-refutation – of Derrida's 'post-Saussurean' position rather than its 'daring' conclusion.

Derrida's conflation of natural and linguistic signs shows how difficult Saussure's central message about the difference between linguistic and non-linguistic signs is to assimilate. It also illustrates the perceptiveness of this passage from the *Course*: 'No one disputes the principle of the arbitrary nature of the [linguistic] sign, but it is often easier to discover a truth than to assign to it its proper place' (p. 68). Derrida's assertion that 'from the moment there is meaning, there are nothing but signs' is, however, baseless even if we confine ourselves to linguistic signs. We are no more entitled to infer from the fact that one sign may lead to another *ad infinitum* that the signified is never reached than to conclude from the fact that since every effect is itself a cause and the causal chain is interminable that there are no effects – that the chain of causes never 'arrives at' effects. Of course, there is no 'transcendental effect' which would bring the causal chain to an end; but this does not mean that there are no effects at all. 'Omne causa de causis' does not imply 'no effects/things/events'.

The transition from Saussure to 'post-Saussurean' thought seems, therefore, to require three dubious moves:

(i) The assumption that since signs form a chain they do not connect with anything other than signs.

    (ii) The claim that since signifiers do not reach a transcendental signified (a place where final meaning meets unmediated presence) they do not reach *any* signifieds at all. The endless chain of signs is an endless chain of *signifiers*.

   (iii) The merging of linguistic value on the one hand with meaning or reference on the other (see Figure 1).

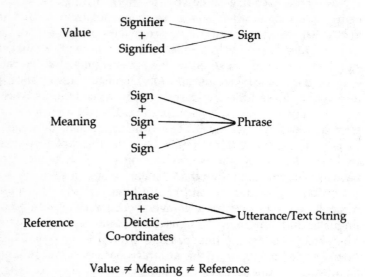

Value ≠ Meaning ≠ Reference

Figure 1   Value, Meaning and Reference

Although we have already discussed (iii) (in Section 3.2) it is worthy of further attention because it is so potent an influence in modern literary theory and implies such a radical misreading of Saussure. The fundamental post-Saussurean confusion is between the signified of a sign and the referent of an utterance or a piece of text. Eagleton, for example, tells us that Saussure argued that the relationship 'between sign and referent' was an arbitrary one;[75] but Saussure's central argument was, of course, about the arbitrariness of the relationship between signifier and signified and the nature of these two notional entities and not about the relation between the sign as a whole in use and its referent.

The signified of a linguistic sign, far from being identical with any referent, is several stages removed from it. That this is often overlooked is the result of an almost unbelievable sloppiness in the handling of key Saussurean terms. Barthes is especially culpable in this regard and it is not therefore surprising that he was so central a figure in the shift of critical interest from structuralist to post-structuralist thought. He treats linguistic signs as if they were the same as non-linguistic ones and the signifier as if it were the same as the sign as a whole and even ignores, when it suits his purpose, the Saussurean claim that the signifier is purely negative and differential, that it is a pure form without substance. Consider this passage from the muddled and grotesquely over-valued essay at the end of *Mythologiques*: 'Or take a black pebble: I can make it signify in several ways, it is a mere signifier: but if I weigh it with a definite signified (a death sentence, for instance, in an anonymous vote), it will become a sign.'[76] Since, for Barthes, semiology, 'the science of signs', is 'a part of linguistics',[77] we must assume that the term signifier has the same force inside language as outside of it. In which case, a black pebble, which provides its own boundaries, has an aseity independent of any system and hardly stands to its signified (a death sentence, for example) as recto to verso sides of a sheet of paper, scarcely counts as a signifier – not at least in the Saussurean sense – or even in the laterally displaced Saussurean sense that Barthes develops later in the essay.[78] If we do extend Saussure's concept of a signifier to include pebbles that have not yet been assigned a definite meaning, then the domain of the signifier is no longer that of language. The 'endless chain of signifiers' starts to look like what the rest of us would call the real world – a world of natural as well as artificial signs and a world in which signs reach beyond themselves – in Barthes's example to death itself. Once we include natural objects, however they are used to signify, amongst the natives of the realm of the Saussurean signifier, then the whole force of Saussure's insights – never mind any radical post-Saussurean conclusions that may be drawn from them – is lost. A black pebble may be used to signify a death sentence; or it may be thrown at someone in execution of that death sentence. A signifier in the Saussurean sense could not have these alternative uses; for it exists purely notionally as a value within a system. Words may be used to pronounce death sentences but not to carry them out. 'The letter killeth' – but not by landing on someone's head.

Let us remind ourselves of what Saussure actually said: 'Although both the signifier and the signified are purely differential and negative when considered separately, their combination is a positive fact; it is even the sole type of facts that language has' (*Course*, pp. 120–1). To proceed from here to post-Saussurean thought, one needs to misread the Saussurean concept of the signifier in two directions at once: to deny its negativity (so that even a pebble can be a Saussurean signifier); and to extend its negativity to the whole sign and on from the whole sign to the referents of discourse.

Once one has identified the steps that lead from the *Course* to post-Saussurean theory it is very difficult, when a literary critic tells us that 'since writers use words, their art must in the end – as Jakobson pointed out – be composed of signifiers without signifieds',[79] to raise even a weary smile.

3.4 POSTSCRIPT: LAPSED STRUCTURALISM

Many of the ideas examined in this chapter are difficult to grasp. This is in part a reflection of the difficulty of thinking (in words) about language and the relation between language and reality. But it is also due to their being profoundly counter-intuitive and thus contrary to our habits of thought. Thinking through such false ideas presents a great challenge to the intellect and to the imagination. If it is difficult to grasp many structuralist and post-structuralist ideas, it is even more difficult to remain within them or to write in a way that is always consistent with them. It would require a superhuman intellectual vigilance to ensure that one was always constrained by ideas that are at once of enormous scope, untrue and absurd – in short to ensure that one was a completely consistent post-Saussurean thinker. Small wonder then, that lapsed structuralism is such a widely observed phenomenon. It could form the subject of a volume on its own.

I ended Section 3.2 by documenting Hawkes's self-contradictions and his abrupt retreat from the assertion that 'language does not construct its formation of words by reference to the patterns of "reality"' to the opposite (common sense) suggestion that 'where the referential function dominates' (and this he tells us is the norm) 'communication is orientated towards context'. Hawkes's is by no means the most spectacular volte-face. Barthes is the supreme master of self-contradiction. The quotations cited on p. 88 remind us how it is possible for a true *maître à penser* to hold both that the signifier and the signified are inseparable and that in the east there are fabled countries that are full of signifiers without signifieds. We also know from Barthes's *S/Z* that a literary text is a galaxy of signifiers.

The case of Emile Benveniste provides us with perhaps the most remarkable example of lapsed structuralism in a field where the competition is fierce indeed. Let us observe his fall during the course of a single, famous essay in his much-admired collection *Problems in General Linguistics*.[80]

Early in the essay, he tells us that

> 'mental categories' and 'laws of thought' in large measure do nothing but reflect the organisation and distribution of the linguistic categories. We imagine a universe which our language has first shaped. The varieties of philosophical or spiritual experience depend unconsciously on a classification which language brings about only for the reason that it is language and that it is symbolic   (p. 6)

This is a fairly standard structuralist version of the Sapir–Whorf hypothesis. A page later, however, there is a significant retreat: 'one is guided by the principle that there is nothing in language but difference and that language avails itself of discriminatory means' (p. 7). This principle is presented not as an objective fact about language but as a *methodological* principle, designed to facilitate recognition of the distinctive units of language: 'and it now becomes possible to recognise the internal organisation and the laws of arrangement of these formal features. Each phoneme or morpheme *becomes* relative to each of the others' (p. 7). 'Becomes' suggests that it is only when we use the guiding methodology of structuralism that the purely differential nature of the linguistic unit comes into being (rather than merely becoming apparent).

The uncertainty – structuralist principles as a method, as a set of discovery procedures, or as body of facts about language – is symptomatic. This is resolved against the earlier structuralism a few pages further on:

> One can then conceive of several types of description and several types of formalisation, but all of them must necessarily assume that their object, language, is informed with meaning,

which gives it its structure, and that that condition is essential to the functioning of language among other systems of signs.   (p. 11)

From the orthodox structuralist point of view, this is out-and-out heresy. It turns on its head the fundamental assumption that meaning arises only out of the system of differences, that the system antedates meaning. Instead we have the claim that language is 'informed' with meaning and that it is *this* which gives it its structure. In short, a recognition of the fact, discussed in Section 3.3, that it is necessary to have intuitions about meaning in order to perceive structure – so that pure uncontaminated structuralism cannot even offer methodological principles.

Even worse heresy is to come. A few lines on from where he enunciates the methodological principle of structuralism, he tells us that

A state of language is above all else the result of a certain balance among the elements of a certain structure, a balance, however, which never leads to a complete symmetry, probably because dissymmetry is built into the very heart of language, through the asymmetry of the organs of speech.   (p. 8)

Now we know why language is unstable, why it evolves! If sufficient ear, nose and throat surgeons were available to correct this (unspecified) anatomical assymmetry in the speech organs, then we could look forward to a time when language might lose its theoretically difficult diachronic dimension. Frivolity apart, it is extraordinary to see one of the great linguists of the present century reverting to primitive conceptions that even Max Muller would have been ashamed to own to.

Almost as remarkable amongst lapsed structuralists, is Todorov. He is associated with the claim that all literary works are self-reflexive: 'Every work, every novel, tells through its fabric of events the story of its own creation, its own history . . . the meaning of a work lies in its telling itself, its speaking of its own existence.'[81] This highly structuralist thesis is overturned elsewhere in his writings. Clearly uncomfortable with the counter-intuitive notion that language is somehow closed off from reality, he tries to propose a way in which the internal laws of language can be reconciled with those of the universe as a whole by appealing to the idea of a universal grammar that somehow coincides with the structure of the extra-linguistic world: 'Not only all languages but also all signifying systems conform to the same grammar. It is universal not only because it informs all the languages of the universe, but because it coincides with the structure of the universe itself.'[82] We seem to be back in a Renaissance world of signatures and resemblances, a seamless unity of words and things.

Hawkes – who quotes this without protest as part of his account of the application of structuralism to literature – tells us that Todorov 'tests this notion by attempting to describe the "grammar" of Bocaccio's *The Decameron*'. One would have thought this was a rather small sample of the universe to check a hypothesis of such scope. But then, since structuralists are born omniscient, empirical testing is probably superfluous anyway. Be that as it may, the idea of a pre-established harmony between external reality and all possible sign systems represents a startling retreat from the 'closed system' conceptions of language associated with structuralism. It is odd that those who advocate the structuralist approach should hardly seem to notice when its adepts forget to be structuralists.

4

Reference Restored

4.1 THE PROBLEM

The anti-realist case thrives on myths about realism. One such myth is that those who write, or attempt to write, realistic fiction imagine they can do so only because they believe that language is a reflecting mirror or a transparent window – at any rate, a passive surface that effaces itself before an extra-linguistic reality which it undistortingly reflects or reveals.[1]

In point of fact, we have little evidence bearing on beliefs the great realistic novelists may have had about language. Tolstoy did not write any treatises on the philosophy of language; and Zola, while he had a marked preference for fiction based on fact rather than upon fancy, and for observation over fabulation, did not derive these preferences, so far as we know, from a consideration of the nature of words.

More specific information is available about the beliefs of one or two minor figures. Perhaps the most simplistic view of the relation between language and reality is to be found in the opening passage of Christopher Isherwood's *Goodbye to Berlin*: 'I am a camera . . .'. And there are naïve contemporary novelist-critics too. Some interesting names appear under this heading. William Gass, who elsewhere attaches himself to the non-referential school, is one example: 'Wittgenstein believed for a time that a proposition, in the disposition of its names, pictured a possibly equivalent arrangement of objects. This is a pleasant fancy, and plainly must be true . . . of fiction.'[2] Some whole-time critics are equally naïve. Todorov, for example, sometimes holds views on the relations between language and reality that, for a structuralist, are really rather surprising: 'Words are to things as desires are to the objects of desire.'[3] But Todorov – like Benveniste – is, as we have seen, prone to startling lapses from Structuralism.[4]

One realistic novelist commonly thought to have espoused a

mimetic theory of language and hence of the aims and possibilities of the novel is Stendhal. In practice, however, many of the chapter headings in *Le Rouge et le Noir* make fun of the idea that the novel can capture reality wholesale, that it can *replicate* a whole world, mocking what Barthes calls 'secretarial realism'. (See, for example, *Men and Manners in 1830.*) As for the famous description of 'a novel as a mirror passing down a road', yes, this is cited by Stendhal – it originates from Saint-Real; but, like many of the epigraphs, is quoted at least in part with irony.

Apart from the examples of one or two minor novelists and a few novelist–critics and isolated major figures misinterpreted by critics, there is little to support the notion that writers of realistic fiction believe in a naïve 'window' or 'mirror' model of language. Nevertheless, it is almost invariably assumed that the realistic novelist must, either consciously or unwittingly, believe that words stand proxy for things; that the relationship between words reflects the relationship between things; or that there is a one-to-one correspondence between language and reality. If, so the (usually unspoken) argument goes, a writer *must* hold these views about language in order to want to write realistic fiction and if, as is surely the case, these views are untenable, then realism itself, as an aim or a particular method of realising that aim, is invalid. If Saussure has shown that language does not mirror a reality that pre-exists it, then the endeavour to let reality into the novel is misconceived and any apparent success must be consciously or unconsciously faked – the creation of a mere 'effet du réel'.

The linguistic argument is rarely spelt out as baldly as this but it is the heart of the post-Saussurean case against realism. We must therefore ask ourselves whether, since language is not (as assuredly it is not) a mirror of reality, and there is no one-to-one correspondence between the elements of a description and the components of the described, it follows that realism is impossible. If language is not structured like extra- or pre-linguistic reality, if there is no isomorphic mapping between words and the world, can texts (including fictional ones) be 'about' or 'refer to' the real world? Can one concede the non-correspondence (in the windowing or mirroring sense) between discourse and the world without being forced to abandon belief in the possibility of reference or realism? Is there a theory of language that can reconcile these apparently inconsistent facts: (i) discourse does not by any stretch of the imagination mirror the world; and (ii) precise reference and accurate description is a normal part of everyday life?

A plausible account of language must take a middle course between the implausible idea that language 'passively' reflects reality and the equally implausible idea that reality is produced by language; between the naïve view that discourse merely replicates the form and content of pre-linguistic reality and the equally simplistic view that reality is differentiated only post- or intra-linguistically. It must be able to accommodate the fact that meaning is articulated (in the sense of being divided up and joined together) by language without making this fact a springboard to the belief that meaning is *created* by language. It must recognise that while the category of 'the edible' does not correspond to a pre-formed natural grouping of objects, to a 'natural kind', nevertheless the ineluctable truth that the difference between 'edible' and 'non-edible' (and so between eating one's fill and starving to death) is not merely a matter of binary oppositions between two values belonging to a language system, is not an internal affair of language.

An adequate philosophy of language must neither aim to correlate words with pre-existing natural kinds (a 'labelling' theory) nor ignore the very real constraints that are placed by extra-linguistic reality upon the manner in which things are linguistically classified. Reality and language are not two rigidly correlated matrices existing in the relationship of, respectively, master and slave; nor is language the only shaper of perceptual reality and the sole determinant of empirical truth; nor, again, are words scattered randomly over extra-linguistic reality. A satisfactory account of language will, at the very least, acknowledge that language stabilises, and to some extent organises, our world in so far as the latter is intelligible, even though it does not itself generate the meanings into which we find ourselves plunged; that linguistic meaning refers us in the end to experiences that go beyond or, more strictly, lie beneath, language.

4.2 THEORIES OF UNIVERSALS

One time-honoured approach to the mystery of the relationship between words and the world is through the problem of universals – of the functioning of general terms (usually nouns and adjectives) and of the nature of reference. Solutions to this problem are traditionally classified into essentialist (or realist), nominalist, conceptualist and resemblance theories.

At the heart of *essentialism* is the belief that common nouns correlate with natural kinds and that material objects are naturally or inescapably classified into those kinds. Essentialists, however, find it difficult to accommodate the everyday observation that an individual object can be classified and reclassified under a multitude of different names; that the same entity, for example, can be validly called 'a brick' or 'a weapon'. They also have trouble explaining the fact that there appears to be no common set of properties linking all the objects correctly made to bear a given name. Nor can essentialists deal with words (such as 'the economy') that seem not to correspond to pre-existing natural kinds, nor to have instances occupying determinate stretches of space–time or to be capable of non-linguistic encounter or ostension. The fundamental problem of essentialism is that it proposes too tight a correlation between types of tokens and types of extra-linguistic objects.

Nominalists take account of the facts that the same term may collect objects that have no evident common property and that a given object may be referred to by a wide variety of terms – of the double dissociation, in short, between words and objects. They have no difficulty with words such as 'or' and 'nevertheless' which do not correlate with objects at all. The trouble with nominalism, however, is that it seems to carry the implication that anything may be called by any name whatsoever and that there is no extra-linguistic basis for the grouping of objects under general terms. In practice, there *are* obvious constraints upon the choice of words by which I refer to an object; and these are not purely a matter of linguistic convention. I cannot, without prior special agreement, call a cat 'dog'. Except for certain special purposes – which require separate explanation (as when, for example, it is decided that a piece of wood shall be called 'The King') – I cannot refer to a brick by the word 'balloon'. The non-random distribution of words over things seems to be a necessary condition of successful verbal communication.

Many of the 'entities' corresponding to words do not seem to have independent material existence outside of language – for example, abstract objects. This observation seems to be the main inspiration for *conceptualism*, which sees universals as essentially *mental* entities and correlates common nouns and adjectives not with types of material objects but with types of perceptions – with, that is to say, *conceptions* abstracted from a multitude of similar perceptions. One of the many problems of conceptualism is that it cannot cope with nouns whose referents could not have originated in an ensemble of percepts (e.g. Africa), with abstract nouns not even remotely rooted in perception or with words that function differently from nouns. It is a genetic theory in so far as it looks at universals through the processes by which knowledge of them is acquired by an individual. It is not surprising, therefore, that it places insufficient emphasis upon the relations between one word and another – upon the *systematic* aspect of language. Empiricist–associationist language *is* 'a word heap'. Conceptualist accounts also face the difficulty of correlating highly variable, accidental, ill-defined concepts with a public language. Language could not be reliably related to public reality by means of essentially private experiences: denotation would be continually threatened by private connotation.[5]

A fourth theory sees universals as inhering in the correspondence between words on the one hand and, on the other, the feature or property by virtue of which the members of the group of objects gathered under the word *resemble* one another. So 'red' is that in virtue of which all red objects resemble one another. Apart from the obvious unsatisfactoriness of a tautological definition, and the fact (pointed out by Russell) that 'resemblance' itself remains as a universal irreducible to resemblance, there is the further problem of non-artificially or non-tautologically finding resemblances between all the members of the class defined by a certain word. In virtue of what property do all 'todays' resemble one another? Even Wittgenstein's conception of family resemblance hardly covers the case which it was introduced to deal with, that of games. To say that 'Ring-a-ring-a-roses', the Olympic games, poker and what a cat does to a mouse are all 'games' by virtue of a family resemblance between them is extending the idea of a 'family' somewhat.

Wittgenstein himself appreciated this

I can think of no better expression to characterize these similarities than 'family resemblances' . . . 'games' form a family.
And for instance the kinds of numbers form a family. . . .

And we extend our concept of number as in spinning a thread we twist fibre on fibre. And the strength of the thread does not reside in the fact that one fibre runs through the whole of its length, but in the overlapping of many fibres.

But if someone wished to say: 'There is something common to all these constructions . . .' I should reply: Now you are only playing with words. One might as well say: 'Something runs through the whole thread – namely the continuous overlapping of those fibres.'[6]

Resemblance theories are really variants of essentialism – essence being sought in resemblance – and they share the latter's difficulties. The error common to both is that of trying to define the semantic catchment area of a word solely in terms of the properties of extra-linguistic objects and without reference to the relations between one word and another – the error, in short, of treating language as a heap of separate words; of trying to explain the relations between words and the world without regard to the *value system* that makes specification of reference possible. And this criticism could, as we have already said, be advanced against conceptualism – which claims that words ultimately owe their meaning to the unstable, private, inner objects with which they are correlated. The opposite mistake of post-Saussurean nominalism is to deny that any correlation exists at all or that it has any pre-linguistic basis, so that the shape of described reality is merely a reflection of the system of the language in which the description is cast.

'The problem of universals' is only one way of approaching the enigma of the relation between language and reality. Most theories of universals, apart perhaps from post-Saussurean system-nominalism, have problems in dealing with language as a *system* and in accommodating terms to which the contrasts particular/general, class/member, type/instance do not apply. It makes intuitive or pre-theoretical sense to talk about the (external) relation between the type 'dog' and the class of entities that are dogs; or between the token 'dog' and a particular dog such as Rover. It makes considerably less intuitive sense to think of the type 'or' as not only being instantiated in tokens used on particular occasions but also as being correlated with a general class of 'ors' whose members are referred to by token-instances of the word.

All theories of universals take hold of one aspect of language, or approach language from one (admittedly very important) direction; but they inevitably fall short of giving a comprehensive account of the relationship between language and extra-linguistic reality. They seem most appropriate in dealing with individual terms and in particular those that appear to have specific reference but less so for those that cannot be said without a good deal of Pickwickianism to have reference. To anticipate distinctions discussed later in this chapter, theories of universals seem to bear more directly upon the referential than the value pole of language – though this distinction is clouded by the fact that reference is achieved, directly or indirectly, only through value. Clearly, the idea of point-to-point correlation between words and world has more intuitive appeal when one is using nouns or nominalised forms of adjectives and verbs.

Another limitation common to all theories of universals is that they tend to treat individual words as if they were typically encountered in isolation. In practice, words occur in strings and even point-to-point reference involves the co-operative activity of many terms, including function words, such as articles, that no theory of universals could accommodate. Moreover, reference is impossible without mobilising the context of the discourse. All reference is situation dependent and without the implied deixis of the present speaker or the surrounding text (and sometimes the surroundings of the text), reference is at best virtual. So, although the burden of specification, of classification-related meaning, is carried by forms such as nouns that theories of universals treat (and to a lesser extent by adjectives and verbs), these are able to operate only in the context of an actual or implied complete sentence; and the latter is itself a communication act possible only in the context of extra-linguistic life.

I am not pretending, therefore, that a satisfactory theory of universals would solve the mystery of the relationship between language and reality. Nevertheless, an anti-nominalist (and, incidentally, anti-essentialist) theory such as will be presented here is a useful corrective to the extreme – and extremely naïve – nominalism of post-Saussurean theory, typified in the Lacanian claim that 'it is the world of words that creates the world of things'.

4.3 WORDS, SENSES, OBJECTS

With few exceptions, all parties to the debate about universals are agreed that words do not stand proxy for material objects in a simple point-to-point fashion. Or at least that words do not secure reference to individuals by virtue of standing proxy for them. Words are not merely 'deputy things'. There are many reasons why this must be so. The most obvious is that, in so far as a token has a meaning, that meaning is general; material objects, on the other hand, are particulars occupying specific regions of space time. The *meaning* of a word cannot be a particular object. So the relation between word and object when the word is used to signify a particular object cannot be a direct correlation. The relation between word and object must be mediated.

In the model I wish to present here, reference to an object is secured by materialising in a sign *one (general) sense* that the object has. The token (or more precisely the referring expression which may be composed of one or several tokens) acts as proxy for *a sense of the object*. A given object may have any number of senses and whether or not the linguistic materialisation of one of the senses secures reference to it will depend upon the context in which the referring expression is used. The context will include what has just been said, what can be assumed in the shared world of the communicants, and the actual physical surroundings of the utterance. Because an object has an indefinite number of possible senses (corresponding to the different relations speakers may have to it, the different ways they may see it, the different uses they may have for it, and so on), then there is room for repeated classification and reclassification.

In reference, word and object meet in the identity of the general meaning of a particular token with one of the (general) senses of an intelligible object. Under this analysis, the sign, or the chain of signs constituting a referring expression, acts as an alternative materialisation of one of the general senses of the object, and 'reference' is the coincidence between the signified of the linguistic sign(s) and the sense of the particular object.

This model makes a clear distinction between the signified on the one hand and the referent of a sign on the other – irt contrast to post-Saussurean theory where the two are persistently confused. In most cases, we referentially take hold of objects in the world via the general senses that they have. Reference resides in the coincidence between the signified of a particular token or group of tokens and one of the senses of an object. The linguistic signified is not the referent; and, outside of the particular occasions when its parent sign is used to secure reference, it is not even a meaning; it is a value, which is best thought of as a 'virtual meaning' realised only when the word type is materialised in a token *in use on a particular occasion*. Correlation between a particular token and a particular object is possible only when the textual and physical co-ordinates of the utterance have been mobilised to secure reference. The relevant noun or noun-phrase – the referring expression – then takes all the credit for what has been a co-operative effort of many linguistic elements as well as involving the implied or explicit deixis of the extra-linguistic situation of the speaker or writer.

This model is consistent with there being constraints upon the choice of general terms by which we refer to an object. These will not be so tight as to imply a rigid correlation between verbal types and natural kinds. The senses of an object – which are potential lines along which it may be classified and narrow the range of expressions that may be used to grasp hold of it linguistically – are determined to a great extent extra-linguistically. But they are not fixed solely by physical properties or by some other 'natural' classifying feature. The sense of an object is potentially as variable as its significance; it is certainly relative to the situation of the individual observing or talking about it. The sense of the object will have historical and social as well as physical determinants. Selection within the range of possible senses of the object will be influenced by the current needs and the past history of the observer. There will be certain circumstances, for example, in which I may be inclined to see a brick as a weapon and so to call it a 'weapon'. Conventions of linguistic behaviour will also be influential on their own account: as discussed in Chapter 2, intertextuality operates even in the most casual conversation; though (as also emphasised in that chapter) at the level of particular conversations it is never the sole and rarely the dominant determinant of how things are named, any more than it legislates over what it is that is said. It is not textual forces alone but also the particular circumstances in which I refer to the animal that make me call it 'That bloody canine' rather than Rover or 'the dog'. All three expressions may be stereotyped – they need to be if they are to be used successfully in reference – but the choice of one in preference to another will be influenced by the unique features of the particular situation of my utterance.

The theory shares the virtues both of essentialism – which takes account of the extra-linguistic constraints upon the choice of the general terms by which we refer to objects – and nominalism – which emphasises that these constraints do not always operate along natural or (even less) physical lines. Physical composition is not the sole arbiter of the *sense* of an object; the theory can accommodate what nominalists point out against essentialists and resemblance theorists, namely that there are few natural kinds based purely on common properties. Physical features alone are insufficient to determine the linguistic classification of an object or, more generally, the emergence of universals. Objects may, for example, be viewed in terms of their uses; in such a case, a log, say, or a boulder, may become a 'seat' though they will bear little physical resemblance to an armchair. Cases like this provide the strongest attraction of nominalism – on the mistaken assumption that if there is no common property shared by all the objects gathered under a given general term, then there is no basis for classification outside of language itself and that anything may be called anything once the appropriate conventions have been set up. But the variability of the application of words to objects (and the influence, that is sometimes apparent, of language on the division of the world into individuals), the differences between objects collected into a single linguistic class and the freedom we have to reclassify objects under different categories do not license the assumption that there is a total arbitrariness in the relations between words and things. The reasons that we are more likely to classify one balloon with another balloon (even though there are no two balloons precisely alike) rather than to classify one particular balloon with other objects classified as bricks are not intra-linguistic. One obvious extra-linguistic reason is that it is possible to substitute one balloon for another in a practical activity but it is rarely possible to replace a balloon with a brick. (Use of course is not the only extra-linguistic basis for the classification of reality.) In summary, the theory fits with the facts: there are constraints upon the manner in which one assigns individuals to classes; they may be very loose but they are real; and they come from outside of language.

It may be thought that the 'object-sense' theory advanced here is merely a variant of conceptualism. This is not so. The senses of the object are external to the psyche of the language user in two respects: firstly, they are tethered to a particular object rather than being abstracted as a result of repeated encounters with supposedly similar objects; and secondly, they owe their independence, their separate and distinct existence, such as it is, to the position they have come to adopt in the language system. It is language, not the psyche of the individual, that confers the edges upon the senses. For this reason, the theory I have put forward is in no way a return to psychologism. The 'sense' retains its attachment both to the public object and to the public language: it is not a private entity. This is worth considering in more detail.

Let us conduct the thought experiment of considering an object being encountered alinguistically. It has a significance which we may characterise as a nimbus around it. This nimbus of unstable or nascent meaning becomes differentiated into stable, denumerable, discrete, hard-edged senses only when they are picked out linguistically. The word freezes one sense of the object from a shifting cloud of significance. Until the relevant terms pick them out, the senses are really 'sense ions' whose distinct or separate existence is only notional.

It must not be thought that language creates or generates either the senses of the object or the object itself. Rather, it confers an *aseity* upon senses that, prior to their secondary materialisation in the signifier of the sign, are confused with other senses. Language does not create differences of meaning; rather it stabilises senses that are pre-linguistically fused in the significance of an intelligible object.

The most important advantage of this model is that it obviates the apparent need for an isomorphism between language and reality. A verbal account of a piece of physical reality does not need to be shaped or structured like reality in order to be true of or to it; for what get expressed – and hence referred to – are not lumps of raw matter but the *senses* of material objects as they appear in particular situations. These senses are not the physical properties of the objects; nor do they necessarily correlate clearly with those objects; for while physical properties place limits upon plausible senses (for example feasible uses), they do not fix those senses completely. The sense of a piece of matter will, as we have already remarked, be highly variable, even when its physical properties remain macroscopically constant. It will depend upon the interests, moods, physiological states and personal history of the individual taking notice of it, as well as, more remotely, upon the history of the society in which he lives. Conversely, the characteristics of all the objects that answer to or materialise a certain sense – let us say that embodied in the word 'table' – cannot be specified in physical terms; we cannot draw a continuous line around the group, class or cluster of properties that would determine whether or not an object could fulfil or carry that sense or not. There is thus a *double dissociation* between senses and physical properties.

One could not therefore hope to embody extra-linguistic sense linguistically by somehow replicating the physical properties of the objects that carry that sense. The sense of things cannot be signified by physical resemblances – one-to-one correspondence of components for example – because sense is not tightly correlated with physical characteristics. A mirror gives the visible appearance of objects but does not replicate or indicate or express their senses. *Sense* cannot be mirrored; so the non-mirror-like nature of language does not have any bearing upon its capacity or otherwise to express reality.

4.4 VALUE, MEANING AND REFERENCE

In some cases it appears to be possible linguistically to isolate objects that could not otherwise exist on their own. Outside of language, 'green', 'haste' and 'smile', to take three examples at random, could not enjoy the spatially separate existence they have in written texts or the temporally distinct existence they enjoy in speech. But this must not be taken to mean that discourse deals with or refers to an autonomous realm populated exclusively by linguistic objects. Though it points to the inadequacies of a naïve realist theory of universals (whether of the transcendental Platonic variety or the immanent Aristotelian type), the existence of smiles, hastes and greens as referents of words does not licence the conclusion that verbal meaning is internal to language; even less that verbal *reference* is to intra-linguistic referents. The smile is out there even if it is separated from the smiling face only by and in the statements that describe smile and face as two mutually external relata. Outside of language, we cannot pick up, or even physically point to the quality green without picking up or pointing to other qualities of a green object at the same time. But green, none the less, remains extra-linguistic; it is a *quale* which is not reducible to its opposition to other colours. It is a positive reality, not a purely differential value. 'Green' may be a verbal type that has token instances; but green itself does not have realisations but spatio-temporally located instances. If this were not the case, it would be difficult to see how language could be used (as it is sometimes used) to redirect someone's attention without physically pointing – as when we say 'Look at that gorgeous green!'

Reference, which is the coincidence of one sense of the object with the signified of a linguistic sign brought down from generality of meaning by tokenisation and the mobilisation of deictic co-ordinates, connects, as we always thought it did, the linguistic and the extra-linguistic realms. The sharp edges of the emergent separate senses are due to the mutual pressure of rival signifieds, as described by Saussure. The sense itself, however, is not intra-linguistic: it still remains tethered to the object as *a sense of that object* and that object comes armed with its own, spatio-temporal rather than semantic, edges, which language cannot supersede or obliterate. The theory shows, moreover, how the *division* of meaning is not the same as the *generation* of meaning. To reiterate what we have said in Sections 3.2 and 3.3: it is values, not meanings, that are purely differential and negative; and it is values, not senses, that are pure form without content.

In so far as language *is* in places an autonomous realm, with its own 'objects', then we are dealing with value rather than reference. Whereas complete statements must, if they are fully intelligible, have reference, individual words may be almost pure value terms, having no other reference than their contrast with, or their effect in modifying the meaning of, other words. We may, if we consider words in isolation, assign them places upon a notional line leading from 'pure value' to 'pure reference' (see Figure 2).

VALUE			REFERENCE
Connectives e.g. 'and' 'or'	Modifiers e.g. 'the' 'a'	Adjectives e.g. 'green' 'surly'	Nouns e.g. 'economy' 'smile' 'cat' 'Rover'

Figure 2

(This metaphorical line must not be taken literally. It is not my intention to ape structuralist scientism.)

'Meaning' of course spans the whole spectrum, encompassing value at the one end and reference at the other. At one end of the axis are connectives, such as 'and' and 'or' that have value with little plausible reference;[7] at the opposite end are the proper names of real objects which may be said to have reference but little value, in so far as they do not belong to a system of oppositional terms.[8] Within these grammatical types, some words are closer than others to one or other end of the spectrum (for example, we could assign nouns places – see Figure 3). The nearer the term is to the left of the spectrum, the more it will seem to conform to the structuralist conception of a word as a value; or rather, the more plausible the structuralist reduction of words to values appears. But even in the case of terms at the far left of the spectrum, the structuralist account does not apply in full because such words do not have definite meaning in isolation. If they appear to do so, this is only because we are used to finding them in the context of other words where they do contribute to meaning, and it is natural to think that that meaning would be preserved even if the words in question alone constituted the vocabulary of a single-term language.

VALUE			REFERENCE
Abstract	'Inseparables'	'Separables'	Proper
e.g. 'health'	e.g. 'smile'	e.g. 'dog'	e.g. 'Rover'

Figure 3

Once the distinction between value and reference is grasped, it is easy to see why there need be no one-to-one correlation between verbal meanings and extra-linguistic objects, or between the elements of language and the elements of reality. Even where there does sometimes appear to be such a correspondence (sufficient to give mirror or picture theories a momentary plausibility),[9] this is only apparent. In the statement 'The dog is in the street', there appears to be a one-to-one correspondence between the (two) components of the described situation (dog, street) and the components of the description ('dog', 'street'). This correspondence, however, operates only in the context of a whole sentence which itself contains several non-corresponding components and is composed of seven, rather than two, words.

There is at best a three-and-a-half-to-one correspondence; and the apparent correspondence is parasitic upon non-correspondence. So there are no *purely* referential terms since all terms have to co-operate with others in order that something can be done with or through them. No word is an island. Even the baldest of referring expressions, such as proper names, are only syncategorematically so; indeed, we could say that, ultimately, proper names are as referentially syncategorematic as determiners such as 'the' and 'a'. No intrinsic grammatical property of a term is sufficient of itself to determine that that term shall count as a referring expression.

Behind the many fallacies of post-Saussurean literary theory may be the assumption that if there is no simple (e.g. numerical) correlation between terms and pre-linguistic entities, then there can be no reference to, or veridical account of, extra-linguistic reality. The post-Saussurean critique of realism may be rooted in the belief that a truly referential language should consist if not entirely of pictures at least of proper names set out in a manner that reflects the arrangement of their referents. The arbitrary nature of individual signs and the systematic features of language are then taken to imply the impossibility of realistic reference. In a sense post-Saussurean literary theory espouses an error opposite to naïve isomorphic theories: instead of seeing all terms as being like proper names and located at the right hand of the value–reference spectrum, it sees all words as if they were function terms, as pure values located at the other end instead.

4.5   THE TRIADIC THEORY OF SIGNIFICATION

The theory of reference advanced in this chapter is triadic and shares many features with the traditional account of linguistic signification which also employs three terms – the sign, the concept and the significatum.[10] It might be thought that these terms could be directly mapped on to those used here and the corresponding entities mutually reduced (see Figure 4). There are important overlaps; but the differences are important, too. The present theory is specifically one of reference rather than of signification as such. This is not simply because reference is what is most at issue in the post-Saussurean attack on realism but also because it is only in reference that one can legitimately separate the three elements. Away from the reference end of the spectrum, concept and signification tend to merge in 'value'; meaning and the thing meant are difficult to extricate from one another.

Traditional account	Present theory
Sign	Referring expression
Concept/signification	Sense (ion)
Significatum	Object/referent

Figure 4

The most important difference between the traditional and the present theory relates to the middle term. In the traditional triadic account of signification,[11] 'words signify [things] by means of mediating concepts'. Now 'concept' is ambiguous. As Lyons points out 'The term "concept" could be used, therefore, in two senses; not only for what we now call mental concepts . . . but also for postulated extramental entities that were apprehended by the mind in its knowledge and perception of the external world.'[12] Lyons uses 'objective concept' to cover both senses of 'concept'. Such a term suggests the possibility of convening the three partners to the classifying enterprise – the mind, language and extra-mental reality. There is a tendency, as we have already discussed, to interpret 'concept' in a narrower sense, as an intra-psychic entity built up out of recurrent experiences. As the immediate signification of a word, 'concept' in this narrower sense would seem to be far too unstable to mediate between language, reality and the individual language user. Alternatively, 'concept' may be used in such a way as to suggest 'mind amongst things' and to imply a mentalistic, and yet realist, account of universals. A doctrine of natural kinds with the linguistically competent mind as a passive mirror or in miraculous pre-established harmony with the natural world would seem then to lie dangerously close at hand.

The theory I have outlined tries to avoid these difficulties. Sense ions remain tethered to individual objects (though the latter are generalised by virtue of being intelligible as 'such-and-suches'); but they are extricated from the significance field of the object and separated out only as a result of the activity of a linguistically competent mind. The present theory, in other words, gives all three elements – language, the individual psyche and the specific object – their due. If, as a result, it only clarifies the traditional triadic account of signification and, in particular, reforms the idea of 'the objective concept' so that it can no longer be used in support of essentialism, nominalism or psychologistic conceptualism, I should be content.

4.6 'A PICTURE HELD US CAPTIVE'

Although the signifier and the signified are values, the sign as a whole *in operation* on a particular occasion is not a pure value. Even so, most referring expressions contain terms that are not themselves explicitly or intrinsically referential: reference is the result of the co-operative activity of a number of elements. There could not, therefore, be a one-to-one correspondence between the components of statements and the components of the realities they are purportedly about. The linguistic capture of an object takes place through one or other of its senses and the latter do not have, nor do they correlate rigidly with, physical properties. There are thus reasons on both sides of the language barrier for regarding the arbitrariness of the linguistic sign and the systematic nature of language as being irrelevant to the question of whether there can be genuine discursive reference to a genuinely extra-linguistic reality.

To put it more bluntly, the presence or absence of physical resemblance or numerical correspondence between discourses and realities does not bear on the question of whether or not the former can really be 'about' or be true of the latter. Physical resemblance between word and object (or the lack of it), or isomorphism between statements and states of affairs (or the absence of it) is quite irrelevant to the truth, the precision or the power of verbal signification. That language does not mirror reality – discourse does not look like, it is not structured like, what it is supposed to be about – is scarcely surprising when we consider that what it is about is the *sense* the world makes to us (rather than the dumb materiality of bits of matter) and sense is not something that can be mirrored. If sense were susceptible of mirror imaging, every puddle in the road would be a continuous source of hyper-realistic discourse.

All of this should be sufficiently obvious. Why then has the opposite view held such sway amongst literary theorists over the last few decades and been so crucial to the contempt in which realistic fiction is held? It is almost certainly because many writers on literature and language have been bewitched by a misleading image of the nature of reference, description and linguistic expression. 'A picture held us captive . . .'[13] as Wittgenstein said – with particular reference to his own theories of verbal meaning. The picture in question derives from the idea that the mechanism and the goal of signification is to *replicate* or to *reproduce* reality in part or in whole – so that to talk or to write realistically about anything is, in some sense, to copy it. Since copying is not possible, then realism (so the, usually unspoken, argument goes) is impossible and descriptions and stories – true or fictional – will seem realistic only as the result of a kind of fraud. Behind this extraordinary prejudice is, curiously, the belief that reality is ultimately pure matter and that the only legitimate, accurate and truthful way of speaking of it would be to deploy an array of signs whose material properties, or at least structural relations, in some degree *replicated* that physical reality. The fundamental belief, 'the picture that held us captive', is that true signification is *physical synecdoche* – that reality is matter and to report on it is to copy it. In the light of this fallacy, spoken or written language, whose signs and sign combinations are arbitrary with respect to the physical properties of the realities referred to, must appear to be a shabby and unreliable instrument of communication.

The 'physical synecdoche' prejudice is well illustrated by Edmund Gosse's century-old argument against the ambitions of the realistic novel and his reference to 'the inherent disproportion which exists between the small flat surface of a book and the vast arch of life which it undertakes to mirror'.[14] This rather literal interpretation of the supposed ambitions of realism is, of course, intended ironically. Nevertheless, the fact that the discrepancy between the physical characteristics of a book (small, flat) and that of extra-literary reality (vast, curved) should count as any kind of argument at all is a symptom of the way in which the project of realism is often conceived. It is as if the aim of realism were a neutral transcription of essentially material reality; and the asymptote of realism were *chosisme*.

A more recent example comes from the prominent anti-realist critic Robert Scholes. Scholes has swallowed many of the standard structuralist reasons for rejecting realism and the implicit claim of realistic writing that it is 'about' something.[15] But he also believes, paradoxically, that literary realism has had its day because it has been superseded – by cine-realism:

The cinema gives the *coup de grace* to a dying realism in written
fiction. Realism purports – has always purported – to subordinate
words themselves to their referents: to the things words point
to. . . . But when it comes to representing things, one picture is
worth a thousand words, and one motion picture is worth a
million. In face of competition from the cinema, fiction must
abandon its attempt to 'represent reality' and rely more on the
power of words to stimulate the imagination.[16]

Realistic literature is assumed to consist essentially of the
'representation' of reality understood as literally re-presenting or
reproducing it. The reality in question is also assumed to be
physical reality; or, more specifically, picturable or visual reality,
because that is what pictures, even moving ones, are restricted to
depicting. This is what the 'competition' from the cinema must be
all about.[17]

Scholes is a highly respected writer on the novel. So my critic
who believes that realistic writers want simply to reproduce the
physical world inside the covers of their books – and who
therefore seem to succeed in fulfilling the aims of realism only by
means of a rather pathetic fraud – is no straw man invented for
my polemic purposes to distract attention from the real opposition
and the real arguments. Moreover, as I have already indicated, it
is not only recent critics who seem to imagine that realism is a
matter of the replication of reality; or that to do justice to reality
one should attempt to duplicate it. The early twentieth-century
writer T. E. Hulme suggested that poetry should aim at 'the
bodily handing over of sensations'. Poetry would seem to be a
remarkably inefficient way of doing this: visual sensibilia could be
better delivered by the cinema; and as for the rest, sexual
intercourse, tourism and the provision of *ex gratia* cash payments
to permit the audience to obtain the sensations first hand
themselves would seem to be more efficient ways of bodily
handing over sensations. At best, language can be an invitation to
recall or to imagine experiences (at the level of perception rather
than sensation): no amount of fiddling with words and meanings
could make the word 'itchy' itself itchy – or not, at least without a
good deal being provided by the reader. Of all activities, the
consumption of words is the most remote from pure or bodily
sensation. This would not, of course, count against language as
an instrument for present reality were it not for the fallacious

belief that all art should aspire to the condition of the cinema or that in order to report truthfully on a part of the world one must duplicate it.

This misconception – wrong both as to the means and the ends of language – has misled many a poetaster into dreary attempts to exploit the physical characteristics of written and spoken words in the hope of making the referents more vividly present and so of intensifying the meaning of the discourses in question. Onomatopoeia is cited as an exemplary poetic technique in classrooms, despite the fact that it rarely – if ever – guarantees a closer resemblance between expression and expressed. Actually, onomatopoeia should be classified along with other devices such as alliteration, assonance, rhythm and rhyme, which serve to draw attention to the material properties of words so that a poem may become what Valéry said it should be – a discourse that hesitates between sound and sense. Such hesitation is, in fact, only an unimportant aspect of most verse (even Valéry's verse) and is certainly not central in the way that those who follow Jakobson assert that it is. Be that as it may, a poem *never* hesitates between *sight* and sense: words make rotten pictures. This explains why so-called Concrete Poetry, in which the visible surface of the written text is supposed to replicate to some extent the visible surface of the referred-to reality, is so uniformly unsuccessful. Since Apollinaire used it to crack a few literary pleasantries, Concrete Poetry has been extensively promoted; it remains, nevertheless, about as poetic as concrete. A picture indeed held us captive: it was the picture of a picture.

4.7 REFERENTIAL REALISM AND FICTION

The theory I have outlined above is not intended to revive a Platonic or even an Aristotelian realism. I do not wish to suggest that universals are real extra-linguistic entities: I am a 'referential realist' not a realist *vis-à-vis* universals. For verbal meaning to result in successful reference, deictic co-ordinates must be mobilised: the spatio-temporal context of the utterance is crucial to the process of identifying the referent and pinning the necessarily general meaning to the necessarily particular object. Only under such circumstances are complete reference, and consequently true or false statements, possible.

The emphasis on deixis may seem to raise insuperable barriers against (realistic) referential *fiction*. The difficulty is not, however, as great as it might seem at first sight. For the situation of realistic fiction is not qualitatively different from that of non-fictional written texts and even non-fictional stories told in everyday life. In the written text or even the spoken tale, the role of deixis may be played by anaphora or the intermediate form of textual deixis.[18] Body-, person- or situation-relative identification is supplanted by text-relative identification. Many referring expressions employed in everyday life are (to use Strawson's term) 'story-relative'.[19] Strawson gives the example of a speaker beginning a story as follows: 'A man and a boy were standing by a fountain.' The story continues: 'The man had a drink.' In the first sentence the article linked to 'man' is indefinite; in the second it is definite, indicating that the second occurrence of 'man' is co-referential with the first. The text establishes a restricted universe of discourse and within this universe the definite article is sufficient to establish unique, numerical identity because no entities of the same type have been referred to and consequently brought into question. Under such conditions, numerical and type identity converge. 'A man' and 'the man' can be assumed, without further evidence, to be co-referential. Since the first encounter was via reference, identity is indistinguishable from the means of identification and repeat reference is the equivalent of reference to an entity that has already been identified by non-referential encounter. Story- or text-relative identification is an essential part of the true telling of ordinary events in everyday life – even of the simplest kind. 'You know that dog that I have been telling you about? Well, he was back in our garden today.' And in fiction, where the object referred to remains absent throughout the reader's textual encounter with it, things are not so different. Just as in the ordinary reporting of true events, encounter followed by reference, followed by repeat reference is replaced by reference followed by co-reference and repeat co-reference.

Novels are usually written rather than spoken and it may be argued that the situation of a text is different from that of a conversation. For speech offers the possibility of at least a remnant of person- or situation-deixis. In practice, this difference has the opposite implication and works to the advantage of fiction. If the story or report is about something that is not in the vicinity of the speaker, his body will offer no spatio-temporal deictic co-ordinates

to help pin down reference to particulars. The only restriction
upon the universe of discourse will be then the sum of what the
speaker is likely to refer to and this must be co-extensive with his
knowledge or experience. In the case of a novel on the other
hand, the universe of discourse will be restricted to the contents
of the book or of the series of books to which the novel belongs.
There is only one Emma in *Madame Bovary* so that we can always
safely assume that all references to 'Emma Bovary' are co-referential with all other references to 'Emma Bovary'.

This raises another problem regarding fiction, however. If the
referents of the expressions used in a novel belong entirely to a
space that is outside of the spatio-temporal nexus of reality, how
can what is said about them be true or false? No experience could
confirm or refute what is said by Shakespeare to be true of
Hamlet. If Hamlet does not even exist, how can it be true that
Hamlet is a man and untrue that he is a woman? The answer is
that this is what consistency demands of us. The list of characters
at the beginning of *Hamlet* tells us that he is Prince of Denmark
and from this we infer that he is male. This inference is supported
by his being referred to as 'he', 'my good lord' and so on, and by
many aspects of his behaviour – for example, his swordsmanship
and his courtship of Ophelia. It is not possible to be both wholly
male and wholly female and since there is no evidence in the play
to suggest that he is androgynous we conclude that it is untrue
that he is a woman.

For a fictional statement to be true, it must, at least, be consistent
with the statements considered to be basic or foundational in the
fictional universe of discourse. But this is not all. There is also
the question of plausibility. Now plausibility is not sharply distinguished from consistency. Whatever is inconsistent at the
level of logic ('not[p·not p]'), must also be implausible. It is
relatively easy to decide that it is inconsistent for Hamlet to be
literally a woman as well as literally a man because most people
are one or the other and, as already noted, there is nothing in the
play to suggest that he belonged to one or other of the intersexes.
Likewise, we would have no difficulty in defending the claim that
it was implausible that Hamlet had four legs, even though there is
no point in the play where the number of Hamlet's legs is
specifically stated; for being four-legged is inconsistent with being
a human being. This is an empirical rather than a logical
observation because being two-legged is an extensional rather

than an intensional property of human beings. A race of four-legged, one hundred per cent human beings is thinkable in the way that a race of female, one hundred per cent males is not. We would, however, have more difficulty in establishing the implausibility of a critic's claim that Hamlet spent a good deal of his time mending roads and that (although Shakespeare suppressed this fact) he used to say 'Yer know' at the end of his every statement. Our objection to these claims would be based in the idea that there should be an empirical as well as logical consistency between the founding statements about Hamlet and any other claims about what he was or did. The appeal to probability would be based on that automatic cluster analysis which takes place as a part of the acquisition of experience of the world. We would then argue as follows:

(i) People of Hamlet's sort (princes) do not usually behave in this way.
(ii) This behaviour is therefore inconsistent with what we have been told about him and which has established the kind of person he is.
(iii) We therefore judge the character of Hamlet (as presented by Shakespeare or developed by a subsequent writer) to be implausible, incoherent, *untrue* to the way people usually are.

In other words, we judge fictions as true or false (or statements made about fictional characters or events as true or false) on the grounds of plausibility, which encompasses logic at one end ('not [p·not p]') and our general experience of the world at the other. We judge fictions, in short, rather in the way that we judge true stories told to us in everyday life; and this is not surprising, since we are not often in a position to test the supposedly true stories told to us directly against experience. We do not experience most facts; and so we deem supposedly factual reports false if they are internally inconsistent or they are externally inconsistent, in the sense of not conforming to the way we have directly or indirectly experienced things usually to be. Enough will have been said to make it clear that the line between internal and external consistency, between *a priori* impossibility and *a posteriori* or empirical improbability, is not sharply drawn and the indications for the invocation of the law of the excluded middle are not precisely defined or definable.

Our assessment of the plausibility or the consistency of a fictional story, therefore, is similar in important respects to the way in which we assess these things in a true story or an ordinary report. There remains a sense, however, in which the referents of fictions are virtual referents. They depend upon us, the readers, to provide the world into which they can be inserted. For, despite what many critics say to the contrary, novelists rarely create worlds – only (if they are very good) plausible tracks through the world the reader brings to his reading. But this dependency is not a matter of the relationship between language and reality; only of the empirical fact that fiction happens to be factually untrue and that, even in the case of true stories, we can invoke a world by referring to it but not replicate it. The trajectory that the story takes through the world (or rather – and this is an important qualification – *a* world) will be new to the reader (as may the world itself, or the level at which the journey takes place); and in this way, fiction may act as a critique of the fossilised world picture, the fixed angle of vision and the calcified conceptions implicit in what the reader brings to the novel. Even so, the worlds in which realistic novels operate are continuous with extra-fictional realities, just as the world of a true story is a real world. For all stories – true or fictional – *make sense* only by virtue of implicit reference to a real world. The latter is the 'horizon', in the phenomenological sense, of the fictional events.[20]

4.8 THE MYSTERY OF REFERENCE

A lack of physical resemblance – both at the level of the individual elements and at the level of their structure and organisation – between discourse and extra-discursive reality does not in any way preclude the former being 'about' the latter, except under the erroneous assumption that all signification must take place by replication of that which is signified. We have, I think, given adequate reasons for maintaining that neither reference nor description[21] could operate through *duplication* of material reality. Reference, far from being made less likely or more difficult by the arbitrariness of linguistic signs and the lack of isomorphism between discourse and reality, is probably dependent upon them.

It is precisely the non-naturalness of the relationship between language and reality that establishes the distance which enables sense ions to be dissected out from a significance field and, ultimately, makes language a means by which man can step back from physical reality in order to refer to and express it and so, in George Steiner's words, 'to talk himself free of organic constraint'. Non-arbitrary signs such as reflections or causal chains, would not embody the wakefulness or the explicitness that, in the last analysis, is what is given expression in language.

Enough has been said to support the claim that it is possible to develop a view of language that adopts a plausible middle way between implausible alternatives: either that language is totally responsible for the differentiation of reality; or that reality is differentiated completely independently of the manner in which it is spoken of. I have further argued that the concept of 'reference' presents no greater difficulties when applied to fiction than it does with respect to the recounting of true events or the production of true descriptions in everyday life.

'Referential realism' would seem therefore to be a tenable position. Nevertheless, I do not pretend that what has been said here amounts to a satisfactory theory of reference. Reference remains one of the great mysteries of language and hence of human consciousness. One, not uncommon, response to the mysterious is to deny that it exists and this refusal to accept the reality of the inexplicable, or the as yet unexplained, may be in the end what lies behind the post-Saussurean denial of the possibility of genuine reference to extra-linguistic reality. Since we cannot yet comprehend how a sculptured puff of air can refer to some object or state of affairs an indefinite distance away, one rather natural response is to deny that the distance is crossed and to assert that the object is either intra-linguistic or the reference is only apparent.

A comparable temptation faces those who are vexed by the mystery of perception; and, indeed, there is an analogy between the denial of reference to discourses and the denial of the objective reality of the intentional objects of perceptions. I offer the following tentative analogy:

SENSATION:PERCEPTION::VALUE:REFERENCE

Since perceptions are not miniatures of the external world, it is argued that they tell us nothing about extra-cerebral or even extra-mental reality. As with language, there is a tendency to think that perceptions would be more accurate and easier to understand if they somehow replicated the reality they are supposed to be 'about' – if there were an isomorphism between percept and object. In accordance with this argument, the best way of constituting a perception of a cup or creating an accurate description of it, would be to place another cup next to it. The analogy between epistemological idealism and the structuralist view of the world is apparent in the parallel between the views that reality is a verbal construct and that material objects are *illogical* constructs out of perceptions. Both views reflect a reluctance to admit to the reality of something that it is difficult to understand. But the fact that we do not understand something is not sufficient grounds for denying its existence unless we adopt the Hegelian principle that the real is always intelligible. Without that evidently false principle, there can be no rationale for denying the existence of things that are beyond the reach of our understanding. Reference is a mystery; but it is not, for that reason, an illusion.

Scepticism about the referential possibilities of language has, of course, a venerable tradition reaching back at least as far as classical times. Cratylus, believing that it was impossible to use words without being misunderstood and without misrepresenting apparent referents, espoused aphasia. For reasons that are fairly obvious, he did not record his own views; they have come down to us through Plato, who tells us that Cratylus declined to used words in philosophical discussion, confining himself to wagging his finger. A discussion with him must have been a rather dull, not to say one-sided, affair; but at least his silent gesticulations were more consistent than the profuse outpourings of his modern successors. Even so, one wonders how Plato came to know of Cratylus's reasons for retreating from language. Cratylus himself must somehow have expounded them at some time and it is difficult to conceive how he could have done so without using words. Finger wagging does not readily lend itself to the expression of complex, abstract and general doubts about language.

One suspects that then, as now, the meta-language used to criticise language was itself granted a mysterious dispensation from the general condemnation. It is, to put it mildly, rather implausible that language should be available to refer to itself and, in particular, to its own limitations *and to no other referent in the world*. Nevertheless, it is usual for those who profess radical doubts about language to suspend those doubts when it comes to using language to express them. But meta-linguistic statements that put the expressive power of language in doubt should not themselves be allowed to pass without critical scrutiny. If discourses cannot reach to a reality outside of themselves, if they cannot be truly 'about' anything, then they certainly cannot be used to comment on the relationship between themselves and reality.

Nor can they be used to pass harsh judgement upon those highly elaborated, ambitious and ordered expressions of parts of reality that we term (realistic) novels. Even if we were to accept the much narrower thesis that it is only literary discourse, uprooted from immediate practical needs, that is self-referential, this would still not release the literary theorist from the charge of pragmatic self-refutation. Barthes, for example, tells us that in (literary) 'writing': 'a fact is *narrated* no longer with a view to acting directly on reality but intransitively, that is to say, finally outside of any function than that of the very practice of the symbol itself'.[22] If 'writing' consists only of the practice of the symbol itself and if the symbols in question consist of signifiers inexplicably uprooted from signifieds (according to Hawkes 'prised utterly free of signifieds'), then writers are condemned to spending their days spinning chains of signifiers that are only meaningless – and certainly referenceless – marks on paper. These are two large and fortunately counterfactual ifs. If, however, these were not counterfactual, then we would have to accept Barthes's claim that when a fact is narrated without a view to 'acting directly on reality', the writer is merely inscribing signifiers without signifieds. And this must cause some embarrassment to literary theorists. For if literature *is* divorced from practical need, so too is literary theory; for the latter is at best second-order or meta-literature. What, therefore, are we to make of apparently realistic literary theory that talks referentially about literature in a way that the theorist forbids the novelist to talk about the world? Is post-Saussurean literary theory merely an *'effet de la théorie'*? I leave the reader to draw his own conclusion, though he may be assisted in his deliberations by considering this passage from Terence Hawkes:

'New' New Criticism would thus claim to respond to literature's essential nature in which signifiers are prised utterly free of signifiers, aiming, in its no-holds-barred encounter with the text, for a *coherence* and *validity* of response, not objectivity and truth.[23]

How is it possible to distinguish a 'valid' response from an invalid one, once one has repudiated *both* objectivity and truth, especially when the thing one is responding to consists only of marks on paper that have been severed from reference and meaning and especially when, as Barthes says, no reading of a work is *wrong* and Racine, for example, consists only of what has been said about Racine?

What seems to be lacking in those who deny the reality of reference is a willingness to recognise the existence of something that they cannot explain. And this is connected with the inability of the structuralist and post-structuralist *terribles simplificateurs* to respond to the inexpressible mystery of language and to see that language cannot be simply modelled. Because words do not mirror the world, it does not follow that discourse is cut off from the world. The correct observation that language is not a heap of labels corresponding to a heap of extra- and pre-linguistic objects does not license the opposite conclusion that it is a closed system. It does not follow from the fact that language is not a mirror that it must be a self-sufficient crystal. It is more likely to be analogous to a heap of spaghetti on a plate or a pile of string vests. More likely still, it cannot be modelled at all: it is a mystery that is exceeded in depth only by that of consciousness itself.

It is possible to subscribe to the aims and hopes of realism while still retaining a sophisticated conception of the relationship between language and reality. The radical nominalism of post-Saussurean literary theory leads directly to a self-defeating linguistic idealism. If in our narratives (or our statements), in our fictions (or our facts), we are confined to the inside of anything, it is not of language but of the sense we make of the world, of consciousness. But to be confined to the inside of consciousness is not to be inside at all, nor to be confined.

Part Two

Part II ...

5

The Mirror Stage: A Critical Reflection

5.1 INTRODUCTION

Over twenty years after the publication of *Ecrits*,[1] the volume in which his major papers are collected, Lacan remains highly influential in certain academic circles on this side of the Channel. Catherine Belsey's *Critical Practice*,[2] Terry Eagleton's *Literary Theory*,[3] and *The Talking Cure* (a collection of essays edited by Colin MacCabe and written mainly by literary critics)[4] – to name only a few out of many recent articles and books – testify to the high standing Lacan still enjoys as a clinician and a thinker in academic departments of English Literature in the United Kingdom. In contrast, professionals in the fields in which he operated, or touched on, are in the main ignorant of his *oeuvre*. Those few who are aware of his writings for the most part consider them to be unnecessarily obscure, self-indulgent to the point of narcissism and even fraudulent. The consensus seems to be that they can be safely ignored. A similar situation prevails in the United States. In 1984, entire issues of *Poetics* and of *Style*, were devoted to 'psychopoetics', an approach to literary criticism currently almost synonymous with the application of Lacanian psychoanalysis to texts. At the same time, Lacan the clinician and theoretician of the human psyche is neglected by psychologists and psychiatrists.[5] His reputation as a philosopher, developmental psychologist and clinician seems to be highest, therefore, amongst those who are trained in the interpretation of literature but who have little or no knowledge of the scientific method and have only a rudimentary appreciation of the nature of clinical practice.

Any attempt to 'refute' Lacan's idea would be doomed from the outset. One cannot refute fog. Many of the theses most associated with his name are presented with little or no supporting evidence, even though they often look like empirical hypotheses. Such arguments as he offers are often carried along on a stream of what

131

in some circles passes for wit; that 'free play of the signifier' which, to dull sensibilities, seems like a succession of rather academic and feeble puns soliciting a donnish smile. The reader will seek in vain the systematic observations, the measurements, upon which the Lacan's conclusions have been based or even indications of the places where such observations are reported or summarised. There is much citation of authorities (Freud, Buhler, Baldwin, and so on) but this is often as imprecisely referenced as name-dropping at an academic cocktail party.

Many of the cases cited in his major papers are taken over from Freud (for example, Wolf Man, Schreber, Rat Man, Anna O.) and the manner in which they are recycled makes it easy to understand why his analyses of them have seemed most convincing to those whose training has been in literary criticism rather than in making and critically evaluating clinical diagnoses. There is little reference to clinical material of his own and, with very few exceptions (such as the report on Aimée, a female psychotic, who was the subject of his doctoral thesis), Lacan's interpretations of his own cases often cannot be assessed because insufficient information is given. If the case histories illustrate anything, it is how not to proceed in diagnostic medicine. The manner in which conclusions are drawn from them is reminiscent of how a first-year medical student, or a hypochondriac, using a few observations to light a gunpowder trail of inference primed with his own preconceptions, might arrive at a wrong diagnosis. The Lacanian *oeuvre* is not unfairly described, therefore, as a huge inverted pyramid of speculation (the words is used deliberately) built upon a tiny apex of fact.

To criticise Lacan on empirical grounds is to play into the hands of his disciples. For Lacan has often indicated his contempt for mere factual truth. Lemaire, in her obsequious and reverential account of the Master's thoughts,[6] refers to the fact that 'some critics have seen fit to use the "factual" insubstantiality' of, say, the mirror stage, as a weapon to 'invalidate it'. She dismisses such pusillanimity as not warranting further attention. 'Factual insubstantiality' does not weigh in assessing the truth of ideas as important as Lacan's; besides, the need to ground hypothesis in observed fact merely symptomatises one's own needs, anxieties and prejudices.

To be fair, Lacan is scarcely unique in exploiting the prestige of the clinic and of scientific diagnostic medicine, while speculating in a manner that patently rejects the rules of clinical inference.

This intellectual vice does not distinguish him from other practitioners in a branch of medicine notorious for its therapeutic inefficacy. Jumping to untested and often untestable conclusions, elaborating without independently corroborating the first diagnosis you thought of, submitting to a wild proliferation of unchecked hypotheses (corresponding to the presuppositions with which each patient is approached) – all things an average medical student grows out of after he has made a sufficient number of mistakes – are the stock-in-trade of the psychoanalyst. They cannot therefore be laid at Lacan's door alone and to encounter his writings on the well-trodden battleground between scientists and clinicians on the one hand and those on the other who claim to be scientists and clinicians while at the same time showing little respect for or understanding of the principles of the basic and clinical sciences, would be fruitless.

Instead, I shall examine some of Lacan's central ideas, the arguments he has put forward for them and the use that has been made of these ideas by literary critics and others who think that what Lacan says about human development has profound implications for the philosophy of consciousness, for linguistics, for literary theory and for literature itself. I shall focus particularly on his theory of the mirror stage in infant development as the view has often been expressed that this above all supports his radical nominalism and that it discredits realistic fiction and the realistic view of the self (or subject) and the world.

5.2 EXPOSITION

(a) Images and the Realm of the Imaginary

The theory of the mirror stage is regarded as the cornerstone of Lacan's *oeuvre*. It has excited an enormous amount of interest amongst his followers and the essay he devoted to it was written and rewritten over a period of thirteen years. It appears at the head of the English translation of his major papers and its conclusions are alluded to or presupposed in nearly all the papers that follow. The mirror stage, Lacan says, is one of those 'critical moments that mark the history of man's mental genesis' (*Ecrits*, p. 17) and it reveals, amongst other things, 'an ontological structure of the human world' (p. 2) and sheds light 'on the formation of the *I*' (p. 1).

From the age of about six months, the child is able to recognise its own image in the mirror. This recognition triggers off a series of gestures

> in which he experiences in play the relation between the movements assumed in the image and the reflected environment, and between this virtual complex and the reality it reduplicates – the child's own body, and the persons and, things around him. (p. 1)

According to Lacan, the child takes great pleasure in the correspondence between its own movements and those of its mirror image. The reasons for this pleasure or 'jubilation' go very deep indeed. The mirror phenomenon is to be understood as a moment of *identification* – 'the transformation which takes place in the subject when he assumes an image' (p. 2):

> This jubilant assumption of his specular image by the child at the *infans* stage, still sunk in his motor incapacity and nursling dependence, would seem to exhibit in an exemplary situation the symbolic matrix in which the *I* is precipitated in a primordial form, before it is objectified in the dialectic of the identification with the other, and before language restores to it, in the universal, its function as a subject.

In other words, the mirror image presents the child with a kind of pre-linguistic, even pre-social 'I'.

But why should this be an occasion for such rejoicing? Because in perceiving, and subsequently identifying with, his image, the infant 'anticipates on the mental plane the conquest of the functional unity of his own body, which, at that stage, is still incomplete on the plane of voluntary mobility' (p. 18). The mirror stage (which lasts until the child is about eighteen months old)

> manifests the affective dynamism by which the subject originally identifies himself with the visual *Gestalt* of his own body: in relation to the still very profound lack of co-ordination of his own motility, it represents an ideal unity, a salutory *imago*; it is invested with all the original distress resulting from the child's

intra-organic and relational discordance during the first six months, when he bears the signs, neurological and humoral, of a physiological natal prematuration. (pp. 18–19)

'Physiological natal prematuration' is an odd phrase but it presumably refers to the infant's immaturity. Being born immature – and hence in a sense prematurely – is uncomfortable; the pleasure afforded the child by its mirror image is due to its anticipating 'in a mirage the maturation of its powers'. As Jacqueline Rose puts it

one of the key factors of the mirror stage is that the child is in a state of nursling dependency and relative motor inco-ordination and yet the image returned to the child is fixed and stable, thereby anticipating along the axis of maturation.[7]

Rose illustrates this connection by referring to Lacan's case of a four-year-old whose 'complete motor and linguistic inco-ordination' is attributed to an inability 'to conceptualise its body as total'.

the rectification of the child's motor inco-ordination during analysis is taken to demonstrate the relation 'between strictly sensorimotor maturation and the subject's functions of imaginary control.'[8]

The logic appears to run as follows: if recovery takes place *during* analysis, then it is *due* to analysis. Analysis is therefore efficacious and the theory behind it must consequently be true. By a similar argument, if I recover from pneumonia after drinking the sacred text of the Koran, the theory that pneumonia is due to possession by evil spirits is upheld. Be that as it may, the claim is that the 'I' or the ego is 'a reflexion of a narcissistic structure grounded on the return of the infant's image to itself in a moment of pseudo-totalisation'.[9] It is this that causes the infant's contemplation of itself in the mirror to be associated with so much pleasure. The infant is jubilant because it *sees* the felt chaos of its existence transformed into the stable image of its physical body.

This image is the basis of the 'Ideal-I' but the latter is 'fictional'. In consequence, while the image 'symbolises the mental permanence of the *I*', at the same time it 'prefigures its alienating destination' (*Ecrits*, p. 2). The mirror stage 'establishes a relation

between the organism and its reality – or, as they say, between
Innewelt and Umwelt' (p. 4). But 'this relation to nature is altered
by a certain dehiscence at the heart of the organism, a primordial
Discord betrayed by signs of uneasiness and motor inco-ordination
of the neonatal months' (p. 4). Since the unified 'I' in the mirror
with which the infant identifies is the first of a series of *fictions*,
the mirror stage is

> a drama whose internal thrust is precipitated from insufficiency
> to anticipation – and which manufactures for the subject, caught
> up in the law of spatial identification, the succession of
> fantasies that extends from a fragmented body image to a form
> of its totality . . . and lastly the assumption of the armour of an
> alienating identity which will mark with its rigid structure the
> subject's entire mental development.   (p. 4)

The infant's 'jubilant' identification with the image of his body
resolves the uneasiness arising from his premature birth but it
does so at a price. The specular 'I' – like all future I's – is founded
upon *mis*-recognition. The reified product of a succession of
imaginary identifications with the mirror image, it is a fiction even
though it is cherished as the stable or would-be stable seat of
personal identity. Stability is borrowed and is consequently
bought at the cost of self-misrecognition, of identification with
something that the infant is not.

> It is in this erotic relationship, in which the human individual
> fixes upon himself an image that alienates him from himself,
> that are to be found the energy and the form on which this
> organisation of the passions that he will call his ego is
> based.   (p. 19)

The subject, as Lemaire says, '*is* his own double more than
himself . . . consciousness collapses into its double without
keeping its distance from it'.[10]

Eventually the price of imaginary identification will be paid.
The alienation implicit in the act of referring oneself to something
that one is not will become paranoia when the image with which
the infant identifies is no longer its own reflection but is another
child of the same age; when, at about the age of eighteen months,
the mirror stage comes to an end and the specular *I* is deflected

into the social *I*. The child will then begin to exhibit 'primordial jealousy' and the phenomenon of 'transitivism'. The jubilant identification of the fragmented and inco-ordinated subject with its totalising mirror image turns sour.

(b) Words

Lacan is a Freudian. Indeed, it is his recurrent boast that he alone has kept faith with the Master's deepest insights. As Malcolm Bowie has said, 'Lacan presents his main task as that of reading Freud well and getting him right'.[11] The mirror stage has therefore to be incorporated into the framework of the orthodox Freudian theory of infant sexuality. The arguments by which this is accomplished are, in those places where they are actually given rather than merely hinted at and the cloud of unintelligible knowingness parts, ingenious in the extreme. The mediator of the processes both by which the infant's specular image gives way to the social 'I' and M. Lacan is united with Herr Freud is, of course, King Oedipus. The Oedipal events mark the transition from a dual, immediate, mirror relationship to a mediate relationship with the other's identification of the self. Successful resolution of the Oedipus complex results in the passage from the imaginary to the symbolic realm, from the world of mirror images to the world of words.

In the mirror stage, the child cannot differentiate himself from the Other with which he identifies himself. Identification with his mirror image will, furthermore, spill over into that of the mother who holds him up to the mirror. This presents no problems until the father appears on the scene. He, of course, disrupts the cosy relationship with the mother and blocks the child's free access to her and certainly prevents his merging with her. The father, in Freudian terms, frustrates the child's wish to become the phallus: the Oedipal conflict begins. Its resolution requires the refashioning of the subject and involves his translocation from the imaginary to the symbolic world; for the Oedipal events are associated with the accession to language. This is explained as follows:

The Father's veto is the child's most fundamental contact with the Law. In order to stand for the Law, the Father must lay it down. Now in human societies, the preferred mode of laying down the Law is speaking it:

The father is present only through his law, which is speech, and only insofar as his speech is recognised by the mother does it take on the value of the Law. If the position of the father is questioned, the child remains subject to the mother.[12]

In the normal course of events, the Father's speech *is* recognised: padre is padrone. And it is speech – and not, as Freud thought, his role in procreation – which confers his privileged status upon the Father:

The existence of a symbolic father does not depend upon the recognition of the connexion between coition and childbirth, but upon something corresponding to the function defined by the Name-of-the-Father.[13]

This reinterpretation of the Oedipal moment requires a parallel reinterpretation of the Primal Scene. For Freud, the crucial event was the child's coming upon the parents engaged in coitus, or imagining having done so, and experiencing his access to the mother being literally blocked by the father. For the Lacanian, the child comes upon the parents talking to one another, engaged in verbal rather than carnal intercourse.

The Oedipus complex is resolved in most children. Painful though it is, the child accepts the Law, renouncing its right of exclusive access to the mother and acknowledging the superior and prior claims of the father. The blow is softened by an ingenious strategy in which the child *identifies* with the father and takes him as his model; in other words, he *becomes* his father by introjection of the paternal image. If you can't beat (or displace) them, then you join them; or if you can't join her, become like him who is permitted to do so. The father's phallus is reinstated as the appropriate object of the mother's desire and the child no longer insists on the fantasy that he is the object of his mother's desire. A symbolic castration takes place, the father separating the child from the mother. (In the ill-lit world of the Freudian pre-nursery, being separated from one's mother and being relieved of one's external or internal genitalia are not clearly distinguishable, even if one is a girl.) The reward for submitting to this operation is to receive a name and a place in the family: the child enters into language, society and culture.

The coincidental resolution of the Oedipus complex and

accession into language, the trade-off between the primal repression of the desire for the mother and gaining a place in discourse, may still seem a little obscure. In the end, it boils down to a tautology (in so far as it can be understood at all) but this we shall discuss in the next section. For the present, let us note some of the ways in which the connection between Oedipus and language has been interpreted by Lacan's followers. The feeblest argument linking the Father and the Law with the acquisition of language and the transition from the imaginary to the symbolic realm appeals to Freud's observation 'that the admonitions of others are conveyed by speech': when father – or the Father – lays down the law – or the Law – he utters rather than mimes it. One would not expect, however, that a list of regulations, a recitation of the rules of the house, of society, would cut much ice with a child who is presumed to be as yet *infans*, outside of language. A better argument originates from the Lacanian A. de Waelhans, who points out that 'primal repression is the act whereby the subject . . . withdraws from the immediacy of the lived experience by giving it a substitute which it is not'. This repression is possible only if the subject has somewhere outside of himself to go to and not be. This place is 'an original signifier of the self which he posits as the negative of his coenaesthesia and which allows him to effect the negation inherent in primal repression'.[14] The child is effaced into language. He has renounced the ambition of being the object of his mother's desire and of having unique access to her; he no longer entertains the fantasy of being the phallus. Instead, he has gained access to the phallus-signifier. Like his father, he *has*, or *has the use of*, the phallus:

> In the quest for the phallus the subject moves from being it to having it. It is here that is inscribed the last Spaltung [splitting] by which the subject articulates himself to the Logos. (*Ecrits*, p. 289)

The phallus-signifier thus symbolises privation or lack of being

> The fact that the Phallus is a signifier means that it is in the place of the Other that the subject has access to it. (p. 288)

> In entering language, one becomes that which one is not; for language above all provides places where one *can* become what

one is not and where, consequently, the primal repression of the desire for the mother can be enacted and the Oedipal conflict resolved. In becoming a speaker, the subject 'crosses himself out'. He suffers the lack of being that necessarily follows from locating one's being where one is not. This is felt most acutely, according to Irigaray, when the child is referred to in the third person. Irigaray's argument has been summarised by MacCabe as follows:

> In the development of the child there is a moment when the infant . . . enters language. In the process of entry he/she becomes aware of certain places which he/she can occupy – these are the points of insertion into language. Crucially this involves the learning of pronouns: the realisation that the 'you' with which the child is addressed by the father or mother can be permutated with an 'I' in a situation from which it is excluded – when the parents speak to each other. This realisation is the understanding that the 'you' with which he or she is addressed can be permutated with a 'he' or 'she' and it is through the experience of this empty place that the child enters language. The passage through this empty place is the exclusion necessary to the proper control of language. . . . It is this which gives language its fearsome quality because the experience of the sign involves a castration at the linguistic level . . .
>
> To accede to the world of absence – to the world of the sign where one thing can stand for another – we must wound perpetually, if not destroy, a narcissism which would render the world dependent on our presence. . . . The name is that which marks the exclusion of the subject from the realm in which he/she is thus constituted.[15]

To enter language is to be decentred; to become a substitutable anyone instead of the centre of the world. The child who has repressed his desire has consented to become a substitutable anyone, a mobile phallus-signifier that will never, except in the symbolic realm, make contact with the object of its desire. A phallus thus cut off from the true or primordial object of its desire is, in the curious linguistics that operate in the pre-nursery darkness, a signifier without a signified. The object of desire has been lost so that it can be conquered only in fantasy by endless expansion along a proliferating chain of signifiers that never touch the ground of the signified. Discourse is, at bottom, the manipulation of the absence of the mother.

Language is the precondition of the process by which the child becomes fully aware of itself as a distinct entity. The linguistic self, the 'I', is a mobile signifier, a fiction even more hollow than the I of the mirror stage. The subject[16] who 'articulates himself in the Logos' (*Ecrits*, p. 277) 'undergoes a split in view of being a subject and only insofar as he speaks' (p. 288). This split – which divides the conscious from the unconscious, the latter composed of the material suppressed at the time of the primal repression – allows the subject to become fully constituted. In the mirror stage, the I discovered itself, acquired unity, only by being translocated outside of itself; it *became* through retroactive displacement. In other words, even as far back as the pre-social mirror stage, the Other was involved; its (strictly *her*) presence was at least implicit

> in the gesture with which the child in front of the mirror, turning to the one who is holding it, appeals with its look to the witness who decants, verifying it, the recognition of the image, of the jubilant assumption, where indeed *it already was.*[17]

Nevertheless, the passage from the Imaginary to the Symbolic involves a more profound emptying of the subject and by the very processes through which the social *I* is constituted. The defining image of the mirror stage had a plenitude that is denied to the self constituted through language. For linguistic signs are constituted through differences; they are purely differential, purely relational – in short, negative. So the self as a mobile signifier is even more deficient than the specular *I* of the mirror stage.

Even so, the mediation of the symbolic is essential if the ordering of the world, of things in the world, of the child's life, is to be ensured. Outside of language, there is only the nameless Real – 'the primordial chaos upon which language operates' which is 'radically extrinsic to the procession of signifiers'.[18] Within the realm of the symbolic, on the other hand, there is the unified self and a world of apparently stable objects. Thus

> It is the world of words that creates the world of things – things originally confused in the *hic et nunc* of the all in the process of

coming-into-being – by giving its concrete being to their essence, and its ubiquity to what has always been.   (*Ecrits*, p. 65)

So much for the theory. On the basis of Lacan's ideas, it has been argued that objects and selves are internal to language and that the fundamental presupposition of both literary and philosophical realism – that there is a language-independent reality, is false. Reference outside of language is not possible because everything that one refers to is intra-linguistic; the reality one would wish to describe is composed of fictions that belong inside the symbolic realm. Even the most painstaking *chosisme* does not provide a window upon an extra-linguistic reality, because the *choses* in question have been created by the world of words. Such conclusions would not in fact follow from Lacan's claims about infant development, even if they were true. But before dealing with these conclusions, let us investigate the extent to which the theories themselves stand up to critical examination.

5.3   CRITIQUE

(a)   Facts

(1)   *Infans jubilans*. Lacan's theory of the mirror stage is offered as an explanation of an *observation*: the 'jubilation' of an infant confronted with his own mirror image. Anyone who has tried the experiment of holding an infant of the appropriate age up to a mirror, however, will find that its response to confronting its own image is highly variable. It may at first take a great deal of interest in its mirror image as, indeed, it takes an interest in most novel sensibilia. But the novelty soon wears off; and anyone hoping to excite a fourteen month old with its mirror image when there is, say, a cat or a moving toy robot in the vicinity, is going to have his work cut out. Even where the child does pay attention, interest is almost as likely to be directed at the frame (especially if it has something, such as a hook that looks as if it could be swallowed, attached to it) as to the image. If the mirror is a small one, the child will often grab it and attempt to bang it up and down in the usual way that tiny children have with delicate objects, as if to torture them into disclosing their name and nature. In any case, attention to the mirror image is usually very

transient and is not often associated with elaborate play and the 'series of gestures' that Lacan refers to. If there is elaborate play, it is usually at the instigation of the parent engaging the child in a game of peep-bo. Moreover, the 'startling spectacle of the infant in front of the mirror', in which he 'overcomes, in a flutter of jubilant activity, the obstructions of his support' and fixes an object 'in a slightly leaning forward position' (*Ecrits*, pp. 1–2) is by no means specific to the mirror experience: it would as well describe an infant confronted by *any* object of interest – a passing cat, or a rustling sweet paper.

(2) *Mothers, fathers and mirrors.* The theory assumes that the child is held up to the mirror by its mother. This is essential if the transition from the specular to the social *I* is also to be associated with resolution of the Oedipus complex and accession to the symbolic realm. The complex mechanism outlined above would be hopelessly deranged if the father were the first to hold the child up to the mirror or if, as presumably happens in most households, mother and father were to divide this particular job between them; or if – and again one has no reason to assume is unusual – sublings, child-minders, aunts and uncles were involved. For the theory requires that mother and child should be glued together at the specular moment when the child identifies with its mirror image – so that the child can suffer subsequent displacement by the father and 'come to realise that he is a third member of the family'.[19] The father has to happen upon a scene where the infant and the mother are united in the infant's fusion or confusion of the mother's image with his own. It is this that triggers the transition from the specular to the social *I*; from the (less hollow) fictional identification with the mirror image to the pure absence of the dispersion of the self into language as an infinitely mobile phallus signifier: 'With the advent of the father, the child is plunged into post-Structuralist anxiety.'[20]

It is extremely awkward both for the child and for the theory, then, if the father is present from the beginning; for the child's imaginary identification with his mirror image would be as likely to spill over into the image of the father as into that of the mother. Indeed, as (according to the theory) the child cannot differentiate himself from the Other with which he identifies himself, nor can he differentiate the components of that other, he would most probably identify with *both* mother and father. Now, except where the father is a sailor, a gaolbird or divorced from the mother, one would expect that both parents, along with anyone who happens to be in the house, would share the task, apparently vital for his metaphysical well-being, of holding the child up to the mirror.

The Oedipal triangle also requires that the child should preferably be male – females can be accommodated only by a scandalous interference with their genitalia – and that he should be an only child, for the second and subsequent children are much more seriously displaced from their mothers by their siblings than by their fathers. But these are difficulties common to all psychoanalytic theories and are not peculiar to Lacan's version of Freud.

(3) *The specific immaturity of human infants.* Lacan contrasts the 'the triumphant jubilation and playful discovery that characterise, from the sixth month, the child's encounter with his image' with the 'indifference' shown by even the highest animals, such as the chimpanzee (*Ecrits*, p. 18).[21] He attributes this difference to the 'specific prematurity of birth in man' and adduces as evidence of this 'the anatomical incompleteness of the pyramidal system and . . . the presence of certain humoral residues of the maternal organism' (p. 4). While it is true that a human infant is helpless for longer than, say, a young chimp or a lamb, the helplessness of the child at birth is no greater than that of a kangaroo and its period of total motor inco-ordination not *proportionally* greater than that of, say, a seal in relation to total lifespan. There is *no* evidence for an *anatomical* incompleteness of the pyramidal tract – all the neurons are present at birth – unless 'anatomical' refers to the *connectivity* of neurons. If that is what is meant, then the argument falls flat on its face, because the immaturity of the perceptual systems is even greater in this respect as the immense amount of research carried out on the visual cortex over the last thirty years has clearly demonstrated.[22] But the interpretation of the significance of the mirror stage depends, as we shall discuss presently, upon the assumption that perception is in some sense ahead of voluntary motor activity. The reference to 'certain humoral residues of the maternal organism' is even less intelligible. Of course the infant carries antibodies which have reached its blood stream by passive transfer from maternal blood across the placenta. But this adaptive response is hardly a sign of immaturity, is not unique to man and has no relevance to the infant's self-

experience, other than protecting it from life-threatening diseases. There is, in short, no evidence to support Lacan's claim (*Ecrits*, p. 137) that 'prematuration at birth' is specific to man, as anyone who has observed blind new-born kittens will agree.

(4) *The totalising image.* The essence of the mirror stage resides in the contrast between the sensed helplessness and inco-ordination of the infant and the wholeness of the image perceived in the mirror. As Lemaire expresses it 'the Mirror Stage is the advent of coenaesthetic subjectivity preceded by the feeling that one's own body is in pieces. The reflection of the body, then, is salutary in that it is unitary and localised in space and time.'[23] *Is* the reflection of the body that infants receive in the mirror thus unified? Is not the image very often only fragmentary, consisting of part of the body – usually the face plus or minus the neck and shoulders? How often does the child see the whole of its body in the mirror? When does it see the back of its head as well as its face, its sore bottom and kicking legs at the same time as its arms and chin? Moreover does not the infant frequently catch sight of its image *en passant*, at times other than when it is being held up to the mirror by its mother? Does it not, for example, receive faint impressions of itself in car, shop and home windows? Or glimpses in car mirrors, saucepans and the backs of watches? In short, is not the infant's entire experience of its mirror image both spatially and temporally fragmented and is not the image it is confronted with also highly variable on account of the variability not only of the surfaces upon which his body is reflected but also of the conditions of illumination in which the self-encounter takes place? Nothing could be less likely to ease 'the feeling that one's body is in pieces' than catching casual glimpses of bits of it. Anyone relying on necessarily random encounters with mirrors to provide an infant with 'its totalising image' is going to have a hard time.

The supposed contrast is between the unitary image and the sense of being in a fragmented body arising out of motor inco-ordination. But surely the sensed helplessness of the child is not constant during the whole period between six and eighteen months. The motor inco-ordination of a six-month-old is dramatically different from the nimbleness of the eighteen-month-old. Nevertheless, the jubilation is supposed to remain undiminished.

(5) *The impotence of factual evidence.* Psychoanalysts have traditionally been unflustered by facts that seem to contradict their theories. Most facts can be reinterpreted so that they appear to confirm rather than undermine the theory. The lack of evidence for the certain processes described by Freud, for example, provides further evidence for the reality of other processes he described – for the universality and omnipotence of repressive mechanisms, for example – and so apparently increases rather than decreases his credibility. The disagreement his theories provoke is interpreted as active resistance to them and taken to be a sign of the very defence mechanisms postulated by his theories and so further proof of the theories themselves. Lacan himself cites the well-known story of the young lady who reported a very unpleasant dream she had had and asked her analyst whether this didn't cast doubt on the Freudian claim that all dreams enact symbolic wish fulfilment. Her analyst replied that she had had the dream in order to fulfil her wish to disprove Freud's theories.

More generally, the ploy is to point out that the person assessing the validity or otherwise of psychoanalytic ideas is himself their subject and therefore not in a position to be objective. The trouble with this ploy is that it tends to rebound on those who advocate the theories because they, too, are encompassed by them. The argument that we reject Freudian ideas because we are in the grip of precisely the unconscious forces that they describe, invites the counter-argument that Freud himself must have put them forward and his followers now support them for the same reason. A more subtle way of dealing with contrary evidence is to suggest that appealing to factual evidence – or referring disparagingly to the lack of it – is to take the theories too literally: the child does not actually *see* his parents copulating; he only imagines that he has done so. Or, if that does not cut ice, to claim that the primal scene stands for some more fundamental relation to external reality and that stumbling upon the primal scene is not a historic event that took place at a certain moment in the child's life; rather it is a *structure* that represents the unconscious of the society to which he belongs. MacCabe, for example, describes Iragaray's 'linguistic' version of the primal scene (referred to above) as 'a diachronic fable of a synchronic functioning'.[24] Thus reinterpreted, the theory is sealed off from any kind of external assessment.

(b) Arguments

The resistance of Lacan's theories to empirical refutation does not prevent one from evaluating them in accordance with 'internal' criteria, assessing their consistency, explanatory power and plausibility. The theory of the mirror stage falls down on all three counts.

(1) *Consistency.* According to Lacan, the mirror stage extends from about six to about eighteen months. The moment when the mirror stage comes to an end

> inaugurates, by the identification with the *imago* of the counterpart and the drama of primordial jealousy (so well brought out by the school of Charlotte Buhler in the phenomenon of infantile *transivitism*), the dialectic that will henceforth link the *I* to socially elaborated situations. (*Ecrits*, p. 5)

Transitivism is an important concept for Lacan and for his literary and psychoanalytic followers. It is a sign of identification with others and evidence that the Oedipus complex has been, or is being, resolved. It is symptomised by the fact that 'The child who strikes another says that he has been struck; the child who sees another fall, cries' (p. 19). According to Lacan, the period in which transitivism 'dominates the entire dialectic of the child's behaviour in the presence of his similars' comes to an end at about the age of two-and-a-half years. Curiously, however, he says – on the same page – that this period begins *at the age of six months*. Few of us will have been lucky enough to overhear a six-month-old complain of being struck by one of his 'similars'. But that is a mere matter of fact. More serious than its mere factual untruth is that it conflicts with what Lacan himself had said a few pages earlier – which was that transitivism *inaugurated* the *end* of the mirror stage. But six months is the age when, Lacan teaches us, the mirror stage begins. No wonder it is so difficult to observe! In the context of such carelessness, the extreme precision of Lacan's claim that mimicry between children is most 'fruitful' if it takes place between 'children whose age differential is no more than two and a half months' is laughable.

(Incidentally, Lacan is completely at odds with Freud in locating the resolution of the Oedipal phase between eighteen months and two years. For Freud, the *pre*-Oedipal phase did not end until the age of three.)

Another key fact invoked by Lacan in putting forward his theory – linking it with his explanation of why man is unique amongst the animals in having a fully developed language and culture – is that the intensity of the human infant's response to the spectacle of its mirror image is of a different order from that of any other animal. In the paper devoted to the mirror stage, however, Lacan adduces the universal importance *throughout the animal kingdom* of the encounter with the mirror image and its connection with socialisation by giving examples of its influence in other species. A female pigeon will not usually ovulate without seeing another member of the species, nevertheless maturation of the gonads may occur as a result of catching sight of its own image in the mirror. Even more startling, the migratory locust can be changed from a solitary to a gregarious form by being presented with a mirror image 'provided it is animated by movements of a style sufficiently close to that characteristic of the species'. So much for the unique responsiveness of the human infant to its mirror image.

(2) *Explanatory power.* A theory that is worthy of the name should not assume all that it is intended to explain. Lacan's theory of infant development is enormously ambitious: it encompasses a genetic epistemology. It claims to have something to say about the genesis of the infant's sense of its self, about its perception of Others as in some fundamental sense equal to itself and about its developing the idea of a world of stable objects. Even more ambitiously, it tries to unpick the origin of the adult world picture, claiming that the real world is either primordial chaos or simply unknown to us and that the world of things (and not merely the infant's access to the world of things) is a product of the world of words.

The ontological thesis is readily dealt with. Although it is suggested that the word of differentiated 'reality' is the product of the world of linguistic 'difference', it has already been assumed that, by the time the child accedes to the symbolic realm, certain differentiated things have been interacting. The mirror stage pre-supposes the existence of at least four separate 'things' – the infant's body, the mother's body, the mirror itself and the mirror image. In addition, a natural standpoint optics ·is presupposed.

How otherwise would the movements of the infant's body be matched by those of the mirror image, and the infant's face be reflected in a consistent fashion in the mirror, so that it could be recognised as being the same on repeated presentation? The pre-linguistic existence of these objects and of the optical relations between them is hardly consistent with Lacan's extreme nominalism or the literary theories that his followers believe his work justifies. If 'the world of words creates the world of things', then we are not entitled to suppose that there are any *things* at all in the pre-linguistic reality of the infant or the extra-linguistic realm of the Real.

Lacan believes he has uncovered the roots of our sense of (unified) self in the infant's identification with his mirror image. To be a self is to enjoy self-recognition mediated through some material or human Other with which one identifies. Since that Other is *not* oneself (by definition), the self or ego thus produced is a fiction. It is a fiction that is cherished, however, because, unlike the unmediated experience of one's bodily being-there, it is stable. The sense of self is consequently founded upon misrecognition. So much for the ontogenesis – and the Lacanian debunking – of the self and the idea of the unified person. How much is this an explanation of the origin of the *I*? How far does it justify the conclusion that the self is a fiction?

It is no kind of explanation at all. In order to construct his theory, Lacan begins with the assumption/observation that the child can recognise his own face in the mirror. This is accepted as a given that requires no further analysis or explanation. He does not wonder what 'own' can mean here where there is no formed conception of the self as being opposed to other human and material objects. Nor does he apparently consider it necessary for his ontology that he should furnish an explanation of the fact that the child can pick out its own image from the background of the person holding it.[25] He also overlooks the extraordinary fact that the child is able to identify its image across a series of transformations and under all sorts of circumstances: he has, in other words, nothing to say about the fundamental puzzle of genetic epistemology, that of object constancy. The self may be a fiction but, if it is, how does the child manage to refer so many different manifestations of its body in the mirror, to the same self? Whence, if the direct, proprioceptive experience of the body is that 'one is in pieces', does the idea arise that 'one is a unity'?

Why should a series of random exposures to quite different images of oneself give rise to a fictitious idea of stability that overrides the more continuous – and according to Lacan true – deliverance that one is fragmented? Whence the belief or feeling that the 'salutary' mirror image is 'unitary' and 'localised in space and in time?'.

Even less satisfactory is the Lacanian account of the genetic epistemology of objects – an account that is ambiguous as to whether or not it is also an explanation of the nature of those objects or a critique of the concept of an object. According to Rose

> The identification of an object world is . . . grounded in the moment when the child's gaze was alienated from itself as an imaginary object and sent back to it the message of its own subjecthood. Access to the object is possible only through an act of self-identification.[26]

The object seems stable because it is fixated by a stable gaze:

> It is from this fixity, and the images that are thus produced, that the subject is able to postulate objects of permanence and identity in the world.[27]

Primordial chaos is brought to heel by the infant's basilisk stare! Rose notes that

> Janet (quoted by Lacan) compared the formal stagnation of the images just produced to the frozen gestures of actors when a film is halted in mid-projection.[28]

We know, of course, that there is no such thing as a steady gaze: the eye is in constant motion and if the image were held fixed on the same point of the retina, it would fade due to bleaching of visual pigments and accommodation of the nervous system. We have also been told that the infant faced with the image of his own body wriggles around in constant play; so there could be no purely specular basis for the sense of one's own body, or the mother's body, as a stable thing. The theory also assumes a synthesis of visual experiences across time and this presumably could take place only within a self or subject that was united with itself over time. Finally, the suggestion that a stable gaze would freeze the object into a stable thing would be tenable only if the object itself were stable, i.e. already frozen; that the ontogenesis of the object had already been accomplished and the child's gaze was encountering preformed objects. In other words, even if the theory of the mirror stage *were* a contribution towards a genetic epistemology of object perception, it would still have nothing to say about the ontological status of apparently material objects. There is a circularity in Lacan's account of the genesis of the sense of a stable self and of stable objects outside of the self. Objects are endowed with a stable identity through identification of the subject with them. Thinghood, in other words, is displaced selfhood. But selfhood is displaced or introjected thinghood . . . all seems to be suspended in the air.

A key assumption of the theory of the mirror stage is that the developing infant is perceptually ahead of its motor capacities: 'The child anticipates on the mental plane the conquest of the functional unity of his own body, which . . . is still incomplete on the plane of voluntary motility' (*Ecrits*, p. 18). We are expected to believe, in other words, that the child *imagines* a unity he has not *experienced*, to accept that his development is governed by the intuition of a oneness to which there corresponds no experience and for which, according to orthodox Lacanian teaching, there is no basis in reality, in the Real. The sense of self – precisely that which it purports to explain – is therefore *presupposed* in Lacan's account of child development, even though the latter claims to show that the self without external foundation – that it is, in short, a fiction.

And what of Lacan's theory of the accession to the realm of the Symbolic and the acquisition of language? Most of the processes by which this is supposed to take place are predicated upon the prior achievement of a fairly advanced level of linguistic attainment. The child who consents to become a signifier must have suffered the experience of hearing the parents talking about him. He must, that is to say, have understood that the sounds emitted by the parents were *linguistic* and that the conversation referred to *him*. 'There is', the reader will recall MacCabe informing us,

a moment when the infant (*infans*: unable to speak) enters language: In the process of entry he/she becomes aware of certain places which he/she can occupy – these are the points of

insertion into language. Crucially this involves the learning of
pronouns: the realisation that the 'you' with which the child is
addressed by the father or mother can be permutated with an
'I' in a situation from which it is excluded when the parents
speak to each other.[29]

An action-packed 'moment'!

There is, of course, no evidence for such a giant intuitive leap
on the part of the child. Indeed, all the evidence is to the contrary.
Although Humboldt and the earliest linguists thought that
personal pronouns constituted the most primitive layer of
language, Jakobson has presented convincing arguments (and
evidence) that their acquisition represents an advanced stage of
linguistic attainment. The personal pronouns are the last elements
to be acquired in the child's speech and also the first to be lost in
aphasia. Their very nature as 'shifters' – their reference depends
upon who is using them – means that they have a double
structure, uniting conventional and existential bonds within the
same sign; and this makes them extremely complex.[30] Pronouns
are an unlikely place for a sensible *infans* to choose to enter
language. And if one assumes, as Lacanian theory does assume,
that the acquisition of language right up to the appreciation of the
shifting reference of pronouns requires no explanation, then one
is (yet again) bypassing all that a theory of its apparent scope
should take account of and try to explain.

Special pleading may save Lacan's theories from the charge of
'factual insubstantiality' but no amounts of such pleading can
save a theory that assumes all the things it pretends to prove or
explain.

(3) *Inherent plausibility.* Enough has been said so far to show that
the theory of the mirror stage lacks empirical support and that as
Lacan presents it even lacks internal consistency. Moreover, even
if it were true and internally coherent, it would explain none of
those aspects of infant development that it purports to explain.
The final point to be made against the theory is that it is not even
inherently plausible.

The basic idea of the mirror stage is that the child's sense of self
is decisively influenced – even created – as a result of the accident
of its catching sight of itself in a mirror. This immediately raises
the question as to what would happen to a child in a household

or a country without mirrors?[31] Supposing mirrors were banned
on the grounds that they encouraged vanity over one's personal
appearance? This is an unlikely state of affairs but the point of this
thought experiment is to highlight the absurdity of a theory that
proposes an *accidental* basis for a fundamental aspect of human
development. One measure of the value, truth or explanatory
power of a theory is its ability to predict novel facts or at least to
accommodate facts that were not taken into account when the
theory was originally formulated. If epistemological maturation
and the formation of a world picture were dependent upon
catching sight of oneself in the mirror, then the theory would
predict that congenitally blind individuals would lack selfhood
and be unable to enter language, society or the world at large.
There is no evidence whatsoever that this implausible consequence
of the theory is borne out in practice.

(c) Style

(1) *The dance of the signifier or Lacan-can.* If my exposition of
Lacan's theory of the mirror stage has made sense, I may be justly
accused of traducing the original which at best consists of tatters
of clearness amidst a general fog. Much discussion of Lacan's
writing – both by his followers and his opponents – is taken up
with his style. This is highly appropriate because without his
distinctive manner of writing, it is unlikely that his *oeuvre* – which
is divided between original ideas which are either baseless or
incoherent and mangled versions of others' ideas – would have
made much of a stir. The Lacanian style – now, alas, widely aped
by literary theorists (especially those of a psychopoetic
persuasion) – has much in common with the verbal chaos of the
usual run of psychoanalytic writing. The addiction to jargon, the
piling up of abstractions and the citation of authorities without
precise reference, the clumsy literary allusions, do not distinguish
him from other meta-theoreticians of the human psyche. On top
of all these vices, however, he has vices of his own that make him
an especially poor writer in a field where competition for the
wooden spoon is fierce indeed.

There are many points where, his apologists explain, he tries to
mimic the mental operations that he is supposed to be talking
about. 'Lacan's own notoriously sybilline style, a language of the
unconscious all in itself, is meant to suggest that any attempt to

convey a whole, unblemished meaning in speech or script is a pre-Freudian illusion.'[32] Random associations, elliptical allusions, puns, deletion of the steps in arguments, and so on all contribute to the opacity of his publications. Word play is especially prominent and many arguments are carried forward through a series of puns on the grounds that the 'free play of the signifier' will show the reader what the unconscious really is. Malcolm Bowie, a writer sympathetic to Lacan, states that

> A complete account of the characteristic features, syntactic and other, of Lacan's style would include: the ambiguous *que*, disturbances of conventional word order, literal and metaphorical senses interwoven, periphrasis, ellipsis, leading notions alluded to rather than declared, abstractions personified, persons becoming abstractions, widely different words becoming synonyms, synonyms being given widely different meanings. . . . All this keeps the signified as a palely fluttering presence behind the rampaging signifier.[33]

To attack this style would be to play into the hands of the Lacanians, by betraying one's inability to handle the anxiety aroused by the suspension of definitive meaning, the permanent deferment of closure of sense. Any such attack would anyway be superfluous, since it would be difficult to formulate a more telling criticism than the inadvertent critique assembled by the contradictory claims of the apologists of his style: *qui excuse, accuse*.

> As contradiction is inherent in language, and as all language thereby becomes, in some sense, self-critical, no external tests are necessary. And to fail a test is, in any case, also to pass it.[34]

> Truth which seeks to remove itself from the contradictory processes of language becomes falsehood there and then.[35]

> Lacan is the originator of a coherent and continuing tradition of scientific enquiry.[36]

> With his very first words, Lacan states his trenchant opposition to the fundamental proposition defended by his follower Laplanche . . . [who goes] . . . directly against the very point

on which his own statements leave *absolutely no possible doubt*, namely that, on the contrary, language is the condition of the unconscious[37] [my italics]

Thus, if one thinks particularly of the Lacanian theory of the relationship the subject has with spoken discourse . . . one is led to recognise in it an astonishingly lucid philosophy of man. Thanks to the efforts of the Lacanian school of psychoanalysis, we can now understand how the unconscious is formed at the beginning of life, what it is composed of, and what its precise modes of arrangement and functioning are. . . . I would be happy to be recognised as possessing the simple virtue of having proposed reasonable and clear explanations [of Lacan's writings] which will in future allow others to go further.[38]

So much for his apologists who, in defending Lacan's right to be obscure and self-contradictory, end up by contradicting themselves. Charles Larmore offers a more plausible explanation of Lacan's style (in so far as the style is deliberate rather than reflecting an intellect helplessly caught up in an interdisciplinary muddle): 'It is difficult to avoid the impression that his stylistic mannerisms are also aimed at covering over difficult theoretical problems by making it hard to pin down just what it is he is saying.'[39]

(2) *Terminology: the slippery phallus.* Larmore's criticism of Lacan's slippery style seems far too restrained when we come to consider the manner in which he uses key terms. In Lacan's writings – and that of his followers – it is true to say that anything can be made to mean anything.

Take, for instance, the phallus. In classical Freudian teaching, the phallus is the part of the anatomy that is threatened during the Oedipal stage. The child fears castration as a punishment for being its father's rival for the mother's love. In his almost impenetrable paper 'The signification of the phallus', Lacan 'rereads' Freud:

the phallus is not a phantasy, if by that we mean an imaginary effect. Nor is it as such an object (part-, internal, good, bad etc.) in the sense that this term tends to accentuate the reality pertaining in a relation. It is even less the organ, penis or clitoris that it symbolizes. (*Ecrits*, p. 285)

What, then, is this phallus, which seems to have taken leave of the infant's body painlessly, and yet without anaesthetic (unless it be the narcotic effect of Lacan's prose style)? The phallus 'is a signifier'. It is not any old signifier – like 'cat' or 'custard'. It is a *privileged* signifier 'intended to designate as a whole the effects of the signified' (p. 285). More specifically, the phallus is 'the privileged signifier of that mark in which the role of the logos is joined with the advent of desire' (p. 287). It is a signifier, in other words, that signifies Lacan's theories about the relationship between primal repression and the accession to language or the Symbolic! We now know that nappy changes may uncover a marvellous little sign that contains, as it were on microfiche, the very essence of the *Ecrits*!

The suspicion arises that Lacan's redefinition of the phallus (in the course of which it acquires and loses a capitalised initial letter, doubtless symbolising its alternation between the erect and flaccid state) makes his theories entirely circular. This is amply confirmed by one of his most admiring commentators who has this to say about the Phallus (which is also here The-Name-of-the-Father): 'The exact nature of this "Name-of-the-Father" or of the "Phallus" remains obscure, but can be thought of as corresponding for the child to his confused and varied intimate experiences which go to make up Freudian thought.'[40] Perhaps it is the amount of 'dissemination' ('a linguistic or textual productivity which escapes the domination of or determination by concepts'[41]) taking place that makes the phallus such a slippery customer to get hold of. No wonder, anyway, that 'Lacan speaks with approval of Humpty-Dumpty as "the master of the signifier".'[42] As Bowie says, 'he proves himself a worthy heir of Lewis Carroll's aggressive talking egg'.

A similar serious inconsistency in terminology is to be found in his commentators. As we noted earlier, Lacan seems to use the terms 'subject' and 'ego' or 'I' interchangeably. And yet the distinction between the two is considered to be one of the great achievements of Lacanian thought. Bowie, for example, points out that, for Lacan,

Whereas the ego, first glimpsed at the mirror stage, is the

reified product of successive imaginary identifications . . . the subject is not *thing* at all and can be grasped only as a set of tensions, or mutations, or dialectical upheavals within a continuous, future-directed process.[43]

And Larmore writes 'Lacan's important insight has been that theories of the constitutive subject fail through not having distinguished between subject and ego.'[44] Lacan himself, however, speaks of the subject 'being a subject only insofar as he speaks' (*Ecrits*, p. 269). The subject then would appear to exist on the far side of the entry into language rather than being merely that which is *behind* the successive identifications that give rise to the ego. The Lacanian subject, in other words, seems to be unable to decide whether it is the shaping spirit – or, rather the shaping emptiness, like Sartre's pour-soi – behind the imaginary or symbolic identifications; or whether, like the *I*, it is a product of those identifications. Whether, in short, it is *constituting* or, like the ego, merely *constituted*. Althusser, of course, assimilated both conceptions of the subject to the political subject and has been criticised by Lacanians for that reason.

5.4   FURTHER REFLECTIONS

The discussion in the preceding section may go some way towards explaining why in the United Kingdom and elsewhere, Lacan's standing as a genetic epistemologist and clinician is higher in departments of English and French Literature than amongst philosophers whose tastes are for more coherent argument, psychologists acquainted with the scientific method and medical practitioners aware of the pitfalls of clinical diagnosis. Some of his ideas – such as, for example, that the infant is comforted by the spectacle of his wholeness in the mirror – have a temporary intuitive appeal and the training of literary critics consists for the most part of learning how to articulate intuitions. That training is less directed towards acquiring proficiency in weighing the competing claims of rival theories, collecting empirical evidence or assessing the extent to which available or offered data support one theory rather than another. Lacan's major metaphysical conclusions seem often to be taken over on trust as *results* by critics who may be unable to follow the steps by which they were derived or to appreciate the absence of such steps. It is of course a good deal easier to take exciting ideas 'on board', as part of one's 'intellectual equipment', than it is to make a responsible evaluation of them.

As a contribution to the theory of child development, Lacan's *oeuvre* has one outstanding virtue: it is in tune with the helplessness and pathos of infancy, with its *difference* from the adult world, with the imperatives of need and desire that drive the little *hommelette* to seek a shape for itself and the urgency with which it tries to find order in its world and the catastrophe of madness that ensues if this fails. The very implausibility of Lacan's theories sharpens one's sense of the inexplicable miracle of infant development. But this single virtue is cancelled out by the many vices I have outlined in this chapter. I should like to end with some general observations: (a) on the character of Lacan's theorising; (b) on the relevance or otherwise his theories may have to realism in fiction; and (c) on what they teach us, by their bad example, about the requirements for any account of child development that has pretensions to being a genetic epistemology.

(a) The Character of Lacan's Theorising

It is frequently unclear whether Lacan is describing, explaining or hypothesising. Consider his account of the stages of self-recognition in the mirror.[45] In the first stage, the infant confuses his reflection and reality: he tries to seize hold of the reflection or find it behind the mirror. At the same time he confuses it with the image of the adult holding him. In the second stage 'he acquires the notion of the image and understands that the reflection is not a real being'. In the third, and final, stage, he realises that the image is his *own* and manifests intense joy.

At first this seems like an intelligible narrative of events based upon observation or the laying bare of a mechanism. It soon becomes apparent that many of the 'observations' are not observations at all but hypotheses; or at least fairly shaky interpretations of what may or may not have been observations in the first place. We are offered something that looks like a 'descriptive explanation'. It is in fact no such thing: it is neither a description nor an explanation but a chain of conjectures presented as pseudo-description. We are told that the child learns: (i) to distinguish between reflection and reality; (ii) to dissociate its own image from that of the adult; and (iii) to identify the appropriate image as being its own. The reader will consult Lacan's writings in vain for an empirical description and even less for an explanation of these fundamental processes. But without an account of *how* the child is able to distinguish between the real and the non-real or between itself and others, the sequence of events outlined above does not amount to an *explanation* of anything. It bypasses the very mysteries it purports to confront. But if it is not an explanation what is it? It is certainly not a set of empirical observations – we are not told of the frequency with which the events referred to have been observed to take place or the conditions under which the observations were made. Lacan's version of the evolution of the mirror stage, in other words, is a patchy rational (or quasi-rational, or semi-rational) reconstruction, supported by a dubious periodisation, that survives precisely by being ambiguous as to whether or not it is a description, an explanation or a series of hypotheses.

(b) Linguistic and Literary Implications

It has often been thought that Lacan's 'discoveries' about the genesis of the self and the acquisition of language have profound implications for our interpretation of the relationship between language and reality and of the nature of the self and that they undermine, on both counts, the pretension of realistic fiction to give an account of how things 'extra-linguistically' are.

According to Lacan, the sense of self is based upon identification with something that is not the self: in the mirror stage there is an imaginary identification with the mirror image; after accession to language a symbolic identification with the father results in a self that is a 'mobile signifier'. In either case, the self is a 'fiction'. Access to objects, moreover, requires identification with them; so, by the same token, things, too, are fictions: they belong to the realm of the Symbolic. The Symbolic realm is composed of signifiers without signifieds since the true signified, the mother as object of desire, has been foresworn, under the threat of castration, in the resolution of the Oedipus complex. Since signifiers cannot exist outside of the linguistic system, everything relating to the Symbolic realm must be internal to language. The self and its world is intra-linguistic: 'It is the world of words that creates the world of things. . . . It is in the world of meaning of a particular language in which the world of things will come to be arranged.'

There is, as we have already noted, not a shred of evidence that the acquisition of language (significantly referred to as 'accession' to the symbolic, as if language were something the child could pick up all at once, or 'entry' into language, as if it were something he could just walk into) is linked in this way to the resolution of the Oedipus complex. Indeed, Freudian theory is against any such link, in so far as the resolution of the Oedipal conflict is supposed to take place between the ages of three and six years, whereas the entry into the symbolic realm apparently occurs at the end of the mirror stage which, we have been told, is at about eighteen months. Let us suppose, however, that Lacan's account of things were true. Would it support the linguistic and literary conclusions that have been drawn from it – that language cannot refer outside of itself and that realism in fiction is a sham? Not at all. For if object perception and the sense of self are based in the first instance upon imaginary identifications of the subject with that which is not itself, then the entirety of human consciousness and experience must be founded upon such fictions. The pre-linguistic world of the infant confronting its mirror image must be as fictitious as the post-linguistic one. If realism is impossible because *all* discourses are founded upon misrecognition, then, by the same token, so is all consciousness. Realistic fiction is no more imprisoned inside an illusion than any other discourse or indeed consciousness; if it is thus imprisoned, the illusion is one to which there is no alternative and the prison one which has no outside. A specifically Lacanian theory of language and, more particularly, a specifically Lacanian case against realism is not upheld. In short, if Lacan's theories were true and they did have the implications his literary followers seem to believe they have, the implications would only be those of any idealistic philosophy which casts doubt on our ability to have access to a 'real' world outside of consciousnesses (cf. Chapter 4).

(c) Genetic Epistemology and Ontology

A further problem relates to *levels* of argument and the validity of drawing ontological conclusions from developmental observations. Lacan's theory of the mirror stage and beyond is immensely ambitious. It purports to explain how the developing infant comes to construct a world of things and a thing-like self as the moving centre of that world. With his emphasis on desire (desire for the Other, desire to be unified, and so on) and on the role of arbitrary signs (in the Symbolic realm), he is presenting an alternative genetic epistemology to those advanced by the cognitivists (who emphasise the interaction between perception, motor activity and innate mental structures in the acquisition of the adult word-picture) and those of associationist or learning theorists (who emphasise non-arbitrary signs and a world picture whose coherence simply reflects the spatio-temporal coherence of the world outside the organism accessed through direct experience and extended through 'stimulus generalisation'). (Although desire in Lacan, rather as in Sartre, is perhaps too self-transparently and continuously metaphysical, lacking in specific, even erotic, detail.) As a contribution to genetic epistemology, Lacan's theories are unsatisfactory for a variety of reasons of which their lack of empirical basis, their internal inconsistency and their incompleteness are foremost. But there are additional grounds for concern.

These further problems cannot be laid solely at Lacan's door but are inherent in the project of genetic epistemology, of describing how the child acquires the adult *metaphysical* world picture. We have to consider our own attitude towards the *endpoint* of intellectual development; to examine whether, when we describe how the child comes to see the world as we see it, we imagine we are explaining how he came to have access to the 'truth' about the world or whether we think we are discovering the aetiology of an *illusion* he shares with us. Our view about the mind-independent reality of material objects, say, may determine our whole strategy in investigating or thinking about the acquisition of object constancy. The very nature of our question will be influenced by whether or not we think of objects as genuinely out there for perception to gain access to or whether they are artefacts of the perceiving subject, constructs out of sense data. It is important that we make the kind of question we are asking quite clear; otherwise we are in danger of conflating two tasks – that of seeing how the child acquires our world picture and that of *evaluating* that world picture – and hence of wobbling between descriptive genetic epistemology and critical epistemology, between ontogenetic psychology and ontology. If we are unhappy with the received world picture, we may find ourselves writing a premature 'teratology' of adult consciousness, a critique of the adult world picture based upon a few conjectures about its genesis in developing individuals. At any rate, we may not be aware of the extent to which our account of the 'metaphysical development' of infants is *tendentious* until we clarify our attitude towards the destination of this process. Only when we have done so will we be able to separate ontogenetic psychology from ontology. For we cannot do developmental psychology *and* ontology at the same time: to try to do so would be rather like using a certain method of measurement to test a particular hypothesis while at the same time using the measurements to assess the validity of the test. The fundamental problems of Lacanian theory are symptomatised in his claim that the mirror stage is both 'one of those critical moments in man's mental genesis' (*Ecrits*, p. 17) *and* that it reveals 'an ontological structure of the human world' (p. 2).

Separating psychological ontogenesis from an evaluative or even revisionary ontology may not be easy. To fail to do so, however, is to succumb to 'the genetic fallacy' that Margaret Boden has defined succinctly as 'thinking that one can justify some belief (or impugn its validity) simply by detailing its history'.[46] Hamlyn has argued that 'philosophical questions about the nature of a certain form of understanding and about its conditions and criteria are utterly divorced and distinct from psychological questions about the conditions under which such understanding develops in individuals'.[47] This is, of course, too extreme, but Hamlyn's further assertion that 'a theory that rests upon both empirical and philosophical considerations must have a degree of incoherence', though directed against Piaget's genetic epistemology, puts a finger upon what is most awry with Lacan's speculations.[48]

Whether or not the genetic fallacy is a fallacy, one should be cautious – as Lacan and the Lacanians have, conspicuously, *not* been cautious – in using conjectural genetic epistemology as a critique of ontology. Once one judges the adult view of 'what kinds of things there are' in the light of psychological ontogenesis, then scepticism is a foregone conclusion. The very process of proposing *mechanisms* by which the developing infant comes, say, to form an idea of a self or acquires the belief that there are mind-independent objects must inevitably cast the validity of those entities into question. For the mechanisms by which the child acquires adult concepts and gains access to the objects and structures of the adult world can never seem less questionable than the grounds for adult belief in them are shaky. There is as yet no philosophical proof of the existence of mind-independent objects; so the infant's grounds for inferring their existence will fall short of absolute proof. If, as Bradley said, metaphysics is 'the finding of bad reasons for what we believe upon instinct', then genetic epistemology must seem like the art of unmasking the child's even shakier reasons for believing what we believe; or reinterpreting those reasons as mere mechanisms or structures within a developing organism, validated only by some unexplained survival value.

By so signally failing to confront the problems implicit in genetic epistemology, Lacan does us the unwitting service – perhaps the only one performed by his *oeuvre* – of emphasising the importance of doing so. Only after these problems have been faced are we in a position to approach infant development with the rigour appropriate to the great intellectual challenge it represents. The challenge – almost as great as that of epistemology itself – is that of uncovering the mechanisms whereby the human infant becomes free of mechanism – or is able at least to rise above it, in part to control it and in part to know it. Of establishing, in short, how it is that an organism comes to live a life that it seems in part to choose rather than merely live. Despite the claims usually originating from academic departments of English and French literature that the Master has 'suggested ways in which intellectual rigour might be possible in branches of psychology where vagueness and guesswork have reigned until now',[49] the Lacanian muddle contributes nothing, apart from its singularly intense vision of the *difference* of infancy, to meeting that great challenge.

6

Walking and Differance: Towards a Reinstatement of Legocentrism

6.1 SPEECH AND WRITING

(a) The Primacy of Speech

At first sight, it seems obvious that speech has priority over writing; that the former is the central linguistic phenomenon while the latter is merely a device for capturing speech in a less transient form and permitting its diffusion beyond the temporal or spatial reach of an individual voice. This is, of course, a simplification. Many texts – for instance this book – are unlikely to have originated first as continuous spoken utterances and then been written down. Because what is written is preserved, it can be revised, collated, organised and connected with other moments of writing to generate a continuous discourse that could not have conceivably been produced in a single stretch of speech. This does not, however, impugn the priority of speech; the written text can still be plausibly regarded as the accumulation of many moments of actual speech (as in a transcript) or of potential speech (as in a text written over many years).

It appears equally evident that without speech there would be no writing: a race or culture all of whose members were literate but speechless would be difficult to imagine. Moreover, while it may be plausibly argued that it is the gift of language, more than any other characteristic, that has distanced man from nature, speech nevertheless originates as a neurobiological function like walking. Writing, by contrast, is a cultural acquisition, an 'optional extra'. While writing has to be *learnt* – through formal instruction – and requires artefacts (pen, paper, ink), speech *develops* and involves no such extra-corporeal elements.

As if these facts were not argument enough, the primacy of

speech is supported by its chronological priority in the history of the human race as a whole and in the lives of individuals. Such evidence as is available indicates that speech antedates writing by nearly a hundred thousand years.[1] Individual children almost invariably acquire speech before they are taught to write. The teaching of writing presupposes speech: it depends on *spoken* instructions. Furthermore, children learn to write ('write down') what is spoken. They may, of course, begin by copying down written material. Nevertheless, these written symbols are from the beginning correlated with spoken sounds; and the ultimate aim is to teach children to write down speech or thoughts that they formulate as speech. (The difference between 'colloquial' speech and 'formal' writing – or between the 'restricted codes' appropriate to domestic exchanges and the 'elaborated codes' of most written discourse – emerges only after the fundamentals of writing have been grasped. The stylistic autonomy of writing does not threaten the priority of speech.)

It is inconceivable that the reverse – with speechless children being taught language by means of written instructions – should become typical. Aphasia for the spoken word is an unusual and tragic pathological condition; whereas illiteracy has historically been the norm. Speech is a human universal, while writing is a specialised – and until recently a minority – skill.

The assumption that speech is the primary linguistic phenomenon and writing a secondary development would seem then to be unassailable. Though the written word now dominates the civilised world, writing remains subservient to speech or, at least, is predicated upon it: we are still primarily speakers and listeners and only secondarily writers and readers.

The commonsense view that the prior existence and acquisition of speech is *the condition of the possibility of writing* has, since the publication of Jacques Derrida's *De la Grammatologie (Of Grammatology)*,[2] been questioned by literary theorists. Indeed the opposite view, that writing is the condition of speech, is now almost commonplace in certain academic circles. The arguments I have rehearsed in the opening paragraphs would be dismissed by many critics as the mere rationalisation of an ancient prejudice against writing that can be traced at least as far back as Plato. This 'phonocentric bias', Derrida and his followers believe, originates from a deep need to conceal the disturbing truth that writing, and not speech, is the primary manifestation of language. For behind phonocentrism – the privileging of the spoken voice over the written text – is 'logocentrism', a belief in the existence of an order of meaning inherent in the outside world and independent of language. Phonocentrics imagine that speech reflects or embodies that order and that writing merely 'represents' (to use Saussure's term) speech. They regard writing as being at two removes from its object; whereas speech is at only one remove: speech is composed of signs, while writing consists of signs of signs.

Derrida denies all this; in particular, he attacks the assumption that the meanings expressed in language are anterior to it. The logocentric prejudice is bound up with the idea that somewhere unmediated being is to be found; that beyond or behind signs there is a fundamental asemic reality that is simply 'there' and with which one can make direct contact. Behind logocentricity, in short, is an implicit 'metaphysics of presence' which Derrida defines as 'the determination of the being of the entity as presence' (*OG*, p. 12). It corresponds to the faith that the trail of signs comes to an end – in unmediated presence.

According to Derrida, therefore, the overthrowing of phonocentricity and the displacement of phonocentric linguistics by a universal 'grammatology' (a term constructed on analogy with 'phonology') has enormous implications. By inverting the hierarchy that gives speech priority over writing, Derrida thinks he has exposed logocentrism and 'the metaphysics of presence' to a destructive critical inspection. He has, it is claimed, confronted a prejudice which is at once so universal and so deeply rooted in Western culture as to be virtually its defining characteristics. 'Phonocentricity' is a vital clue to the nature of Western culture, its pathognomonic sign.

(b) Irrational Phonocentricity

Before engaging with Derrida's well-known beliefs about 'language' and 'presence', it is necessary to strip them of a spurious authority they derive from being presented as consequences of, or part of, a *diagnosis* reached by an exhaustive examination of the history of Western culture. I say 'spurious' because it is considerably easier to give the impression of an established diagnosis and to imply that certain ideas are confirmed by that diagnosis than it is to prove those ideas directly by valid, explicit arguments. And when, as is so often the case in Derrida's writing, argument towards a conclusion is interwoven with exposition of that conclusion as if it had already been established and with description of an already diagnosed condition, then it is possible to present even the most paradoxical results as firmly established, even though they are ill substantiated and have been put forward on the basis of arguments that are not infrequently self-contradictory and usually fall short of final proof.

To establish his diagnosis of Western culture, Derrida needs to present phonocentrism as both *universal* and *irrational*. By a careful selection of examples (Saussure, Rousseau, Lévi-Strauss in *Of Grammatology*; Husserl in *Speech and Phenomena*[3]) and by an often unscrupulous manipulation of their views, he endeavours to suggest that phonocentricity is not only a constant theme in Western philosophy, but, indeed, an unbroken and central tradition. He also insinuates that wherever phonocentrism is most vociferous (if this word is not overdetermined) it is also irrational.

His method with his chosen examples is to 'deconstruct' their writings. Deconstruction dismantles implicit or explicit philosophical positions by showing how the texts in which they are advanced undermine themselves from within and betray an unconscious commitment to views precisely opposite to those which they overtly propound. Deconstruction in Barbara Johnson's succinct formulation involves a 'careful teasing out of the warring forces of signification within the text'.[4] So Derrida sets out to catch notable phonocentrics actually preferring writing to speech.

One such specimen, dissected in *Of Grammatology*, is Rousseau. Rousseau, Derrida tells us, dismisses writing as a mere supplement to speech and condemns it as 'a destruction of presence and as disease of speech' (*OG*, p. 142). Nevertheless, we are informed in Rousseau's *Confessions*, he prefers to hide himself away and present himself to society through writing because 'If I were present, one would never know what I was worth' (*OG*, p. 142).

Although Rousseau sees writing as 'a destruction of presence', as unnatural and artificial, it is still apparently the medium through which he chooses to make his essential or natural self present to others. Derrida believes this inconsistency to be very revealing indeed: it betrays an irrational hostility to writing.

Derrida thinks that he observes a similarly inconsistency in Saussure. 'Language and writing' Saussure writes 'are two distinct systems of signs; the second exists for the sole purpose of representing the first. The linguistic object is not both the written and the spoken form of words; the spoken forms alone constitute the object.'[5] Indeed, 'writing obscures language; it is not a guise for language but a disguise' (*Course*, p. 30). But Saussure then appears to contradict himself by employing illustrations drawn from writing in order to clarify the essential nature of linguistic units.

Another recipient of Derrida's deconstructive attentions is Husserl who, it is claimed, has deeply metaphysical reasons for preferring speech to writing, the voice to the text. This preference however turns out to originate in a conception of signs that actually undermines the metaphysical difference between these two modes of linguistic communication. Derrida's critique of Husserl (see note 3) is sympathetic and in parts truly illuminating; it raises issues that are central to this chapter. I shall therefore devote a separate section (6.3) to it. There is considerably less to be said for his deconstructions of Rousseau and Saussure and I shall deal with them briefly here as part of the process of removing the *diagnostic* force of Derrida's assertions so that they may then be examined solely on the strength of their supporting arguments.

What Derrida believes he has identified in those writers who most vociferously privilege speech over writing is a process of pragmatic self-refutation. Their assertions, he thinks, are undermined by the positions implicit or explicit in their texts. In fact, things are not as simple as Derrida believes them to be and whereas these writers may nibble at the edges of their own arguments, they do not actually gnaw at their roots. Unlike Derrida himself, Saussure, Rousseau and others are rarely in the position of having already sawn off the branch they claim to be sitting on.

When Rousseau derogates writing as 'a destruction of presence' and yet prefers it to speech as the best means of displaying himself in a true (or advantageous) light in society, he is not being inconsistent. In the artificial society in which he feels uneasy – a society that hides itself behind manners and mannerisms – a blundering child of nature (such as Rousseau romantically conceived himself to be) may find it impossible to give authentic expression to what he regards as his true self. 'Real-time', 'on-line', self-presentation may prove impossible in a hostile environment. Writing in the security of his own hide-away, he may find it easier to present an external surface of himself that conforms more closely to that which he thinks he is. In a diseased society, writing – 'a disease of speech' – may be the best medium to which an individual may present himself. Anyone with a stammer, anyone lacking stage presence when exposed to the public gaze, will not unnaturally prefer writing to speech as a way of communicating himself, although he may at the same time recognise that writing is an indirect method of communication and for that reason unsatisfactory. One might be cynical about Rousseau's self-image; but his self-deceptions do not undermine the phonocentric position, nor do they have any metaphysical significance. What we see in Rousseau is not pragmatic self-refutation, but compromise.

It is really rather odd that Derrida should choose not to see Rousseau's inconsistency in this light as this is precisely how Jean Starobinski, to whom he seems to have been indebted for drawing this passage to his attention, convincingly analyses it (*OG*, p. 142). 'Deliberate misinterpretation of compromise as self-refutation' could also summarise Derrida's handling of Saussure. Saussure is not necessarily being inconsistent when he looks to writing for illustrations of the nature of linguistic units – despite his assertion that writing 'exists for the sole purposes of representing speech' and is a secondary, not a primary, linguistic phenomenon. As he himself says, it is only through writing that he can get a grip on the object of linguistics:

> Whoever consciously deprives himself of the perceptible image of the written word runs the risk of perceiving only a shapeless and unmanageable mass. Taking away the written form is like depriving a beginning swimmer of his life-belt. . . .

> To substitute immediately what is natural for what is artificial would be desirable; but that is impossible without first studying the sounds of language: apart from their graphic symbols, sounds are only vague notions, and the prop provided by writing, though deceptive, is still preferable. (*Course*, p. 32)

The reasons for Saussure's inconsistency are obvious. Graphic signs are more tangible than vocalic ones; the latter do not stay for inspection, vanishing as soon as they are spoken. So if I wanted to demonstrate how the different material realisations of the phoneme 't' do not alter its value (because the value of linguistic signifiers is purely negative and differential), it will be easier for my audience to grasp my point if I *write* it in three different ways (as indeed Saussure does) than if I *say* it in three different ways. It is easier to hold together in one's mind and to compare the members of a spatio-temporal series (an array of letters simultaneously present before the eye) than the members of a purely temporal series (a succession of sounds). Furthermore, *The Course in General Linguistics* comes down to us not as a spoken lecture but as a written text. All the more reason then, that Saussure's examples should be written rather than spoken. Even those who are suspicious of writing are obliged to record that suspicion *in writing*. Writers writing against writing must seem to be caught up in pragmatic self-refutation even if they are not. If Saussure had rigorously confined himself to the spoken word, his ideas would have faded with his death in 1913 and the fruitful intercourse of subsequent minds with his *Course* would not have given rise to the semiotic explosion of the sixties and the dissemination that followed it. (No great loss, perhaps.)

The examples studied so far give some idea of the nature of Derrida's much-vaunted 'close readings'. They are often characterised by his alighting upon a small part of a text – frequently a throwaway remark – and inflating its significance out of all proportion. The material with which he does the inflating is Derrida's own preconceptions and ideas. For example, he misrepresents Saussure's concern that writing should not seem to be the primary linguistic phenomenon as an hysterical antipathy towards it. When Saussure observes that writing 'is not a guise for language but a disguise', Derrida glosses this to imply that, for Saussure, writing

> is even a garment of perversion and debauchery, a dress of corruption and disguise, a festival mask that must be exorcised, that is to say warded off, by the good word.   (*OG*, p. 35)

Saussure's concern to set aside writing becomes

> Less a question of outlining than of protecting, and even of restoring the internal system of the language in the purity of its concept against the gravest, most perfidious, most permanent contamination which has not ceased to menace, even to corrupt that system.   (*OG*, p. 34)

Anyone going back to the original will be disappointed to find Saussure's mild animadversions against those who try to pronounce words as they are spelt rather than vice versa is all that Derrida's talk of 'perfidy' and 'corruption' amounts to. It is easy to see, however, how, by distorting Saussure's rational views about the respective relations of speech and writing, Derrida is able to transform certain petulant and pedantic remarks into the symptoms of a universal hysterical aversion to writing within western culture.

It will be clear that even Derrida's carefully chosen sacrificial victims cannot be plausibly charged with pragmatic self-refutation on this matter of the relative status of speech and writing. They prove resistant to his deconstruction. Or, rather, their inconsistencies are more amenable to a non-deconstructive reading. So even if one were to accept his few selected examples, his straw men, as being necessarily representative of western philosophy or western culture, the assumption that phonocentrism is always held irrationally (so that it can be regarded as a disease to be diagnosed rather than a position to be argued with) is not supported. Rousseau disliked writing because it was a *secondary* manifestation of language, it involved yet another intermediary between one person and another, it was artificial rather than natural. It is perfectly possible to regard writing as a mere supplement to speech – for the obvious and good reasons given in the opening section of this chapter – without developing a hysterical mistrust of it. *A fortiori* it must be rare for someone to use these reasons as a way of rationalising a hysterical prejudice.

Even if there are instances where phonocentricity does have an irrational origin, it does not follow that the belief itself is necessarily irrational. Because, for example, Plato's phonocentricity seems to stem from an original dislike of writing, it does not follow that *my* phonocentricity arises in the same way. To blacken a perfectly reasonable point of view by drawing attention to the fact that it is held by (amongst others) unreasonable people is unfair because it suppresses the fact that the same view might be held by reasonable people for good reasons. History can furnish us with examples of an almost infinite variety of views held for an almost infinite variety of reasons and motives. It would be no great feat to demonstrate, by appropriate selection, that phonocentrism was universally and irrationally held. It is all the more surprising then that Derrida hasn't succeeded in falsifying history more convincingly!

(c) Rational Phonocentricity

How often *is* phonocentrism irrational? One could easily cite writers who have seen speech as the natural, primary mode of linguistic communication without as a result becoming hysterically suspicious of writing. Why indeed should the 'naturalness' of speech justify distrust of writing? Men do not question the nutritional value of bread because it is 'less natural' than corn: quite the reverse. So while 'cool' or rational phonocentrism may be quite widespread (not surprising if it were true and reasonable), irrational hysterical phonocentricity is probably rare. Suspicion of writing *per se* is a minor tradition as Derrida himself acknowledges (*OG*, pp. 92–3 – discussed below). There is a much stronger tradition – extending from Cratylus to Artaud[6] taking in Apuleius and Somerset Maugham – of equal hostility to both speech and writing. Even more widespread is the elevation of writing *above* speech, of the written document above the oral report. This Derrida himself explicitly acknowledges when, as Norris reports, 'He agrees with Saussure that linguistics had better not yield uncritically to the "prestige" that written text have traditionally enjoyed in Western culture.'[7] This might suggest that Western culture is *not* synonymous with the few western philosophers Derrida chooses to examine; and that a few moments of Saussurean petulance or apparent self-contradiction cannot symptomatise Western philosophy.

The *prestige* of writing is easy to understand. For obvious practical reasons, important agreements are often accepted as valid only when committed to paper. Contracts and treaties, depositions and bills are legally acceptable and legally binding when written down. As writing has spread, so has the custom by which the outcomes of negotiation and discussion are defined by what has been signed or sealed on paper or parchment. History itself is almost synonymous with written history; the history of the pre-literate world, a history that has to be deduced from artefacts, is annexed as 'pre-history'. The real is the minuted or the documented; the best version of what took place is the written account; and the best history of the real is the history of marks on parchment and paper. (In consequence, the illiterate have been almost 'hidden from history'. The recent proliferation of technologies – photography and cinephotography, tape recording and the storage of digitised information on magnetic media – has not liberated historiography from its base in signifying artefacts from which the inscriber is absent at all times, except, in some instances, at the moment of inscription.)

Even in the religious sphere, there is no noticeable hostility towards the written word: the Holy Bible is no less sacred for being a *book*; the gospels have not been despised for failing to be the oral reminiscences of the Apostles; the Sermon on the Mount is not dismissed because it was 'unfortunately' preached centuries before the invention of the tape recorder. The most decisive transaction between God and Man resulted in writing: when Moses came down from Mount Sinai, he brought back not verbal reports, but 'tablets of stone, *written* with the finger of God'.[8]

Interestingly, Derrida himself bears testimony to this:

> The fact that access to the written sign assures the sacred power of keeping existence operative within the trace and of knowing the general structure of the universe; that all clergies, exercising political power or not, were constituted at the same time as writing and by the disposition of graphic power; that strategy, ballistics, diplomacy, agriculture, fiscality, and penal law are linked in their history and in their structure to the constitution of writing; . . . that the possibility of capitalisation and of politico-administrative organisation had always passed through the hands of scribes who laid down the terms of many wars and whose function was always irreducible . . .; that through discrepancies, inequalities of development, the play of permanencies, of delays, of diffusions etc, the solidarity among ideological, religious, scientific–technical systems, and the systems of writing which were therefore more and other than 'means of communication' or vehicles of the signified, remains indestructible, etc.   (*OG*, pp. 92–3)

In this interminable sentence, Derrida gives confused but persuasive witness to the prestige of writing and to the *trust* – rather than distrust – that was laid in it.

Not even Derridan history, therefore, by any means yields a uniform picture of irrational phonocentricity and associated graphophobia. It is speech, rather than writing, that has been the object of more widespread mistrust – for the obvious practical reason that spoken words, unlike written ones, fade on emission. Committing oneself in writing means that one cannot so easily forget, or, if one does forget, withdraw: the written commitment is independent of the vagaries of memory and the fluctuation of feelings. Where there has been a traditional preference for speech over writing – as in court proceedings – this has been in order to make it possible for an individual to be questioned on-line in real time. It is perhaps easier to lie in a written statement (which can be checked before submission for internal consistency and plausibility) prepared in the calm of the study than in a public inquisition. But this has much more to do with the conditions of preparation than with the medium one is using. There is no metaphysical issue at stake: a defendant dealing with the cross-examination on-line by means of written answers will be in the same position as the speaker, except that he will have a little more time to think. Contrarywise, a speaker giving a rehearsed answer will be in the position of a defendant submitting a written testament. Moreover, when it comes to the question of perjury, what is said is identified as that which has been recorded by the clerk of the court: the definitive account of the court proceedings is the written account.

In summary, there is considerably more evidence for a graphocentric bias than for a phonocentric one in Western culture.

(d)　Historical Diagnosis versus Rational Argument

Why should Derrida be at such pains to misreport and misrepresent history? It is my belief that it is because he is excited by an idea he has about the nature of Western culture triggered by his reading of certain philosophers – notably Husserl, Heidegger and Hegel. He wishes to prove that the impossible quest that these philosophers set themselves is symptomatic of a universal project implicit in Western culture. Husserl's tortured pursuit of 'presence', which we shall discuss in Section 6.3, is considerably more exciting if it is symptomatic of Western culture than if it is merely the egregious problem of a small group of philosophers. Diagnosing history and cultures is a relatively simple matter: it is always easier to insinuate and then to assert a diagnosis than to clinch a difficult argument. Strong diagnoses and weak argument can act synergistically and may together carry conviction that neither alone would warrant. Derrida's need to diagnose Western culture, then, is based upon a wish to find the easier way to prove the validity of certain insights he feels that he has had as a result of his philosophical studies.

Of course, Derrida's preference for diagnosis over rational argument – or for insinuation over analysis – is also connected with his notorious repudiation of logic. Since, according to the fundamental principle of deconstructionism, logical arguments will inevitably generate conclusions that conflict with their premises – and the more powerful they are, the more it is likely to happen – it is acceptable, even preferable, to be illogical. Some of Derrida's followers, in particular the 'wild' deconstructors of the Yale school – and most notably amongst them Geoffrey Hartman – have taken this to mean that anything goes (so long as it goes into print).

Until the short final section of this chapter, I shall resist the Derridan temptation to *diagnose*, rather than to analyse, and attempt to assess Derrida's arguments and assertions on the basis of their internal consistency and their plausibility. Though they are ultimately misleading, one has to admit that they take their rise from interesting observations and traverse exciting realms of thought. Once we have set aside Derrida's *diagnoses* and uncovered the weakness and absurdity of his *arguments*, it will become clear that his importance does not lie in his celebrated assertions about 'language' and 'presence' or in his deconstruction of philosophy 'as a form of writing'. On the contrary, the interest of his works lies in his, largely unconscious, performance as a spokesman of the tragically flawed human condition.

6.2 THE ILLUSION OF PRESENCE

(a) The Aetiology of Phonocentricity

According to Derrida, phonocentrism originates from a deep impulse to suppress the truth about writing and, ultimately, about language, reality, meaning and ourselves. For to acknowledge that writing is the condition of possibility of speech and not vice versa would threaten much more than the 'privileged' status of speech. Writing, one of Derrida's commentators tells us 'is a threat to the deeply traditional view that associates truth with self-presence and the "natural" language wherein it finds expression'.[9] Or, as Derrida himself has expressed it

> phonocentrism merges with the historical determination of the meaning of being in general as *presence*, with all the subdeterminations which depend on this general form and which organise within it their system and their historical sequence (presence of the thing to sight as *eidos*, presence as substance/essence/existence [*ousia*], temporal presence as point [*stigme*], of the now or of the moment [*nun*], the self-presence of the cogito, consciousness, subjectivity, the co-presence of the other and of the self, intersubjectivity as the intentional phenomenon of the ego, and so forth).   (*OG*, p. 12)

With so much at stake, it is small wonder that there is something of a rush to keep writing in its place.

Phonocentrism is a symptom of the logocentric epoch. The temporal boundaries of this epoch are somewhat ill-defined. They seem to reach back as far as the origin of writing. Since, according to Derrida, Heidegger was a representative figure (*OG*, p. 12), we must still have been in this epoch in the seventies. I suspect it is synonymous with Western history (plus or minus a bit of pre-history). Its spatial boundaries are even less sharply defined. Where does the West end and the East begin? It may be that these terms have conceptual rather than spatial boundaries and that 'Western culture' is a term with value but no reference (value, that is to say, for Derrida). Alternatively, it may be the case that the logocentric epoch (or culture) is really 'the world' under another name.[10]

Be that as it may, Derrida thinks that the characteristic belief of this epoch is that meaning is 'out there', external to language, situated either in the consciousness of the speaker/writer or in the world that his discourse is 'about', or in the coincidence between the two that is called 'reference'. Logocentricity in turn is an aspect of 'the metaphysics of presence' – 'the historical determination of the meaning of being in general as *presence*' (*OG*, p. 12).

Phonocentrism has its roots, then, in the metaphysics of presence; but it is not a mere passenger. It actively supports logocentric metaphysics. Phonocentrics believe not only that speech has priority over writing, but that there is a profound difference between these two modes of communication. While the speaker is invariably present in his voice, the writer is usually absent from his text. My speech does not outlive the moment of my speaking, whereas the purpose of my writing something down is that my text *does* outlive the acts by which I committed it to paper. Writing permits communication in the absence of the communicator: Homer can communicate with me millennia after his death. The speaker, in contrast, until the very recent development of means of recording the human voice (which is, anyway, really a means of inscription or 'writing down' of the voice), has to be present to talk to me.

Derrida denies this apparently fundamental difference between speech and writing. We are, he asserts, no more absent from our writing than from our speech because 'presence' is itself an illusion. (It is an illusion that, as we shall see, curiously arises out of the accidental properties of speech.) Being absent from, or non-present in, what we communicate is the *normal* state of affairs. For this reason, writing, far from being a mere supplement to speech, is closer to the heart, the truth, the reality, of language because it gives no support to the illusion of presence. Writing is nearer to that proto-writing which is the condition of the possibility of *both* voice and text. And this is a disturbing truth that phonocentrics, unlike Derrida, cannot face and why writing 'has the power to dismantle the whole traditional edifice of Western attitudes to thought and language'.[11] It is this that lies at the bottom of the hysterical, as opposed to rational, phonocentricity Derrida has found everywhere in Western culture by so assiduously mis-reading one or two philosophers.

(b) Present Speaker, Absent Writer

In what sense, according to phonocentrics, is the speaker 'present' in his voice? The illusion of vocal presence encompasses many connected beliefs. Here are a few:

(i) there is a self behind the voice that authenticates or endorses what is said;

(ii) the self is the point of origin of the speech;

(iii) the voice is animated by the consciousness of the speaker and expresses what he 'has in mind' at the moment of utterance;

(iv) the meaning of the words used by the voice are what the speaker means by them – in other words, there is a more or less

complete coincidence between signifying intention and verbal
meaning;

(v) expressed meaning matches a meaning inherent in the
extra-linguistic world so that the voice refers outside of itself to
an external state of affairs of which its utterance may be true.

The relationship between the writer and what is written does
not feed such illusions of origin, presence, reference, meaning
and truth. When we come across a copy of *The Iliad*, we do not
imagine that Homer is in the page authenticating what is written
on it. He is not currently the origin of what we are reading: the
words are not animated by his consciousness, nor do they express
what 'he has in mind'. The text, moreover, does not refer to a
world currently surrounding Homer's body in which the meaning
of his words is to be found.

Thus common sense. Derrida, however, disputes the validity of
this sharp contrast between speaking and writing:

> The thesis of the *arbitrariness* of the sign . . . must forbid a
> radical distinction between the linguistic and the graphic
> sign.   (*OG*, p. 44)

Writing is *not* exterior to language proper

> from the moment one considers the totality of the determined
> signs, spoken, and *a fortiori* written, as unmotivated institutions,
> one must exclude any relationship of natural subordination,
> any natural hierarchy among signifiers or orders of signifiers. If
> 'writing' signifies inscription and especially the durable
> institution of a sign (and that is the only irreducible kernel of
> the concept of writing), writing in general covers the entire field
> of linguistic signs. In that field a certain sort of instituted
> signifers may then appear, 'graphic' in the narrow and derivative
> sense of the word, ordered by a certain relationship with other
> instituted – hence 'written', even if they are 'phonic' – signifiers.
> The very idea of institution – hence of the arbitrariness of the
> sign – is unthinkable before the possibility of writing and
> outside of its horizon. Quite simply, that is, outside of the
> horizon itself, outside the world as a space of inscription, as the
> opening to the emission and to the spatial *distribution* of signs,

to the *regulated play* of their differences, even if they are 'phonic'. (*OG*, p. 44)

Or, as Jonathan Culler has glossed it, 'writing-in-general is an archi-ecriture, and archi-writing or proto-writing which is the condition of both speech and writing in the narrow sense'.[12] The fundamental difference between speech and writing is therefore apparent rather than real; and speech is a subdivision of writing. In so far as there *is* a difference between these two modes of communication, it is that speech conceals its true nature better than writing does. To see speech as a natural, direct mode of communication and writing as artificial and oblique – 'the representation of a representation' – is therefore to see things upside down. It is in writing rather than in speech that we find language in its most artless state: writing is language wearing its essence on its sleeve. For linguistic signs are *essentially*, rather than *accidentally*, devoid of the presence of a signifying agent.

(c) The Origin of Presence

Since speech is a form of writing and writing is characterised by the absence of an originating consciousness, how are we to account for the belief that we are present in our voices? What is the aetiology of this illusion of presence? Or indeed of any sense of presence? According to Derrida it is, astonishingly, the result of a trivial accident whereby speakers hear themselves speak.

When I utter a remark, I hear and understand what I have said. 'Presence' is an effect of this closed circuit of auto-affection constituted by the phenomenon of 's'entendre parler' (where 'entendre' means both 'to hear' and 'to understand').

Speech and the consciousness of speech – that is to say consciousness simply as self-presence – are the phenomenon of an auto-affection lived as suppression of difference. That *phenomenon*, that presumed suppression of differance, that lived reduction of the opacity of the signifier, are the origin of what is called *presence*. (*OG*, p. 166)

(We shall come to 'differance' in due course.) As a result of the happy accident of hearing oneself speak, conversation seems to be

a communication between two absolute origins that . . . auto-
affect reciprocally, repeating as immediate echo the auto-
affection produced by the other. Immediacy is here the myth of
consciousness. (*OG*, p. 166)

It would be no exaggeration to say that the consequences are
enormous

> The system of 'hearing (understanding) oneself-speak'
> through the phonic substance . . . has necessarily dominated
> the history of the world during an entire epoch and has even
> produced the idea of the world, the idea of world-origin, that
> arises from the difference between the worldly and the
> nonworldly, the outside and the inside, ideality and nonideality,
> universal and nonuniversal, transcendental and empirical,
> etc. (*OG*, pp. 7–8)

'These are large claims' Jonathan Culler comments with massive
understatement and no evident irony.[13] They are indeed; so large,
one is curious to know what could be left over for the 'etc.' to
refer to. That the claims are not only large but implausible, we
shall discuss later.

Presence, it would seem, is an effect of the afferent feedback
that makes us feel that we are where our words are, that we
inhabit our voices, that we put our meaning where our mouths
are. We also convey this feeling to our listeners: to them, the
voice is the obvious point of intersection between linguistic
signification and the physical body – though, as we shall see, the
Husserlian reason for singling out the *voice* as the bearer of self-
presence is that sounds are spared the degradation of traversing
the opacity of the body and hence of having location in external
space.

Compelling though it is, the illusion of presence remains an
illusion; for in so far as he is deposited into language the speaker
is absent from himself. What he says does not embody some
meaning anterior to language – a piece of his consciousness, or of
the physical world, or the meaning the latter has to or in the
former. On the contrary, meaning is an effect of language; it is
generated within language. If meanings are extrinsic to language
users and internal to language, then depositing oneself in language
cannot be a way of being present to oneself or 'coming to oneself'.

The self-presence of the speaker is an illusion. Speakers are no more present in what they say than writers are in what they write or have once written. Only a groundless logocentricity leads speakers to believe in the existence of a realm of pre-existent, extra-linguistic meaning.

(d) The Absent Speaker

Derrida's reason for denying presence, or self-presence to the speaker are invariably badly presented. It is often unclear where he is putting forward an argument and where he is making an assumption. Presuppositions, premises and conclusions are mixed together in the seamless muddle of his prose. Often one does not know when he is presenting his own views and when he is presenting (or misrepresenting) the views of others.[14] Nevertheless, it is possible to identify three major strands to his dissent from the idea that a speaker is present in his discourse. They relate to: the notion of differance; the 'boundless context' of the speech act; and the iterability of the linguistic sign.

(1) *Differance*. Derrida takes his cue from Saussure. Although I summarised the relevant aspects of Saussure's thought in Chapter 3, I shall reiterate the fundamental principles here, for the reader's convenience. For Saussure, the arbitrary nature of the linguistic sign is the primordial fact of language. The actual material composition of individual linguistic units is irrelevant to their signifying functions. Linguistic signs are not, for example, 'motivated' by a physical resemblance to that which they signify. Linguistic signs are not only arbitrary, but also unable to operate in isolation: the essence of language lies in the *relations* between these arbitrary signs. The individual unit owes the specificity of its function to the *system* to which it belongs.

The sign is a fusion of the signifier and the signified – of a 'sound image' and a 'concept' – and both signifier and signified are relational entities. The essence of the signifier

> is not the sound alone, but the phonic differences that make it possible to distinguish this word from all others, for *differences* carry signification. (*Course*, p. 118)

Phonemes are not characterised by their own positive qualities, but simply by the fact that they are distinct. Phonemes are above all else opposing, relative and negative entities. (*Course*, p. 119).

The signified, too, is a relational entity. Signifieds do not precede language; prior to their incorporation in linguistic signs, there are no discrete signifieds, no discrete 'ideas' (as Saussure calls them) only 'an indefinite plane of jumbled ideas'. Signifiers and signifieds are picked out only in relation to each other and they exist in mutual definition

> A linguistic system is a series of differences of sounds paired with a series of differences of ideas.   (*Course*, p. 120)

It is differences that carry signification:

> in language there are only differences. Even more important: a difference generally implies positive terms between which the difference is set up; but in language there are only differences *without positive terms*. Whether we take the signified or the signifier, language has neither ideas nor sounds that existed before the linguistic system, but only conceptual and phonic differences that have issued from the system. The idea or phonic substance that a sign contains is of less importance than the other signs that surround it.   (*Course*, p. 120)

Derrida seizes upon Saussure's insights and, in his belief, draws out the radical consequences implicit in them, implications that Saussure himself shied away from.

> The first consequence to be drawn from this is that the signified concept is never present in itself, in an adequate presence that would refer only to itself. Every concept is necessarily and essentially inscribed in a chain or system, within which it refers to another and to other concepts, by the systematic play of differences.   (*Speech and Phenomena*, p. 140)

The efficacy of a particular linguistic sign depends upon the implied presence – that is, the absence or non-presence – of the other linguistic signs with which it has an oppositional relationship. Linguistic signification and verbal meaning are thus inextricably interwoven with non-presence. Saussure, Derrida says, reminds us

> that the play of differences was the functional condition, the condition of possibility, for every sign; and it is itself silent. The difference between two phonemes, which enables them to exist and operate, is inaudible. (*SP*, p. 133)

Linguistic meaning, moreover, is not only founded upon 'the systematic play of differences' but also upon deferral. Meaning – the ultimate target of the sign – is always deferred. Every signified may itself be a signifier, so that there is no closure of meaning, no final or transcendental signified. As was discussed in Section 3.3 (and we shall return to this in Section 6.3(c)), Derrida cites C. S. Peirce in support of this view. According to Peirce, a sign is

> anything which determines something else (its interpretant) to refer to an object to which itself refers (its object) in the same way, this interpretant becoming in turn a sign, and so *ad infinitum*. . . . If the series of successive interpretants comes to an end, the sign is thereby rendered imperfect, at least. (*OG*, p. 50)

Derrida interprets this to imply that 'from the moment there is meaning there are nothing but signs'.

> *We think only in signs.* Which amounts to ruining the notion of the sign. . . . One could call *play* the absence of the transcendental signified as limitlessness of play, that is to say as the destruction of onto-theology and the metaphysics of presence. (*OG*, p. 50)

Linguistic signification, whether it is in speech or in writing, being founded upon the play of differences between signs and haunted by deferral of the closure of meaning, is riddled with 'differance'. 'Differance' – a neologism intended to carry the fused concepts of difference and deferral – is

> the movement of play that 'produces' (and not by something that is simply an activity) these differences, these effects of differences. . . . Differance is the nonfull, nonsimple 'origin', it

is the structured and differing origin of differences. (*SP*, p. 140)

Differance looks remarkably like Sartre's for-itself, the Néant that woke Être out of coma. At times, it even looks a bit like what other philosophers might call consciousness. But of this more later.

Verbal meaning – and hence speech acts and speaking subjects as much as written texts – is shot through with non-presence. How can a speaker be *present* in his meaning when meaning itself is entwined with *absence*? Furthermore, since meaning is an effect of language, it cannot be pre-linguistically embodied in the outside world or the intentions of a speaker. Saussure has apparently shown us that

'language [which consists only of differences] is not a function of the speaking subject'. This implies that the subject (self-identity or even consciousness of self-identity, self-consciousness) is inscribed in language, that he is a 'function' of the language. He becomes a *speaking* subject only by conforming his speech . . . to a system of differences . . . to the general law of differance. (*SP*, pp. 145–6)

Derrida forsees an objection to this radical conclusion

to be sure, the subject becomes a *speaking* subject only by dealing with a system of linguistic differences; or, again, he becomes a *signifying* subject only by entering into a system of differences. . . . In this sense, certainly, the speaking or signifying subject would not be self-present, in so far as he speaks or signifies, except for the play of linguistic or semiological difference. But can we not conceive of a presence and self-presence of the subject before speech or its signs, a subject's self-presence in a silent and intuitive consciousness? (*SP*, p. 146)

Derrida's answer to this question is negative. His reasons for denying the possibility of an 'asemic consciousness', a pure presence of the self to itself, unmediated by signs, are given in his essay on Husserl and we shall discuss them in Section 6.3. For the present, we shall allow his claims that differance is primordial, and that the self-presence of the speaking subject is an effect of differance, to pass unchallenged.

(2) *Speaker's intentions and the boundless context of speech acts.* Phonocentrics believe that the meaning of a well-formed utterance will embody, or will be animated by, a signifying intention present in the consciousness of the speaker. In opposing this view, Derrida uses, and then uses against him, Austin's speech act approach to verbal meaning.

According to Austin, the meaning of an utterance is not determined solely or even primarily by the words of which it is composed. Utterances are *acts* and the meaning – or force – of any act is at least in part determined by its context.[15] Features of the context will be utilised in the conventions that determine the nature and guarantee the success or (to use Austin's word) the 'felicity' of the speech act. Felicity conditions and truth conditions are almost inextricably interwoven. The same words will have a different force – or no force at all – in a different context. For example, the success – and the existential truth – of the utterance 'I do' as a marriage vow will be crucially dependent upon its taking place in a church under the appropriate conditions. It will not be fixed solely by the meaning its speaker intended it to have. In order (successfully) to mean what one says, it is not enough to say what one means – to choose the correct form of words. If the aim of the philosophy of language is (as Austin said it was) to elucidate 'the total speech act in the total speech situation' then such a philosophy must attempt to specify completely the context which will determine the felicity of individual speech acts. This however, is impossible. As Derrida points out, meaning is context-bound, but context is boundless: 'This is my starting point: no meaning can be determined out of context, but no context permits saturation.'[16] The context of a speech act opens on to the boundless text of society.

Since it is impossible to specify the context that determines the success of our speech acts, it will *a fortiori* be impossible to *intend* or to choose that context. We can scarcely intend that which we cannot even specify. We cannot choose or intend all of the factors that control or influence the meanings of our utterances. It follows from this that anyone who has successfully made, say, a promise, has executed a speech act that far outreaches his ability to intend. If we think of all the different ways in which an attempted promise may fail – the recipient is deaf, the speaker is (unknown to himself) no longer in a position to make a promise, and so on – and if we think, too, of all the traditions, conventions, concepts, etc. that are implicit in a promise, we shall be forced to conclude that the speaker can legislate over little of that which determines that his promise should have the meaning which he intends it shall have. None of this is likely to be 'in his mind' at the time of promising. Even in those cases, therefore, where we communicate successfully, we are not fully present in our utterances. Their meaning is more than or different from whatever it is we are capable of 'actively' meaning.

(3) *Speaker's intentions and the iterability of the sign.* Absence, in the form of differance, haunts the linguistic system as a whole. Absence, in the form of the boundless unspecifiable context of their success, haunts individual speech acts. Finally, absence penetrates even the individual sign. Speech is not only differance-ridden from within and context-haunted from without; it is also impersonal. Words, phrases, verbal responses are not personally 'owned' by the voices that use them. It is obvious why this must be the case: signs need to be recognisable as signs – and as signs of a particular class – if they are to signify at all. A particular token must therefore sacrifice its particularity in order to be a mere instance of a type. Signs are the inherited treasure of a language that antedates my very existence, and even more so, my present intention to speak.

This is true not only at the level of individual signs, but at higher levels of verbal response. We operate with clichés, catch-phrases, standard formulae, routine questions and answers – with prefabricated speech modules that have a connotative overlay transcending the particular uses to which we as individuals wish to put them. We are obliged to choose our words off the peg; they are not tailor made. Even in 'engaged' conversation, we sometimes seem as speakers to be mere echo chambers of oral intertextuality. Much of what we say appears to be citation, quotation from a verbal bran-tub, rather than an original use of words chosen to fulfil an independently conceived signifying intention. Even 'I love you' may, Culler says, partake of a quotation, a citation, rather than an originating utterance.[17] My very signature – as personal or personalised a sign as can be imagined – does not carry with it the guarantee of my personal signifying intention.

This is in part because signing is an act of signification whose felicity will depend upon conditions I cannot specify (and so, as noted above, can scarcely intend or have in mind) but also because

> In order to function, that is to be readable, a signature must have repeatable, iterable, imitable form; it must be able to be detached from the present and singular intention of its production. It is its sameness which, by corrupting its identity and its singularity, divides its seal.[18]

As Derrida points out, a *machine* can reproduce my signature and so 'sign' on my behalf.

It appears then that the very conventions which must be respected to ensure that a speech act is successful and its component linguistic signs are intelligible, divide the speaker from his speech. This has been well stated by Norris:

> This 'iterability' or power of being transferred from one specific context to another, is evidence that speech acts cannot be confined to the unique self-present moment of meaning. They partake of the differance or distancing from origin that marks all language in so far as it exceeds and pre-exists the speaker's intentions . . . The 'iterability' of performatives can be explained and located only within a larger system of non-self-present signification. They belong to *writing* in Derrida's sense of the word: an economy of difference nowhere coinciding with the present intentions of individual speech.[19]

There is one final related point to be made. According to Saussure, 'The idea or phonic substance that a sign contains is of less importance than the other signs that surround it' (*Course*, p. 120). If this really is the case, then the words we select to express 'ourselves', 'our meaning', and so on, owe *their* meaning to the words that we do *not* choose. Since we do not explicitly or deliberately unchoose or delete the entire system of opposing terms from which our chosen words derive their differential, specific meaning, then the meaning we choose is not chosen by us. Intention cannot therefore even penetrate our discourse at the level of word choice. We cannot possibly say (or intend) what we – or rather our words – mean.

(e) The Collapse of Presence

'Presence', then, is an illusion. Or rather a nexus of illusions. 'The metaphysics of presence' presupposes or provides a framework for several loosely associated ideas about external reality, consciousness, signifying intentions, speech acts and reference:

- (i)   There is an external world of present objects that impinges on the subject and gives rise to an image of itself. The process by which external world and subject are linked is called perception and the latter gives us access to the presence of the Other.
- (ii) On the basis of perception, the subject develops the idea of an external world and of a self that confronts that world.
- (iii) Part of the speaker's consciousness is incorporated into a signifying intention, is formulated.
- (iv) The signifying intention gives rise to an utterance as a result of the embodiment of the intention in signs; and the intention animates these signs.
- (v)   The resulting utterance refers to the outside world. Reference is the consequence of a coincidence between a meaning inherent in the outside world and a meaning inherent in a signifying intention embodied in an utterance. Or reference *is* that coincidence.

Derrida repudiates every aspect of this view of the relationship between language, reality, meaning and consciousness. Our utterances do not embody, nor are they animated by, our signifying intentions; nor, again, do they refer to a pre-existing extra-linguistic external reality. We can neither say what we mean nor mean what we say; and the meaning of our utterances does not lie outside of the language in which they are embodied. The critique of 'presence' goes further than this however. The very idea that there is an external world – from which meanings ultimately arise – simply present to consciousness is also repudiated. The presence of the 'other', as the meaning of being, as presence, is unintelligible and is an illusion – the byproduct of hearing oneself speak. With the abolition of the opposed presences of oneself and external reality comes the elimination of meanings 'out there' embodied in that external reality; and of language as the passive transmitter (as opposed to the source) of those meanings. More specifically the collapse of reference must eliminate the difference between referential and self-referential or non-referential utterance. There are no meanings 'out there' for language to receive, transmit or reach for.

The dismantling of presence takes us beyond purely linguistic considerations and to Derrida's critique of Husserl and the phenomenological quest for unmediated presence.

6.3 THE CRITIQUE OF HUSSERL

(a) The Phenomenological Project

Derrida's dazzling critique of Husserl (see note 3), by turns sympathetic commentary and beady-eyed man-hunt, is conducted at times with uncharacteristic fairness. It starts out from a detailed examination of *Expression and Meaning* (part of the first of Husserl's *Logical Investigations*) and proceeds to uncover internal conflicts within the phenomenological enterprise. These conflicts, Derrida argues, arise inevitably out of the Husserlian notion of 'Presence'.

'Presence' is the asymptote of the phenomenological quest for unmediated reality, for the apodeictically self-evident, for the primordially given. Derrida's deconstruction of the Husserlian idea of 'Presence' and – by a giant metonymy – of the 'Western Metaphysics of Presence' aims to demonstrate the hopelessness of this quest. Husserl, he believes, was under the spell of precisely the philosophical tradition from which he was most concerned to distance himself. By accepting as 'real', as 'indisputably there', the absolutely self-given, by assuming the primordiality of *immediate* presence, Husserl's phenomenological vigilance is controlled by the very metaphysical heritage he rejects.

Phenomenology starts by shedding all that cannot be known with absolute certainty. It is inaugurated by the so-called *epoche* or phenomenological reduction that brackets off all constituted knowledge whether it comes from metaphysics, psychology, the natural sciences or common sense. The naïve ontology of the natural standpoint, which accepts as given an external world, is not disputed but suspended: the 'external world' is seen merely as an object of belief, as being constituted in consciousness, the product of an active constitution of sense and value, of the activity of a *life* which produces truth and value in general through its signs. After the *epoche*, there remains only original self-giving objects – those that are present to sense in a full and primordial intuition. The immediately given, which lies on the hither side of signification, is the ultimate court of appeal as to what is really there.

The claim of phenomenology is that it puts to one side all that previous metaphysicians have previously taken for granted. It is neither confident of the truth of the common-sense world-picture, nor is it confidently sceptical. It simply suspends judgement about all that is not immediately given to consciousness. That, at least, is the claim. According to Derrida, however 'The phenomenological critique of metaphysics betrays itself as a moment within the history of metaphysical assurance' (*Speech and Phenomena*, p. 5). That assurance resides in the assumption that the being of the entity is determined as Presence (*Of Grammatology*, p. 12) and that reality consists of a succession of nows, of present moments. *Speech and Phenomena* deals with the contradictions inherent in the idea of an 'immediate' – or unmediated – absolute Presence (especially apparent in the light of phenomenology's own avowed aims); with the conflicts internal to the idea of the temporal present; and with the manner in which the idea of Presence originates out of the experience of the speaking subject.

(b) The Mediation of Signs

In *Expression and Meaning*, Husserl distinguishes between indicative and expressive signs. An indicative sign is something that moves 'something such as a "thinking being" to *pass* by thought to something else'. Its meaning lies outside of itself and so does not belong to the absolutely ideal objectivity that is allowed and retained after the phenomenological reduction. The signified of an indicative sign is not indubitably there; it is not guaranteed to exist. One can be misled by indicative signs into believing in the existence of something that does not in fact exist. For Husserl, the realm of the indicative sign is precisely that of those things that fall victim to the phenomenological reduction, that are bracketed off by the *Epoche*. They do not belong to the self-presence of transcendental life.

An expressive sign, on the other hand, is 'charged with its meaning' and is consequently not separated or separable from it. Such a sign is animated through and through by the signifying intentions of the subject. In expression, as opposed to indication, the signifying intention is absolutely explicit because it animates a voice which may remain entirely internal (as when one thinks to oneself – *vide infra*) or because what is expressed is a meaning that is an ideality 'existing' nowhere in the world. In contrast with the indicative sign – that is external, opaque and has a dead husk which would be pared away by the phenomenological reduction – the expressive sign is internal, 'lived' through and through, transparent. It remains intact, on the hither side of the phenomenological reduction.

So much for the apparent distinction between indicative and expressive signs, between the inferred and the immediately given, between that which is and that which is not bracketed off by the moment of philosophical doubt. The distinction, however, does not seem to withstand further examination. We have no primordial intuition of another's lived experience. Signs involved in communicating such experiences must, therefore, be indicative and consequently entrain an inexpressive component. Pure expression without indication is possible only when 'effective' communication is suspended; when, that is, there is no physical *mediation*. Such pure unity of the expression with the expressed is possibly only in solitary mental life where signs do not have to traverse the opacity of the body. But there is no use for signs in such inner life. The certitude of inner experience does not need to be signified: it is immediately present to itself. In solitary discourse, the subject learns nothing about himself, manifests nothing to himself. The process of purifying signification to its expressive core seems liable, therefore, to cause the very notion of a sign to collapse in on itself.

Moreover, the difference between 'mental speech' and external or 'effective' communication may not be as clear-cut as first appears. Even if we conceive of a pre-expressive stratum of sense, the content of genuinely solitary communication would still be *imaginary speech*. In order for expressive signs to make sense to us even in such speech, they are required to conform to a general form. So conformity to a general form is as much a property of expressive signs used in solitary communion as of indicative signs used in effective communication. Ideality, therefore, is a feature as much of imaginary as of external speech. Speech belongs to the order of ideal representation; or to look at things the other way round, effective language is as imaginary as imaginary speech: 'If every sign whatever is of an orginally repetitive structure, the general distinction between the fictitious and effective usages of the sign is threatened' (*SP*, p. 56).

This is the first move in Derrida's deconstruction of Husserl; Husserl's pursuit of the immediately given, as opposed to mediately presented being, presupposes an irreducible distinction between indicative or mediate signs on the one hand and expressive or immediate ones on the other. But it appears that there can be no unmediated signs. Once you pare an indicative sign to its expressive core, you are left with nothing. The unmediated sign is a nothing. Furthermore, in order to make sense to ourselves, even in solitude, we have to 'come to ourselves' through the mediation of signs that signify, by virtue of their generality, their antedating the present moment of consciousness. There is no 'language of the self' such as Paul Valéry dreamt of, no idiolect composed entirely of *hapax legomena*, no private language of self-communion.

The self cannot, therefore, manifest itself to itself through signs purified of indicative component. Are we then entitled to start off from the assumption that there is an asemic consciousness that is simple and simply present to itself and which would reflect its own presence in silence? Is there a self-presence produced in the undivided unity of a temporal present that would have nothing to reveal to itself through the agency of signs? Is there a consciousness to which language is merely *added on*? The answer to this question is no; though it is not always clear in *Speech and Phenomena* from whom that negative answer is originating. The basis for this negative answer comes from a consideration of Husserl's conception of the temporal present.

(c) The Temporal Present

No 'now' can be isolated as a pure instant. There is an irreducible 'spreading out of the "now"'.

> It belongs to the essence of lived experiences that they must be extended in this fashion, that a punctual phase can never be for itself. (*SP*, p. 61)

> The now-apprehension is, as it were, the nucleus of a comet-tail of retentions. (*SP*, p. 62)

The actual *now*

> is necessarily something punctual and remains so, a form that
> persists through continuous change of matter. (*SP*, p. 62)

According to Husserl, the temporal present is the 'source-point' of
primordial presence. But the analysis of the 'now' indicates that
the latter, far from being a bedrock given, is curiously elusive: a
form that continuously returns to itself. It is constitut*ed* rather
than constitut*ing*. The apparent immediacy of the self-given
present – the very touchstone of immediacy in phenomenology –
is *derived*. The privileged position of the present is consequently
undermined: the now of self-consciousness, of self-presence, of
perception through which presence is revealed, is a form that
comes to itself, or is realised, through that which is not itself. At
best, presence is a self-conscious consciousness constituting itself
via repeated return to itself, to a form that persists through a
continuous change of matter.

If self-presence is repeated presentation or *re*-presentation to
the self, it must be mediated – through signs. Presence is
consequently the continuous pursuit of the traces of itself. As
Derrida says

> the presence of the present is thought of as arising from the
> bending-back of a return, from the movement of repetition, and
> not the reverse. Does not the fact that this bending-back is
> irreducible in presence or in self-presence, that this trace or
> difference is always older than presence and procures for it its
> openness, prevent us from speaking about a simple self-identity
> . . .? Does this not compromise the usage Husserl wants to
> make of the concept of 'solitary mental life' and consequently of
> the rigorous separation of indication from expression?
>
> (*SP*, p. 68)

A continuous transition from perception to retention to protention
defines the now. 'Now' is therefore continuous with 'not-now',
perception with not-perception. Non-presence and non-evidence
are admitted into the instantaneous present. Presence itself is
mediated; immediacy is derived; immediate presence, originary
perception is a mirage.

There is no final home of meaning where the trail of indicative signs yields to the expressive core and the last sign is cashed as a meaning that does not point elsewhere. Presence is not a primordial given, existing prior to signs or to language. Language is not surpassed, extinguished in pure self-presence. On the contrary, self-presence is derived from or is an effect of language. Presence resides in the sign-mediated pursuit of itself; and it *is* that pursuit.

(d)   Phonocentricity and the Metaphysics of Presence

The phenomenological enterprise is, therefore, riddled with contradiction. The immediately given, the absolute now, the transcendental signified at which the trail of signs comes to an end, are themselves constituted out of signs. Why then is the idea of presence so powerful? Why is there a privilege attached to the here and now, to the present indicative? Why, in particular, is *speech* bound up for Husserl, with the idea of a 'perfect expression' whose telos is 'the total restitution in the form of presence of a sense actually given to intuition'? Derrida's study of Husserl's treatment of speech and presence reveals the origin of some of his own extraordinary ideas.

The reader will recall that Derrida attributed the origin of the illusion of presence to the closed circuit of auto-affection whereby the speaker hears and understands himself speak. It is evident from *Speech and Phenomena* that it is in Husserl rather than in Western culture that phonocentricity is so closely linked with the metaphysics of presence. For absolute presence to be mediated by signs it

> must be constituted, repeated and expressed in a medium that does not impair the presence and self-presence of the acts that aim at it, a medium that both preserves the presence of the *object* before the intuition and *self-presence*, the absolute proximity of the acts to themselves. The ideality of the object . . . can only be expressed in an element whose phenomenality does not have worldly form. *The name of this element is the voice. The voice is heard.* Phonic signs . . . are heard (and understood) by the subject who proffers them in the absolute proximity of their present. The subject does not have to pass forth beyond himself to be immediately affected by his expressive activity. My words

are 'alive' because they seem not to leave me; not to fall outside me, outside my breath, at a visible distance. (*SP*, p. 76)

Hearing oneself speak is quite different from, say, seeing onself write. In writing, the sign is external to the writer and is distinct from, and outlasts, his expressive intention, indeed is a dead product of it. The spoken word on the other hand does not outlast its being said, its being *meant*:

the phenomenological 'body' of the signifier seems to fade away at the very moment it is being produced; it seems already to belong to the element of ideality. It phenomenologically reduces itself, transforming the wordly opacity of its body into pure diaphaneity. This effacement of the sensible body and its exteriority is for *consciousness* the very form of the immediate presence of the signified. (*SP*, p. 77)[20]

The signifier, animated by my breath and by the meaning-intention is in absolute proximity to me. The living act, the life-giving act . . . which animates the body of the signifier and transforms it into a meaningful expression, the soul of language, seems not to separate itself from itself, from its own self-presence. It does not risk death in the body of the signifier that is given over to the World and the visibility of space. (*SP*, p. 77)

Hearing oneself speak is an 'auto-affection' and of a unique kind:

the subject can hear or speak to himself and be affected by the signifier he produces without passing through an external detour, the world, the sphere of what is not 'his own'. Every other form of auto-affection must either pass through what is outside the sphere of 'ownness' or forego any claim to universality. (*SP*, p. 78)

This auto-affection requires 'the intervention of no determinate surface in the world' unlike, for example, seeing myself in the mirror. The unity of sound and voice

which allows the voice to be produced in the world as pure auto-affection, is the sole case to escape the distinction between

what is wordly and what is transcendental; by the same token,
it makes that distinction possible. (*SP*, p. 79)

No consciousness is possible without the voice:

> the voice is the being which is present to itself in the form of
> universality, as consciousness; the voice *is* conscious-
> ness. (*SP*, pp. 79–80)

The absolute proximity of signifier to signified

> is broken when instead of hearing myself speak, I see myself
> write or gesture   (*SP*, p. 80)

Derrida contests the privileged status that Husserl attributes to
the voice, using Husserl's own arguments.

> taking auto-affection as the exercise of the voice, auto-affection
> supposed that a pure difference comes to divide self-presence.
> In this pure difference is rooted the possibility of everything we
> think we can exclude from auto-affection: space, the outside,
> the world, the body etc. As soon as it is admitted that
> auto-affection is the condition for self-presence, no pure
> transcendental reduction is possible. (*SP*, p. 82)

Auto-affection is the curious process by which consciousness
comes to self-presence by affecting itself, that is to say, by being
different from itself. This difference – or rather differance (because
it is both differing in space and deferring in time) – is

> not something that *happens* to a transcendental subject; it
> *produces* a subject. Auto-affection is not a modality of experience
> that characterises a being that would already be itself (*autos*). It
> produces sameness as self-relation within self-difference; it
> produces sameness as the non-identical.   (*SP*, p. 82)

How then does speech usurp this privileged position and give
rise to the fallacious idea of pure auto-affection?

> What constitutes the originality of speech, what distinguishes it

from every other element of signification, is that its substance seems to be purely temporal. (*SP*, p. 83)

But the idea of temporalisation is inextricably woven in with that of spontaneous auto-affection: the now is that which is always returning to, seeking out, representing itself.

The intuition of time itself cannot be empirical; it is a receiving that receives nothing. (*SP*, p. 83)

It is, as Husserl himself says, 'primal creation', underived, spontaneous.

Towards the end of *Speech and Phenomena*, Derrida gradually drifts from exegesis towards an advocacy of his own views. This will be apparent from the following:

The word 'time' itself, as it has always been understood in the history of metaphysics, is a metaphor which *at the same time* both indicates and dissimulates the 'movement' of the auto-affection. All the concepts of metaphysics – in particular those of activity and passivity, will and non-will and, therefore, those of affection or auto-affection . . . – *cover up* the strange 'movement' of this difference.

But this pure difference, which constitutes the self-presence of the living present, introduces into self-presence from the beginning all the impurity putatively excluded from it. The living present springs forth out of its non-identity with itself and from the possibility of a retentional trace. It is always already a trace. This trace cannot be thought out on the basis of a simple present whose life will be within itself; the self of the living present is primordially a trace. The trace is not an attribute; we cannot say that the self of the living present 'primordially is' it. Being-primordial must be thought on the basis of the trace, and not the reverse. This protowriting is at work at the origin of sense. Sense, being temporal in nature . . . is never simply present; it is always engaged in the 'movement' of the trace, that is, in the order of 'signification'. It has always already issued forth from itself into the 'expressive stratum' of lived experience. (*SP*, p. 85)

According to this highly Derrida-ised Husserl, the trace is not the trace of something that is simply present. There are always everywhere only traces.

(e) Primordial Supplementation

Indication is not simply 'added' to expression and the latter not merely 'added' to an inexpressive stratum of primordial experience. Nevertheless, with regard to indication and expression 'we can speak . . . of a primordial "supplement": their addition comes to make up for deficiency . . . to compensate for primordial non self-presence' (*SP*, p. 87). The paradoxical idea of 'primordial supplementation' (paradoxical because that which is supplementary cannot be primordial) feeds back into the concept of differance. Primordial supplementation

> not only implies non-plenitude of presence . . . but [the] function of substitutive supplementation in general, the 'in place of' structure which belongs to every sign in general. . . . The *for-itself* would be an *in-the-place-of-itself*: put *for-itself* instead of itself. The strange structure of the supplement appears here: by delayed reaction, a possibility produces that to which it said to be added on.   (*SP*, p. 88)

The very process of paring off what is non-essential to expression causes Husserl, Derrida claims, to put out of play the acts of intuitive cognition which 'fulfil' meaning. The fulfilling intuition cannot, therefore, be essential to expression, to what is aimed at by meaning. An expression can be absurd, without possible object, without thereby becoming meaningless. Consider, for example, the Golden Mountain, or the Square Circle. Since the absence of object does not imply an absence of meaning,

> we might be tempted to maintain not only that meaning does not imply intuition of the object, but that it essentially excludes it. What is structurally original about meaning would be the *Gegenstandlosigkeit*, the absence of any object given to intuition.   (*SP*, p. 92)

It is difficult to know who is meant here by 'we'. Whether 'we' means Husserl, Derrida, the philosophically trained reader or the

man in the street is uncertain; it could certainly not apply to a
reader who has an elementary grasp of the philosophy of language
and is able to appreciate the distinction between meaning and
reference. It is not, however, any part of the purpose of this essay
to discuss the accuracy of Derrida's exegesis of Husserl. Our
concern in presenting the argument of *Speech and Phenomena* is
only to establish the provenance of the ideas through which Derrida has achieved his reputation.

The possibility of speaking in the absence of the object or of an
expression making sense in the absence of the object or of the
speaking subject 'should structure the very act of him who
speaks' – even, Derrida claims, if the speaker is actually perceiving
the object that is spoken of.

> Let us consider the extreme case of 'a statement about
> perception'. Let us suppose that it is produced at the very
> moment of perceptual intuition: I say 'I see a particular person
> by the window' while I really do see him. It is structurally
> implied in my performance that the content of this expression is
> ideal and that its unity is not impaired by the absence of
> perception here and now. Whoever hears the proposition,
> whether he is next to me or infinitely removed in space and time
> should, by right, understand what I mean to say. Since this
> possibility is constitutive of the possibility of speech, it should
> structure the very act of him who speaks while perceiving. My
> non-perception, my non-intuition, my hic et nunc absence are
> expressed by the very thing I say, by that which I say *because* I say
> it. This structure will never form an 'intimately blended unity'
> with intuition.   (*SP*, pp. 92–3)

It is as if the fact of speech retro-acts upon the subject so that
speech and indicative signs become necessary not only to assert
what is there but to supplement it and to confer presence upon it:

> The absence of intuition – therefore of the subject of intuition –
> is not only *tolerated* by speech, it is *required* by the general
> structure of signification, when considered *in itself*. It is radically
> requisite: the total absence of the subject and object of a
> statement – the death of the writer and/or the disappearance of
> the object he was able to describe – does not prevent a text from
> 'meaning' something. On the contrary, this possibility gives

birth to meaning as such, gives it out to be heard and read.   (*SP*, p. 93)

We understand what someone has said even when they are dead.

Whether or not perceptions accompany the statement about perception, whether or not life as self-presence accompanies the uttering of the I, is quite indifferent with regards to the functioning of meaning.   (*SP*, p. 96)

'I' cannot, therefore, mean 'I' as the living present person, otherwise it would become meaningless as soon as I was absent or dead. To say 'I' is to absent myself in speech; for when I tell myself 'I am', this expression, like any other, according to Husserl/Derrida, has the status of speech only if it is intelligible in the absence of its object, in the absence of intuitive presence – here, in the absence of myself. Writing ('the common name for signs which function despite the total absence of the subject because of or beyond his death') is, therefore, 'involved in the very act of signification in general and, in particular, what is called "living" speech' (*SP*, p. 94).

The argument is faulty in at least two respects. First of all, the possibility of speaking of something that is not present does not imply that, when we speak of an object that *is* present, the latter is in practice absent. We could just as well argue that the possibility of speaking of an object in its presence implies that when we speak of it in its absence, it is really present. The same counter-argument applies to the living and dead subjects of the personal pronoun 'I'. Moreover, the fact that 'I' preserves its meaning when the person who used it is dead does not imply that 'I' could *never* have a living referent. Meaning and reference must be kept distinct. Clearly, to use Wittgenstein's example, the meaning of the expression "Mr N. N." could not be Mr N. N. himself, otherwise the expression would become meaningless whem Mr N. N. died. The statement 'Mr N. N. is dead' would then be meaningless – which patently it is not. The problem disappears once one perceives the elementary distinction between meaning and reference. (A difference that Derrida himself must be aware of in view of his references to Frege.[21])

It is on the basis of such arguments, however, that Derrida's fundamental claim that writing, which is usually thought of as merely supplementary to speech, is the primordial linguistic phenomenon, and that speech is predicated upon a proto-writing, has been advanced.

(f) Summary

Phenomenology begins with the idea of 'the living present', that which is 'immediately given', as the touchstone of reality. In pursuit of that immediate present, Husserl separates indicative from expressive signs, the former pointing beyond themselves to their significations, the latter being 'charged with their meaning'. Only expressive signs seem likely to give access to, or to reveal, immediate presence. Even expressive signs, however, will necessarily entrain an indicative husk if they are to be used in effective communication. It might seem, however, that in solitary communion, where they do not have to traverse the opacity of the body, they retain their expressive purity. If, however, they are to *mean* anything – even to a self communicating with itself – they must conform to a general form so that they may be recognised as signs. They must, therefore, move outside of themselves in order to signify themselves. Even within the context, then, of solitary self-communion, expressive signs still retain an indicative residue. Moreover, indicative signs are effective only in virtue of conforming to a general form. They, therefore, share the ideality of expressive signs. Husserl's initially confident distinction between expressive and indicative signs, between immediate and mediated signification, consequently undermines itself.

(Immediate) presence cannot be given through or carried by signs. Does it reside in an asemic consciousness that is simple and simply given to itself? The answer to this is no: self-presence inescapably involves the mediation of signs since it is a relation of the self to the self under the aspect of generality. The irreducibility of presence as a *relation* is illustrated by temporal presence and the inescapable 'spreading out of the "now"'. Now is a continual retention of, and return to, itself. It is infected by mediation.

Presence is not, therefore, a primordial given existing prior to signs. On the contrary, it is an illusion *arising out of* language; more particularly out of speech. The speaker, who is connected to himself in the closed circuit of hearing-and-understanding himself speak, is connected thus through the mediation of signs which fade away at the very moment of being produced. It is *this* that gives the speaking subject the character of being in a state of pure auto-affection and thereby creates the illusion of self-presence.

If presence and self-presence *were* primordial, they would scarcely need supplementation with speech or some other form of communication in order to be completed. They are not, however, primordial. Furthermore, not only is the presence of the speaker and of the object of his speech unnecessary for successful communication but, on the contrary, his absence is implicit in all such communication. Since I can mean an object that does not exist (such as the Golden Mountain), or which could not exist (such as the Square Circle), meaning is possible in the absence of that which is meant. Meaning in the absence of the speaker or his referent is possible only because verbal meaning necessarily presupposes those absences even when a present speaker is talking about a present object. This structural absence, according to Derrida, derives from that deferring and differing which he calls 'differance'.

6.4 THE ILLUSION OF THE ILLUSION OF PRESENCE

(a) The Giant Synecdoche

It is a commonplace of deconstructive criticism that it is the hostile critics of a text who are most likely to have fallen under its spell and to have accepted its presuppositions. Even – or especially – an adverse reading will imply complicity with the text that is attacked. As Culler writes, 'The transferential structure of reading . . . involves a compulsion to repeat, independent of the psychology of individual critics, based on a curious complicity of reading and writing.'[22] Barbara Johnson's critique of Derrida's study (of Lacan's analysis) of Poe's 'The Purloined Letter' aims to demonstrate this 'transfer of the repetition compulsion from the original *text* to the scene of its *reading*'.[23] The irony of Derrida's deriving his notion of 'presence' from Husserl could, therefore, have already been anticipated from 'the transferential structure of all reading'. Nevertheless, it cannot be allowed to pass without comment especially as it provides the key to much that is strange and absurd in Derrida's writings.

Throughout *Speech and Phenomena*, Derrida alternates between Husserl and 'Western philosophy' or 'Western metaphysics' and between these two and 'Western culture'. He treats them as if they were interchangeable. The breathtaking synecdoche Husserl = Western metaphysics = Western culture appears to cause him little embarrassment. Equating Husserl (and a few other philosophers) with 'Western culture', however, is no more bold than Barthes's dismissive definition of the 'bourgeoisie' in a few derogatory sentences or Foucault's confident, if opaque, assertions about 'the Classical episteme'. (See also note 10.) Whether or not Husserl's views are identical with, or diagnostic of, 'Western culture' is a position too implausible to be worth debating. For Derrida it is an *a priori* assumption not an empirical observation and an appeal to historical fact would be unlikely to yield decisive refutation. It is more important for the purpose of the present discussion to show the extent to which Derrida is under the spell of Husserl's strange and interesting ideas – to the point where he mistakes them for the framework of Western culture. Derrida's response to Husserl exemplifies in an extreme form the tendentious history writing (historiography that consists of wrapping up history in sweeping historical asides) we discussed in the first section of this chapter.

The unmediated presence that Husserl seeks to uncover by the *epoche*, and from which he wishes to derive the structures of everyday consciousness, proves to be extraordinarily elusive. And no wonder. The Husserlian quest is for a 'pure' presence uncontaminated with non-presence. Unmediated presence is either a paradox or a tautology. Presence is presence *to* and as such it must reveal itself to that which it is not via signs of itself. It cannot, therefore, be immediate. If, on the other hand, unmediated presence is *self*-presence then it must become present to itself without being or becoming other than itself. The idea of self-presence as a non-mediated relation to the self involves the paradoxical idea of a non-mediated relation; of a relation without distinct relata. So, if 'conciousness' means 'nothing other than the possibility of the self-presence of the present in the living present' (*SP*, p. 9) it is scarcely surprising that there is not much of it about. It is even less surprising that there is a shortage of it in the subject as speaker; for to communicate ourselves we must exteriorise ourselves, yield ourselves to the body and language. This must imperil the condition of absolute transparency or total interiority that Husserl demands for self-presence, and Derrida requires after him – especially since Husserl–Derrida believes that 'all speech, or rather everything in speech which does not restore the immediate presence of the signified content, is inexpressive' (*SP*, p. 40).

It is easy to see why the phenomenological project must be doomed from the outset. It can never restore all that has been 'put out of play' by the *epoche*. Intersubjectivity and the outside world presupposed in the natural standpoint cannot be derived from the solipsist or quasi-solipsist meditations of the philosopher. I say 'quasi-solipsist' because the *epoche* puts everything in brackets *except* the language that the philosopher uses in his meditations. This latter, if the meditations are to make sense to the philosopher, must be laden with inherited presuppositions. The vigilance that Husserl's quest demands is, in other words, impossible because the quest has to be conducted in a language which necessarily disarms vigilance at source. (Derrida himself almost sees this when he makes the Fregean point that it is an *assumption* that the theory of signs can be derived from epistemology and not vice versa.)

Derrida identifies 'Western culture' most closely with Husserl (and vice versa) when he considers Husserl's phonocentricity. The special status of the voice in Husserl becomes the rationale for the supposed privileging of the voice over written text in Western culture. Husserl's (and possibly Hegel's) ingenious interpretations of the impact of non-spatial signs upon the self-consciousness of those who use them is transformed into the presence itself:

> speech and the consciousness of speech – that is to say, consciousness simply as self-presence – are the phenomena of an auto-affection lived as suppression of differance, . . . that presumed suppression of differance, that lived reduction of the opacity of the signifier, are the origin of what we call presence.   (*Of Grammatology*, p. 166)

Consciousness of speech equals consciousness; self-presence in speech equals presence: the synecdoches are almost as breathtaking as Husserl = Western philosophy = Western culture. They would lead us to infer that the congenitally stone deaf, denied the happy accident of hearing themselves speak, would be denied self-presence. (Out of sound, out of mind, perhaps?) Not only would they be non-present to themselves (or lack the illusion of presence to themselves) but they would also be deprived even of the idea of the world. For, as the reader may recall

> The system of 'hearing (understanding)-oneself-speak' through the phonic substance – which *presents itself* as a nonexterior, nonmundane, therefore nonempirical or noncontingent signifier – has necessarily dominated the history of the world during an entire epoch, and has even produced the idea of the world, the idea of world-origin, that arises from the difference between the worldly and the non-worldly, the outside and the inside, ideality and nonideality, universal and nonuniversal, transcendental and empirical, etc. (*OG*, pp. 7–8)

Rampant, unchecked synecdoche can take one far into absurdity.

(b) Absolute and Ordinary Presence: A Confusion of Levels

Husserl's conception of presence is of an extraordinary tautology: something that is given to, or returns to, itself without being 'mediated'; an absolute proximity of acts to themselves. It is scarcely surprising, then, that there is nothing in ordinary experience answering to it. The real may not be rational (as Hegel would have us believe) or even intelligible; but it is not self-contradictory. We would not therefore expect to encounter many examples of Husserlian presence in daily life since the former is not only unintelligible but also self-contradictory. Unfortunately, Derrida takes the impossibility of Husserlian *metaphysical* presence to imply the impossibility of presence *tout court*. His most celebrated positions derive from a confusion of Husserlian absolute presence – the asymptote of phenomenology – with ordinary presence meant in the ordinary sense.

The failure of the phenomenological quest to find absolute presence does not imply that presence in the ordinary sense is a concept riven by contradiction or that presence itself is an illusion or myth. The confusion of Husserlian absolute presence with ordinary presence not only involves large synecdoches but also a serious mixing up of levels. An examination of ordinary presence makes it clear that it could not be eliminated by philosophical analysis. The fact that we, objects and meanings are not present

in the Husserlian sense does not imply that we are not present in
our speech acts or that we are not their authors or that they do
not embody a signifying intention on our part. We may not be
'absolutely present' in anything we say or do but we are certainly
more present in some linguistic acts than others, in linguistic acts
rather than non-linguistic ones and in our own acts rather than
those of other people. And this remains true even when we
consider almost formulaic utterances such as 'Thank you'.

The meaning of this phrase is dependent upon the mobilisation
of the system of differences that is linguistic value and it is
deferred in the Derridan sense that it does not touch down upon
some transcendental signified that would bring the chain of signs
to an end. No-one imagines that 'Thank you' effects closure on
the sense of the world. So it is differance-ridden. 'Thank you',
moreover, is iterable, off-the-peg, rather than specially made for
me to express an original gratitude. Furthermore, its context,
when I use it, is boundless and unspecifiable by me: I cannot state
or make explicit the social framework of my act of expressing
gratitude. Nevertheless, I am present in the usual sense in my act
of saying 'Thank you' in a way that I am *not* present in any of the
following:

   (i) another person's saying it;
  (ii) yesterday's tape-recording of my saying it;
 (iii) my not saying it;
  (iv) my mumbling the words in a coma or a dream or during brain
       surgery when I am having my speech centre stimulated;
   (v) a letter saying 'Thank you' that I wrote ten years ago;
  (vi) your letter saying 'Thank you' that you wrote many years ago
       when you were alive.

To be more specific, consider the situation where my toddler
and I purchase some bubble-gum from a machine. 'Thank you' he
says indistinctly, as he fills his mouth with the over-large coloured
ball. The words 'THANK YOU' are also incised on the steel upper
lip of the machine's mouth, stamped thereon when the machine
was manufactured. 'Thank you' is also printed on a notice
hanging in the shop door, asking me to call again. The same
phrase is to be seen on an empty paper-bag originating from a
supermarket and bowled down the street towards my feet by a
breeze. Is it unreasonable to suppose that my toddler is more

present in his mumbled formula than the machine, the shop door or the paper-bag are in the 'Thank yous' they 'proclaim'?

Similarly, there is more of an individual presence in a personal statement of thanks than in a pre-printed 'Thank you' card. Attempts to personalise pre-printed cards are doomed from the start – doomed not by the iterability of the signs they use or by the non-specifiability of the context necessary to make them intelligible but by the absence of the thanker. Indeed, if there is an attitude of suspicion towards writing, it is most evident when attempts are made to mass-circulate, by means of writing, the simulacrum of personal presence. Even so, spoken gush may strike us as less sincere, less authentic, less informed by personal presence, than a thoughtful letter. (The attempts to automate the courtesies of daily life, using the mass-duplication of written signs is reminiscent of those prayer mills that lazy monks employed to automate prayer. The formulaic nature of prayer was mistakenly construed – Derrida fashion – to mean that the personal presence of the worshipper, his engagement in a time-consuming act, was a superfluous addition to the reiteration of the formulae. Driven by the wind, the prayer mills left God to pray to Himself, without the intervention of human beings who were otherwise engaged.)

Only a perverse conception of presence could lead one to deny that a speaker talking now is present in his speech to a degree that a writer who wrote many years ago is not present in his text. The speaker and his words are in the same place and the spoken words do not outlast the act by which they are produced. In order to speak, I have to be 'here and now'. The 'here and now' is only the origin of the written text which then outlives the act of its production, permitting it to continue to signify in the absence of its author. What the speaker is saying to me now is informed by his presence, by a current signifying intention, in a way that what he wrote many years aso is not now so informed. Texts outlive signifying intentions and they may (as in the case of a deceased author) outlive the writer himself. The author, moreover, simply could not be present in a duplicated, mass-reproduced, widely circulated work. No one in his senses would deny that I am more present in my most routine, automatic verbal responses than Homer is in any of the hundreds of thousands of copies of the English translation of the *Iliad* currently scattered up and down the bookshops of the land.

If speech acts were riddled with absence (or 'non-presence' –

see Section 6.4(e) below), then the very acts by which we asserted our presence would be pragmatically self-refuting. If, in response to my name being called out from a register, I were to say 'present', I would (according to Derridan analysis) be absenting myself. I would vanish into the differance-ridden world of iterable signs with their boundless unspecifiable context, at the very moment that I was asserting my presence. It seems, to say the least, implausible that the utterance in which I assert my presence should involve my absenting myself. How could I be said to be absent? What part of me, when I am saying that I am present, is non-present? Not my body. Not my voice. Not my consciousness in so far as I am attending to the part of the world in which my name is being called. It is more plausible that my assertion that I am here (present) is the assertion of something that actually is the case.

What Derrida seems to be unable to accept is that, in ordinary experience, presence (to) and self-presence are not absolute but matters of degree. I can be more or less present to something, more or less absent from it – in terms of the sharpness of my attention to it, the collectedness of my consciousness. For Husserl, there are no degrees of presence; one can no more be a teeny-weeny bit present to one's surroundings, say, any more than one can be a teeny-weeny bit pregnant. Presence for him (and consequently for Derrida whose critique takes place from within the Husserlian framework) is all-or-nothing, non-graded. And since presence is an unachievable absolute, it must be nothing. Disbelief in Husserl's absolute presence, however, does not license dissent from belief in ordinary conceptions of presence and absence. Likewise, uncovering the paradoxes in Husserlian presence does not necessarily undermine 'the Western metaphysics of presence'. It may undermine Husserl's (or even Hegel's) metaphysics of presence but not the notion of presence implicit in everyday life.

Curiously, much of Derrida's argument (and certainly the arguments of some of his followers) depends upon distinctions that would be intelligible only if presence – or at least the expectation of presence – *were* graded. In his analysis of signatures, Derrida appeals to the fact that a machine can sign on one's behalf as evidence that one is not present (*in propria persona*, as it were) even in the act of signing one's name. The force of this observation, however, presupposes the idea of graded self-presence – where a machine is already assumed to be less self-present than a human being. Similarly, Culler's remark, quoted earlier, that *even* 'I love you' is really a quotation also implies the idea of graded presence, the graded animation of speech acts with speaker's intentions. The fact that most of our talk consists of standard phrases and responses (so much so that an original phrase stands out), that as speakers we are (to use computer jargon) menu-driven so that even attitudes may be dictated by and structured by the available talk, is taken to confirm our non-presence. But, such comparative, empirical data cannot settle a metaphysical issue especially when what is at stake is an absolute. Besides, originality and degree of presence are independent variables: I can make a novel remark absently or a standard remark (such as 'Thank you') with a good deal of self-presence.

Derrida is caught up in an absurd confusion of levels – between metaphysical absolutes and the ordinary senses of words; or between the absolutes of the metaphysician and the facts of daily experience. This becomes particularly evident when specific conclusions are drawn from his positions. The most deliciously absurd examples come from those philosophically incompetent literary critics who are his most vigorous advocates.

How should literary criticism be conducted in a world without presence? Since there is no primordial given, since there is no transcendental signified and the chain of signifiers never comes to an end, we cannot trace a written text, for example, to an extra-linguistic origin in an individual. We must not approach it as if it had been written by someone – whose name appears on the cover – who has inscribed his expressive intentions in it. The text is only the trace of other traces. For how could anyone be the author of a given book when no one can even be the author of his own signature? We must not think of Jacques Derrida as the origin of *Of Grammatology*; nor must you think of Raymond Tallis as the originator of this page. This creates difficulties. Surely, Derrida is more the author of *Of Grammatology* that Raymond Tallis is; and Raymond Tallis is more the author of this page than is Jacques Derrida. And neither of us is the author of *War and Peace*; or not at least as much the author of *War and Peace* as Leo Tolstoy. Or, to pursue this point further, it is surely not unreasonable to believe not only that I wrote this page (I thought it up, I wrote down the words, and so on), but also that what I wrote was influenced by my biography. If I were a Kalahari bushman rather than a university-educated western European, it is unlikely that I would have penned this critique of Derrida. It is even less likely if I had died in 1820. Moreover, my writing about him is contingent upon the biographical accident of my hearing of Derrida's works through reading the kind of books that I do and meeting the kind of people I run into – upon having the types of interests and education that I do have. The Raymond Tallis to whom I attribute the writing of this page has so many features in common with the Raymond Tallis that I call 'I', it seems not unreasonable to imagine that he is the same Raymond Tallis and for me to call him 'I' and to say that 'I' wrote and was the origin of this page.

Even greater difficulties arise when the literary critic tries to found his specific practices upon Derrida's ideas. Since the notion of an external world is only an effect of language, and since meaning also is an effect of language rather than something merely transmitted by language, language does not refer to an outside world where its meanings existed prior to it. ('Il n'y a pas de hors-texte', *OG*, p. 158.) If all language is non-referential then the distinction between referential and non-referential, or referential and rhetorical, modes of discourse collapses. A literary critic should not therefore attempt to interpret a text as if it referred to something outside of itself. All texts are self-referential. If they have reference outside of themselves it is to other texts. Every text is at best an echo chamber of intertextuality.

That a literary critic should have his daily practice influenced by the 'discovery' that the external world is only an effect of language, and consequently write and try to publish one kind of article rather than another, is rather like a sports commentator deriving the superiority of cricket over football from the discovery that 'the outside world' (including playing fields) is a mental construct. Even more absurd confusions of levels are evident when feminist critics, taking their cue from a strikingly opportunist Derrida, see the dismantling of logocentrism as being connected with the deconstruction of the complicity between logocentrism and phallocentrism, otherwise known as 'phallogocentrism'. The feminist case is far too strong to require this kind of dubious metaphysical patronage. The metaphysics of presence and the metaphysics of penises are liable to be unhappy bedfellows and their unequal marriage seems likely to suffer from its grotesque asymmetry as well as from its implausibility.

(c) Misreading Saussure, Peirce, Austin and Others (see also Chapter 3, Section 3)

We have already noted Derrida's unreliability as an exponent of other writers' work – although in much of his remarkable account of Husserl he can be exempted from this charge. Indeed, misreading and misunderstanding have been elevated to the status of a critical principle especially by some of Derrida's disciples.[24] We have seen how he focuses on remote and dusty corners of a writer's *oeuvre* in order to catch him in self-contradiction. We have observed, too, how he manipulates many writers' statements to make them sound like things that Derrida would like them to have said. Where this tactic fails, he simply passes over, seamlessly, from exegesis to statement of his own views. This last ploy is evident even in his (comparatively fair) critique of Husserl. Once he has made his sacrificial victims say what he wants them to say, he proceeds to claim that what they say is symptomatic of an entire historical trend. In the first section of this chapter we saw how Saussure's pedantic or donnish quibbles about pronunciation were transformed into a hysterical hatred of writing which was then seen as symptomatic of a world-historical trend. Sometimes, he doesn't stop at mere distortion and passes on to frank misrepresentation or elementary error. This becomes especially important when he cites writers whose contradictions seem to substantiate his own views.

(1) *Saussure.* According to Derrida, Saussure either did not see or shied away from the conclusions that would follow from his insights into the nature of language. Saussure failed to realise that the arbitrary and differential nature of the sign inevitably meant that the speaker could not be present in the signs he uses because those signs themselves are essentially negative. Signs, Derrida would have us believe, are the product of a system of differences, mere effects of difference. Let us, however, look what Saussure actually said.

In the section 'The Sign Considered in its Totality', he writes

> but the statement that everything in language is negative is true only if the signified and the signifier are considered separately; when we consider the sign in its totality, we have something that is positive in its own class. . . . Although both the signified and the signifier are purely differential and negative when

considered separately, their combination is a positive fact: it is even the sole type of facts that language has, for maintaining the parallelism between the two classes of differences is the distinctive function of the linguistic institution. (*Course*, pp. 120–1)

It is difficult to see how this could have been put more clearly. Although the *institution* of language consists of 'classes of differences', actual speech is composed of signs which are not merely differential but also positive. In speech we deploy not signifiers or signifieds in isolation but signs in which they are fused. Differences are used to establish positive, present meaning. Which is precisely what we might have thought all along. A particular speech act is not all a matter of difference (or form); it is also a matter of presence (or content). *The sign in use* is not purely differential, non-substantial.

These points are missed or confused by Derrida. In his essay 'Differance', he writes,

> As the condition for signification, this principle of difference affects the *whole sign*, that is, both the signified and the signifying aspects. (*SP*, p. 139)

So, if in the linguistic system there are only differences,

> the play of differences . . . prevents . . . there from being at any moment or in any way a simple element that is present in and of itself . . . (*SP*, p. 139)

Yes, difference does affect both aspects of the sign; but *not* the sign *as a whole*. One of Derrida's commentators, Culler, develops Derrida's error even further

> but it follows from the purely differential, non-substantial nature of the sign that the difference between signifier and signified cannot be one of substance and that what we may at one point identify as a signified is also a signifier.[25]

In other words, he starts off from the non-substantiality of the sign and concludes (presumably as one lot of nothing is the same as another lot of nothing, nothing being identical with itself) that the difference between the signifier and the signified is also non-substantial. Saussure could not be more completely misread.

It is of course obvious that *the system* should be purely negative and differential although the signs *in use* are positive. A sign may derive its specificity from the other signs that surround it and define its territory. These other signs are absent. This does not, however, mean that the sign in use is absent. Nor must it be taken to imply that the user of the sign, engaging an absence, must be himself absent or, at least, non-present. Meaning may be carried by difference but it is not carried away by difference.

(2) *Peirce*. Peirce is cited at a critical point in *Of Grammatology*, where the concept of deferral is added to that of difference to create that of differance. We saw (in Chapter 3, Section 3) how Derrida develops Peirce's observation that one sign leads to another. If a sign makes sense, then it will signify another sign which will, in turn, signify another sign and so *ad infinitum*. The chain of signs never comes to an end. This implies, Derrida says, that the chain of *signifiers* never comes to an end; more specifically, that the signifiers never reach the plane of the signified. Discourses, texts, utterances, are strands of an 'endless chain of signifiers'.

Derrida's conclusion is invalid for many reasons, some of which have already been discussed. At the risk of repetition, however, I should like to go over some of the crucial points again here. First of all, it is important to appreciate that Peirce was not talking specifically about linguistic signs, but about signs in general – grey clouds as much as black ink. Moreover, he was speaking of *whole* signs; and, as such, his remarks are unexceptionable and do not bear the interpretation Derrida puts upon them. Even natural signs do not produce a total closure of meaning: when grey clouds signify rain, this is not the end of the matter. The sense of the world is not rounded off. No sign is an island, able to solve the world one and for all.

Derrida misinterprets this. First, instead of seeing the endless chain of signs as the guarantor of the openness of consciousness, he interprets it to imply the closed-off-ness of language. Secondly, Peirce was talking about the relationship between one sign and another. Derrida misreads him as referring to the relationship between signifier and signified. The endlessness of the chain of signs is read as 'the absence of the transcendental signified' (*OG*,

p. 50) and consequently 'the destruction of ontotheology and the metaphysics of presence'. He confuses, in other words, the relationship between whole signs with the relationship between the signifier and the signified of an individual sign. 'One sign leads to another' becomes 'one sign refers to another' becomes 'one signifier refers to another' or 'the (exclusive) referent of a signifier is another signifier'.

It is out of such elementary errors that 'the non-referentiality' of language and the endless deferral, as opposed to the endless development, of meaning arise. We have of course no better reason for regarding linguistic signs as being self-referential than we have for regarding grey clouds as being self-referential.

As we noted in Chapter 3, Section 3, no sign is ever purely or exclusively a sign. Objects and events *are* (in themselves) as well as having significance. The fact that the chain of signs never comes to an end does not mean that there is only an interminable trail of traces and that presence is never reached. For presence does not lie at the *end* of the trail of signs; rather, it is there from the beginning; the sign is present as well as signifying. For it can signify only if it is present – present to me for whom it is significant. A sign may signify an absence; but only in virtue of being itself present.

The double negation that brings 'differance' to birth is not 'difference' and 'deferral' but 'Not Saussure' and 'Not Peirce'.

(3) *Austin*. The misreadings of Austin are less serious. Perhaps the most significant arises from a confusion in Derrida's mind between what is necessary in order to intend a given utterance and what would be necessary to complete what Austin considers to be the aim of the philosophy of language, namely the elucidation of 'the total speech act in the total speech situation'.[26] Austin pointed out that the meaning of an utterance was not identical with the meaning of its propositional content understood as the sum total of the meanings of its component words. An utterance is an act and the success of the act depends upon the non-verbal context in which it takes place at least as much as upon the choice of words used. It is very difficult to define the limits of this context. To understand why a certain speech act counts as a promise or a vow of marriage would ultimately require an elucidation of the whole of society. Every framework refers us to a wider framework. This may reasonably be taken to

mean that the project of speech act analysis is doomed to be interminable from the outset. It must not, however, be interpreted as implying that we cannot mean what we say because we cannot intend all the conditions that determine the meaning of our utterances or which must be fulfilled in order that they should have the meaning that we wish them to have. Nor does the impossibility of completing the task of the philosophy of language as Austin understood it does prove that that task is self-contradictory. No one could complete an inventory of the grains of sand on a beach but it does not follow that the attempt to do so is self-contradictory – even though it may be futile.

(d) Walking and Differance

The Street
Here is a long and silent street.
I walk in blackness and I stumble and fall
And rise, and I walk blind, my feet
Trampling the silent stones and the dry leaves.
Someone behind me also tramples stones, leaves:
If I slow down, he slows;
If I run, he runs. I turn: nobody.
Everything dark and doorless,
Only my steps aware of me,
I turning and turning among these corners
Which lead forever to the street
Where nobody waits for me, nobody follows me,
Where I pursue a man who stumbles
And rises and says when he sees me: nobody

(Octavio Paz)

If we are not present in our speech acts then, surely, we cannot be present in any other acts; indeed we must be non-present in our entire lives. For deliberate speech acts are the very paradigm of self-conscious behaviour, of self-expression, or embodied self-presence. They seem to be intentional to a degree exceeding all else that we do; for the primary purpose of such an act is the production of meaning whereas other acts serve non-signifying intentions and only secondarily or incidentally convey meaning. If we cannot mean what we talk we certainly cannot mean other things that we do. If we deny intentions to speech then we must banish them from our lives.

Consider a non-linguistic act such as walking. If I believe that I am present in my act of walking, it is because that act is informed by an intention that it may also incidentally signify. I know what I am doing, in so far as I have some notion of a goal towards which I am progressing and it is this notion of a goal that directs and co-ordinates the many separate movements of my limbs. Of course, my knowledge of the purpose and nature of my own actions will inevitably be generalised or abstract: the intelligible is necessarily general; and the more explicit that intelligibility, the more abstract my knowledge will be. My recognition of what I am doing – 'that I am doing *this*' – will be mediated by universals. An action will be recognised for what it is in so far as its profile is congruent with the silhouette of its general kind. Walking, analysed as a set of physical events, may not have discernible formal properties. The individual movements comprising my journey to the pub cannot easily be related to 'movement-types' whose successive realisations amount to a 'sentence' whose resultant meaning is 'arrival at a pub'. I may dawdle on the way, deviate to avoid a particularly unpredictable dog, pause to look at some flowers, and so on. There will be, in other words, continuous, non-systematic variation in the physical elements that go to make even such a stereotyped act as my nightly visit to the same local. Nevertheless, inasmuch as my journey makes sense to me, my walking can be analysed as the realisation of a series of elements, though it is not sufficiently segmented to make a formal '-emic' analysis anything other than strained and implausible. Recognition of such elements as they are realised, however, is the middle step in the organisation of the afferent feedback from my walking into a sign of what it is, of the process that it was intended to be. Nothing could be more conventional or more ready-made than the signs that give me on-line reassurance that I am doing what I think I am doing and what I intended to do. Walking, then, if it is recognised by the walker for what it is, is composed of iterable signs.

My sense of the meaning of my action, my confidence in the coincidence between intention and action, the process by which the action is informed by its intention, will be mediated by more indirect, more abstract, more complex signs. Such signs derive their meaning from the boundless context of my current location; ultimately from the limitless horizon of my consciousness and its history. For the meaning of my action will be context-dependent and in a way that I will certainly not be able to specify. The meaning of a walk to the pub may plausibly be related to everything that I have been up to that moment. In so far as any action is meaningful, its meaning is differentiated. An action implies choice and implicit in any given course of action are the many alternative actions that have been rejected. The meaning of my action therefore also depends upon the opposition of at least some of its elements to other actions that have different meanings. Choice implies differentiation and exclusion.

Differing and *differance* are therefore intrinsic to non-verbal meaning as well as to verbal meaning. (This is in addition to the verbalised meaning that many actions have and to the fact that perception itself is language- and theory-ridden.) Furthermore, the meaning of an action such as walking always points to a future – the future in which the action is completed and the goals attained. That future, however, point to another future and so on. The meaning of walking escapes the present in so far as it refers to this elusive future. Non-verbal meaning, too, is therefore characterised by *deferral*. Walk-acts as much as talk-acts exhibit the features of iterability, context dependency, difference and deferral. It is not only speech that is riddled with differance.

Must we conclude that we are really or typically absent in our walking? Is a man who is deliberately walking to the pub self-deceived when he believes that his action is expressing his intention to walk to the pub? It is certainly true that when we are walking we may forget what we are doing; our intentions may occultate and our intending selves may temporarily absent themselves from what we are doing. We do not continuously intend even our most deliberate actions throughout their duration. On the way to the pub I may become totally absorbed in the conversation I am having with the person who is walking with me. There is often a time-sharing of attention, whereby we switch from one on-going action to another. For part of my journey to the pub, I may walk deliberately; at other times I may delegate my walking to the automatic pilot while I turn my attention (and so my intentions) to other things. It does not, however, follow from the fact that my intention sets my action in motion, rather than being necessarily present throughout, that I am non-present in my action. Even less does it follow that my walking is entirely without authorship. Fluctuating attention and braided intentions do not imply non-intention. A man who is walking and talking at the same time is not, from the point of view of his walking, a headless automaton.

It is perfectly obvious that we are present in our walking. Nevertheless, the reasons for denying presence in our speech acts seem to be equally applicable to other flesh acts such as walking. Indeed, they seem to be more applicable to the latter. And this already fits with ordinary intuitions: speech acts, in addition to having the features shared with other voluntary acts of being purposeful and deliberate, also have as their primary intention that of conveying meaning. We would therefore expect speech to include those acts in which we are most present and self-present; within which it is most easy to discriminate grades of automaticity, or stereotyping – and hence of conviction, sincerity and so on. Speech acts are the flesh acts in which we are most present. If we are absent from our speech then we must be absent from our lives and we must abandon the notion that we are present in any of our purposive acts.

Can I intend what I walk? Well, what would count as intending my walking? If we require that 'the intention animating (the walking) should be through and through present to itself and to its contents', could we ever intend walking? All bodily actions have physiological, psychological and social causes or frameworks wholly or mainly inapparent to the actor. Must we then conclude that we are not the authors of our actions, that we are non-present in them? I could not run my body for ten seconds if it did not run itself. My most deliberate acts are predicated on the unwilled health of my body and operate through mechanisms of which I am unaware. Can I therefore in any sense be entitled to believe that I intend any of my life? So much of what I *am* is *given*. And what could be more general – and more particular – than the body and its functions?

Since every argument Derrida uses to 'prove' that we are non-present in our speech acts could be equally well applied to other flesh acts, must I conclude that walking is a kind of writing; indeed, that writing is the condition of possibility of walking? And if I do not, indeed cannot, will not, accept this, am I the hopeless victim of a 'legocentric' fallacy? Is my belief that I am present in my walking an illusion generated by the circuit of 'se regarder marcher' or 's'entendre marcher'? (Cf. the 'I' of Octavio Paz's poem.) Since every act is a sign of itself – and it is by virtue of this sign that the actor recognises what he is doing so that he is able to continue doing it – walking is haunted by differance. Should I not believe that walking has differences but no positive terms? Should I not therefore deny that there is a walking subject? Would it not be reasonable for me to maintain that a falling corpse reveals the true nature of walking more than ordinary ambulation, that a headless hen shows us what ambulation really is?

These questions are not frivolous or unfair. The extension of Saussurean analysis to the whole of experience was at one stage the goal of structuralism and, more specifically, of the '-emic' analysis of behaviour that was so fashionable in the fifties. Moreover, Gayatri Spivak, Derrida's translator, tells us that 'according to Derrida, Husserl's text is tortured by a suppressed insight that the Living Present is always already inhabited by differance' (*OG*, Introduction). So it is not just speech but consciousness itself that is hollowed by non-presence. As we walk, our feet may touch the ground, but the play of signs that is our walking will never touch the ground of meaning, the transcendental pavement.

A *reductio ad absurdum*. Non-verbal acts and even the world of natural signs such as grey clouds are as differance-ridden as speech and writing. Differance, therefore, doesn't seem to make much difference. And for this reason, where Derrida's dazzling gnomic darkness has caused others to defer, I beg to differ.

(e) Mr Pickwick to the Rescue

> *Pickwickian sense. In a technical constructive or conveniently idiosyncratic or esoteric sense; usually in reference to language 'unparliamentary' or compromising in its natural sense.*
>
> (*Oxford English Dictionary*)

> *The chairman felt it his imperative duty to demand . . . whether he had used the expression . . . in a common sense. Mr Blotton had no hesitation in saying that he had not – he had used the word in its Pickwickian sense.*
>
> (*Pickwick Papers*)

There are signs that Derrida himself has never been entirely comfortable with some of the ideas most associated with his name. Though he usually manages to avoid drawing conclusions that can be readily tested against experience, he does feel the need to use more than obscurity to elude or baffle his readers and to deflect the sceptical astonishment of those who might be inclined to dismiss his views as nonsensical.

In a characteristically caustic passage, Austin writes as follows:

> One might well want to ask how seriously this doctrine is intended, just how strictly and literally the philosophers who propounded it mean their words to be taken. . . . It is, as a matter of fact, not at all easy to answer, for, strange though the doctrine looks, we are sometimes told to take it easy – really it's just what we've believed all along. (There's the bit where you say it and the bit where you take it back.)[27]

Austin is here referring to the doctrine that we never *directly* perceive or sense material objects; but he could well have been speaking of many of Derrida's claims; for Derrida spends a good deal of time retreating from things we might think he may have said. (Though it has to be admitted that many of the positions most notoriously associated with his name are vulgarisations of his views by his less gifted but more publicity-conscious followers.) The process by which he executes his U-turns and wriggles out of positions that seem, on the surface, to be an affront to common sense and ordinary experience involves a continuous redefinition of words that would seem not to require definition in the first place. This is the Pickwickian method and we shall examine how it is applied to 'writing', 'presence' (and 'absence'), 'intention' and 'auto-affection', though many other key words are handled with equal unscrupulousness and cunning.

(1) *Writing.* According to Derrida, 'To affirm . . . that the concept of writing exceeds and comprehends that of language presupposes of course a certain definition of language and of writing' (*OG*, pp. 8–9). So, for Derrida, writing is not merely

> the penning or forming of letters or words; the using of written characters for purposes of record, transmission of ideas etc.; the action of composing and committing to manuscript; the expression of thoughts or ideas in written words. (*Oxford English Dictionary*)

That is the narrow 'graphic' acceptation of the word. Derrida interprets writing in a more generous sense:

> and thus we say 'writing' for all that gives rise to inscription in general, whether it is literal or not and even if what it distributes in space is alien to the order of the voice: cinematography, choreography, of course, but also pictorial, musical, sculptural 'writing'. One might also speak of athletic writing, and with even greater certainty of military or political writing in view of the techniques that govern these domains today. All this to describe not only the system of notation secondarily connected with these activities but the essence and content of these activities themselves. (*OG*, p. 9)

If writing *were* all of these things, then it would be scarcely surprising if it were to exceed, indeed encompass, speech.

This greatly expanded definition of writing has not been arrived at as the result of a careful examination of the object in question. It is to be found at the very *beginning* of *Of Grammatology*. As Derrida himself admits, the belief that 'oral language already belongs to this language presupposes a modification of the concept of writing that we for the moment merely anticipate' (*OG*, p. 24). It proves, in fact, difficult to anticipate what directions this modification will take. 'Writing' acquires a larger and larger catchment area and Derrida cites Plato and Hegel in support of an extraordinary extension of the concept of writing. (The citations are, to put it mildly, imprecisely referenced so that the reader is not in a position to evaluate the Platonic or Hegelian uses of the term. But the names invoked are so big that the ordinary reader is disinclined to do anything other than take what is said on trust.) For Plato, Derrida tells us, writing is at once mnemotechnique and the power of forgetting; whereas for Hegel, writing is 'that forgetting of the self, that exteriorisation, the contrary of the interiorising memory, of the *Erinnerung* that opens up the history of the spirit' (*OG*, p. 24).

The most powerful redefinition of writing, and the one from which most of Derrida's most striking positions have been derived, is insinuated and developed intermittently in the early pages of *Of Grammatology*:

> If 'writing' signifies inscription and especially the durable

institution of a sign (and that is the only irreducible kernel of
the concept of writing), writing in general covers the entire field
of linguistic signs. In that field a certain sort of instituted
signifiers may then appear, 'graphic' in a narrow and derivative
sense of the word, ordered by a certain relationship with other
instituted – hence 'written', even if they are 'phonic' – signifiers.
The very idea of institution – and hence the arbitrariness of the
signs – is unthinkable before the possibility of writing and
outside of its horizon.   (*OG*, p. 44)

Even before it is linked to incision, engraving, drawing, or the
letter, to a signifier referring in general to a signifier signified by
it, the concept of the *graphie* (unit of a possible graphic system)
implies the framework of the *instituted trace*, as the possibility
common to all systems of signification.   (*OG*, p. 46)

The 'if' at the beginning of the first quotation is characteristic,
indeed pathognomonic, of the post-Saussurean style of argument –
as we discussed in Chapter 1. It is not clear why, if writing *does*
signify the durable institution of a sign, it should cover the entire
field of linguistic signs. The force of the argument, such as it is,
seems to depend upon confusion between the 'durability' of the
institution – presumably 'langue' as opposed to 'parole' – and the
durability of the particular signs that are used. Naturally, a written
word is durable in the way that a spoken one is not. In either
case, however, the institution – the system of differences in the
Saussurean sense – is durable. So much is clear, if of dubious
validity.

Once, however, linguistic signs are related to 'the framework of
the instituted trace', the gates of obscurity are flung wide open:

The instituted trace cannot be thought without thinking the
retention of difference within a structure of reference where
difference appears *as such* and thus permits a certain liberty of
variation among the full terms. The absence of *another* here-
and-now, of another transcendental present, of *another* origin of
the world appearing as such, presenting itself as irreducible
absence in the presence of the trace, is not a metaphysical
formula substituted for the scientific concept of writing.   (*OG*,
pp. 46–7)

Perhaps not, but absence has insinuated itself into the concept of writing which, as we have been told, encompasses the whole of the linguistic institution. The space of writing 'constitutes the absence of the signatory, to say nothing of the absence of the referent. Writing is the name of these two absences' (*OG*, pp. 40–1). Writing as the name of the absence of the subject and the absence of the referent of writing strikes one as curious; but the 'modification of the concept of writing' is still not complete. In the essay on 'Differance', writing (or proto-writing) conquers yet more territory:

> and it is this constitution of the present as a 'primordial' and irreducibly nonsimple, and, therefore, in the strict sense non primordial, synthesis of traces, retentions and protentions . . . that I propose to call protowriting, prototrace, or differance. (*SP*, p. 143)

Culler accepts this quite without protest and asserts baldly that 'writing in general is an *archi-ecriture*, an archi-writing or protowriting which is the condition of both speech and writing in the narrow sense'.[28]

Long live the narrow sense! If we read 'proto-writing' as 'Pickwick-writing', then we should be in a position to see some of Derrida's more extraordinary positions for what they are.[29]

(2) *Presence/absence.* If we are not present in what we say, it might be reasonable to suppose that we are absent from it. But things are not so straightforward in Derrida's writings (or protowritings): 'nothing, either in the elements or the system (of language) is anywhere simply present or absent. There are only, everywhere, differences and traces of traces.'[30] Derrida frequently uses the term 'non-presence' to signify the middle position between presence and absence. 'There is the bit where you say it and the bit where you take it back.' (Or: one can write – or speak – 'sous rature'.) Derrida says it by asserting that we are not present in our speech but takes it back by saying that we are not absent either – rather non-present. Supposing we were to say that that which is non-present is also non-absent, would we not deprive Derrida's conclusions of much of their power to astonish? Few people would object to being told that they were 'non-absent' from their speech. Or does 'non-absent' mean something

different from 'not-absent'? In the dazzling chaos of Derrida's gnomic texts it would appear to be possible to deny the presence of something, to deny also its absence, and also to give slight preference to the denial of presence over the denial of absence.

(3) *Intention*. One not unreasonable reading of Derrida is that we cannot, indeed we do not, mean what we say. But, as pointed out earlier, if we cannot mean what we say, we certainly cannot mean what we walk. By abolishing intention from speech – or treating the idea that what we say is informed by our intentions as an aspect of the logocentric fallacy – then we must abolish intention from our entire lives. This conclusion must be unpalatable to Derrida himself. After all, he must have, in some sense, intended to write *Of Grammatology* rather than to earn his living as a harpooner or a tattooist. And he must take a far greater share of the blame for that book than either Queen Elizabeth I or myself can be expected to do. His recognising this may be why he smuggles intentions back into ordinary life:

> the category of intention will not disappear: it will have its place, but from that place it will no longer be able to govern the entire scene and system of utterance . . . the intention animating the utterance will never be through and through present to itself and to its content.[31]

But whoever thought that 'the intention animating the utterance' *would* be 'through and through present to itself and to its content'? As the ever-helpful Culler says, 'it is not a matter of denying that signatories have intentions, but of situating those intentions'.[32] So that's what it is all about! On closer inspection, Derrida's conception of intention is no more subversive of ordinary understanding than those of a Marxist or a psychoanalyst; and they are considerably less radical than those of a physiologist[33] – or a social psychologist such as Mead.[34]

(4) *Auto-affection*. In the essay on Husserl, auto-affection almost evaporates before the demonstration of its own impossibility. As a condition or criterion of 'full' presence, it proves a major stumbling block to the phenomenological enterprise. Elsewhere, however, it seems to be flourishing to an extraordinary degree:

Auto-affection is a universal structure of experience. All living things are capable of auto-affection. And only a being capable of symbolizing, that is to say of auto-affecting, may let itself be affected by the other in general. Auto-affection is the condition of an experience in general. This possibility – another name for 'life' – is a general structure articulated by the history of life, and leading to complex, hierarchical operations, etc. (*OG*, pp. 165–6)

By an inexplicable miracle, Husserl's impossible dream becomes life's inescapable structure.

(5) *Conclusion.* The continuous process of on-line redefinition of crucial terms is the key to Derrida's ability to arrive at astonishing conclusions. It is blatant enough to cause Mr Pickwick himself to cry out in protest. Those of us who still think of 'writing' as typically something that is committed to paper and who insist that absence is different from – indeed the opposite of – presence and vice versa, may remain unimpressed. Even less impressive is Derrida's habit (cf. Hawkes as discussed in Chapter 3) of blurring elementary distinctions – such as between type and token in order to sustain the idea that all communication is 'the durable instituting of signs'.

It might be appropriate to end this section by introducing a new term of my own. It is intended to encompass the misreading and miswriting necessary to pull off the Derridan conjuring trick. I shall christen this process (in memory of one of Derrida's most fervent disciples who has made much of the 'fruitfulness of misreading') *léger de Man*.

6.5 THE TRAGIC META-PHILOSOPHER

> [*Differance*] *must be conceived without* nostalgia; *that is, it must be conceived outside the myth of the purely paternal or maternal longing belonging to the lost fatherland of thought. On the contrary, we must* affirm *it – in the sense that Nietzsche brings affirmation into play – with a certain laughter and with a certain dance.*
>
> (*Speech and Phenomena*, p. 159)

It is tempting to dismiss Derrida's attacks on phonocentrism, logocentricity and the metaphysics of presence as merely misconceived, muddled and fraudulent. But we must look beyond his tendentious accounts of 'Western Culture' and 'Western philosophy', his misrepresentations of individual philosophers, his cavalier use of certain key terms, his tendency to confuse and conflate issues and arguments that are most fruitfully kept apart and his many stylistic vices, to the intuitions that may lie behind his *oeuvre*. These are considerably more interesting than the texts to which they have given birth. His is in some ways a tragic case: a man of immense talent and massive erudition, gifted with profound insights, who could not say the things he most wanted to say but who, nevertheless, has built a huge *oeuvre* out of his circlings round them. The publicity his ideas have attracted has only deepened the tragedy: the bad influence of those he has himself influenced has added frivolity to the obscurity; the ridiculous, indeed despicable, response to John Searle's criticism of his views is a characteristic production of recent years.[35]

Derrida would be quite comfortable with the charge that he is no philosopher. He anyway undermines the claims of philosophy to be more than mere writing, to be free of the influence of the textual forces that govern other, more explicitly literary, modes of writing. Nevertheless, he is, whether he likes it or not, a meta-philosopher – of a certain tragic strain in post-Kantian philosophy. Derrida's refusal to accept the reality of ordinary presence stems from his refusal to settle for less. This is a hunger he shares with Hegel, Husserl, Heidegger and Sartre. Behind the more technical arguments of these philosophers' writings is a disappointed longing for the union of absolute lucidity and undeniably sub-stantiality, of thing-like thereness with thought-like transparency, for an absolute coincidence of knowing and being. The latter is impossible: as being or presence moves towards transparency, it attenuates to insubstantiality; as it gains substance, it thickens to opacity. The actual cannot be both absolutely general and utterly particular.

He has very stringent criteria for what may be accounted 'real' presence and these explain why he denies presence to the speaker; why presence for him, as for Husserl, Hegel and Heidegger, must be absolute or nothing; why he overlooks or dismisses the graded presence of everyday reality and diagnoses non-presence. Since, according to his analysis, absolute presence is impossible, the idea of it being riven by contradiction, ordinary presence as it is given to daily experience must be a mirage. It is not 'the absolute matrix form of being but rather . . . a "particularisation" and "effect". A determination and effect within a system that is no longer that of presence but of difference' (*SP*, p. 147). Presence is not an autonomous given, a primordial, primitive fact that both faces consciousness and is the givenness of consciousness to itself. The concept of the temporal present, too, is riddled with absence and contradiction. The idea of a current event seems to presuppose a synthesis across two absences – the no longer of the past and the not yet of the future. The present as the seat of change, of activity, of events, the temporal seat of presence, of what is actually there, incorporates self-differing, differance. The very notion of the present is an effect of differences or (since the notion of change involves the future and hence deferral) of differance.

Derrida denies that the speaker is present in his speech act – or, indeed, in any signifying or even significant act – because, like so many philosophers before him, he will accept nothing less than an absolute coincidence within voluntary acts of consciousness and meaning. Self-presence *chez* Derrida requires total self-possession. If the signs I use do not originate with me and if I do not explicitly intend all the conventions and, indeed, all the utterance-conditions, that make meaning possible, then I am not present in my act. Since what I say to some degree escapes my control, exceeding or falling short of any formulated or formulable signifying intention, since it is not inwardly lit through and through by such an intention, I cannot be said to have intended the meaning of my utterance.

The disappointed vision behind these impossible criteria for presence is of a self entirely given over to its intelligible acts, without any residue of opacity – either of disengaged self or of unintended meaning. Derridan presence implies total self-knowledge, a consciousness utterly turned over to explicit meaning, fully signifying itself to itself, rendered without remainder into transparent signs. A sign, however, must be iterable to be intelligible, that is to say general. To be present or self-present on Derrida's terms we should have to be given over entirely to generality. Our acts would have to become the universal profiles of themselves, to be entirely silhouette. It would not be sufficient that they should become, like structuralist signs,

all form and no content; they must also be independent of any
system that is not fully on display. At the very least, the actor
should shed his particularity, including his specific locations in
space and time and all the deictic co-ordinates that constitute
'being here'. Presence in the Derridan sense would demand
replacement of localised bodily being by pure generality; the
shedding of particularity, because particular being always exceeds
the saturation of a finite number of variables and so falls short of
full articulation.

Even if this were possible, we still could not possess ourselves
through the signs we use in speech acts. No actor could ever
achieve total coincidence within his act of being, consciousness
and meaning. He could not dissolve, without residue, into a kind
of pure semantic light; for some of him would have to remain
undissolved in order to receive that light and be lit by it. The
project of absolute self-knowledge is frustrated by the need for
that knowledge to have a knower, itself not contained within that
knowledge. In the case of a speech act, the speaker could not be
present in the Derridan sense in the meaning of the utterance
because the meaning would have to mean to someone: the
speaker would have to be, at least in part, the consumer of the
meaning of his utterance as well as the meaning itself. If total
coincidence between being and meaning is the criterion for being
present in a speech act, it is scarcely surprising that such presence
proves impossible.

Much of Sartre's philosophical megalith *Being and Nothingness*[36]
is devoted to agonising over this: 'The being of consciousness
does not coincide with itself in a full equivalence' (p. 74). Worse
still, 'consciousness – the for-itself – is a being which is not what it
is and which is what it is not' (p. 79). But of course 'the *phenomenon*
of the in-itself is an abstraction without consciousness' (p. 658).
Because consciousness is consciousness 'of' – of something other
than itself – it has to be distanced from itself in order to be, in
order to have content. If Husserlian immediate presence is
impossible it is not because speech is riddled with differance but
because consciousness is necessarily an intermediary; because
self-presence is necessarily indirect. One cannot, to use Sartre's
example, be oneself as an oak tree is an oak tree. Put another
way, one cannot become a word – confined to its borders, filling
its semantic catchment area uniformly with one's self-presence.
Even less can one achieve this state by filling out the contours of

an act to which a word can be attached in absolute definition or rigid designation.

The presence that Derrida denies is a special type of metaphysical self-presence that goes even beyond Husserlian absolute presence. His assertion that meaning and presence are effects of language rather than existing prior to them are really reformulations of ancient worries about agency – the feeling that even in our apparently voluntary actions we are not fully the agents of what our actions mean. We are not, and cannot be, transparent to ourselves and the significance even of our speech acts cannot be 'rounded up' in our intentions or our consciousness of them. There is nowhere where we can coincide with ourselves – certainly not in our perceptions where we are given up to that which is not ourselves – and equally certainly not in our actions, where we engage an outside world through the mediation of a body that is other than the moments of our consciousness. The world we experience and act on always exceeds in weight, and falls short in purity, of the world of our articulate imagination or our explicit recollection.

The double 'failure' of language – as a vessel in which we can deposit and so repossess ourselves and as a means of expressing extra-linguistic reality – the lack of coincidence between word and self, and between word and world – is a dominant theme in Proust. Recollection and anticipation are closer to names; the present moment, unconfined by words, laden with a particularity that exceeds language, is, by comparison, flawed. Unexpressed even in our speech acts, we are 'never quite there': in the present, we elude ourselves and the world eludes the grasp of a fully self-possessed experience. For Proust, as for many continental philosophers, 'the systematic elusiveness of the I' is a consequence of the nature of time itself which denies us total self-possession, rather than being merely a consequence of the grammar of the word. The flawed present is like music; it inheres in hastening away from itself and towards itself.

The elusiveness of the present and the unattainability of undivided self-presence have been fundamental preoccupations of thinkers over the centuries. An impatience at 'never quite being there', at not being identical with oneself, marks a point where the artist and the mystic meet. Hunger for sharper, more continuous self-presence, for a shadeless internal lucidity, for a more acute realisation of the world and the fact that one is in it,

lies at the root of many spiritual quests. Ouspensky has expressed
this very clearly, in his reporting of Gurdjieff's teaching:

> 'Not one of you has noticed the most important thing that I
> have pointed out to you' he said. 'That is to say, not one of you
> has noticed that *you do not remember yourselves*. . . . You do not
> feel yourselves; you are not conscious of *yourselves*. With you 'it
> observes', just as 'it speaks', 'it thinks', 'it laughs'. You do not
> feel: *I* observe, *I* notice, *I* see. Everything still 'is noticed', 'is
> seen'. . . . Only those results will have any value that are
> accompanied by self-remembering. Otherwise you yourselves
> do not exist in your observations . . .'
>
> I said that we have overlooked a fact of tremendous importance,
> namely that *we do not remember ourselves*; that we live and act
> and reason in deep sleep, not metaphorically but in reality . . .
> we *can* remember ourselves if we make sufficient efforts, we *can*
> awaken.[37]

A less tragically inclined thinker than Derrida might accept that
presence and self-presence could never be established through
acts because they are presupposed in the very concept of an act.
The generality and the iterability of the signs we use do not
undermine that ordinary presence – just as the stereotyped or
even ritualistic nature of much human behaviour does not absent
us from that behaviour. Generality is essential for self-recognition;
for it is under the aspect of generality that we recognise ourselves
and so 'come to' ourselves. Even – or especially – the objects of
our desires are socially coded – that may be how we recognise
that we desire them, recognise them as desirable[38] – but the
desires are no less fiercely felt for that. That desires are
differentiated as values belonging to a system is not the end of the
matter.

The question of the context of acts can be approached in a non-
Derridan spirit. The boundless text of society which no one can
fully specify but which is requisite for acts to have their specific
meanings is not necessarily alien to the actors. It is arguable that
the sum of our contexts, of circumstances, is what we are; or
rather we are that in virtue of which all of these loci are specified
or designated *as* contexts. There is no absolute difference between
the self that has a context and the context that surrounds it. The

ultimate context from which my speech acts derive their felicity is myself; only that self can change a material or social reality from the status of virtual contexts to that of being the actual conditions of a particular utterance. My presence, in short, is that in virtue of which my utterances have deictic co-ordinates to anchor them – is that in virtue of which their transformation from general values to specific assertions, from non-specific possibility to determinate meaning is possible. My presence, my being here-and-now, furnishes the necessary deictic input required to give my words specificity. Without the opaque residue of unexpressed self or context behind my signs, the latter would drift in a void of generality; my particular existence is what saturates the truth conditions of my utterances.

Of course, we are never 'there' in the absolute Hegelian or Husserlian sense. Complete coincidence of being and knowledge, of explicit self-presence and facticity, is not possible. The for-itself is fatally divided and Derridan presence is therefore inachievable. We cannot be totally rendered up to ourselves without remainder; we cannot unite within ourselves the solidity of thing-like existence with absolute transparency of consciousness, perfect lucidity with complete changelessness. These demands are conflicting. We are not made in the image of Rilke's angel 'a perfect consciousness . . . a being in whom thought and action, insight and achievement, will and capability, the actual and the ideal are one'.[39] For we 'when we feel evaporate; oh we breathe ourselves out and away; from ember to ember yielding a fainter scent'.[40] The angels, on the other hand, 'only catch up what is theirs, what has streamed from themselves'. Accordingly, we are doomed from the start if we wish to be what we know and do and to know what we do. In Sartre's vision, we are given over to a lifelong futile passion to be God, to become a self-founded self, the for-itself-in-itself:

> Every human reality is a passion in that it projects losing itself so as to found being and by the same stroke to constitute the in-itself which escapes contingency by being its own foundation, the *ens causa sua*, which religions call God.[41]

Octavio Paz's poem is aware of this futile passion, this doomed attempt to found oneself. The walker through the deserted street discovers the non-coincidence of the self with the self through the vertigo of solitary, uninterrupted self-awareness, the vortex of auto-affection.

This is perhaps Derrida's inaugural, and unacknowledged, insight. He shares the Hegelian/Husserlian dream of absolute self-presence, of the self-world 'coming to' itself without ever going outside of itself. Why otherwise would he move from the impossibility of absolute self-presence to denying the reality of ordinary presence? His position is reminiscent of those who will not settle for less than total wakefulness and, when they fail to find any state of consciousness answering to this notion, denounce all of life as a dream.

No one would dispute that absolute presence in the Derridan sense is impossible. It does *not* however, follow from this that:

(i) We are no more present in one activity than in any other. Or, more specifically, that speech is a type of writing so that we are no more present in what we say now than Homer is now in the epic poems he wrote millennia ago.

(ii) We cannot intend or mean what we say and that meaning is an effect of language (bits of extra-linguistic reality having no intrinsic difference in meaning) so that what we say is no more true of one bit of external reality than of another and what we say does not refer to one bit of external reality rather than another.

(iii) There is no difference between use and mention, assertion and quotation, being a reader and being a writer.

Likewise, it does not follow from the fact that we are not Rilkean angels or Sartrean Gods that we do not or cannot mean what we say; that we cannot mean to say one thing rather than another; or that dead authors are as present in their texts as living speakers are in their utterances.

It would be rather extraordinary if such highly *specific* conclusions as that writing has priority over speech should follow from such profoundly metaphysical premises – as surprising as if a decision for or against the mind-independent reality of space–time could enable one to decide whether or not cricket had priority over football. Since differance is supposed to be primordial, since it haunts not only language but also 'The Living Present', its discovery should hardly influence our decisions about the relative status of speech and writing.

So rational phonocentricity may still be regarded as rational after the 'discovery' of differance. And so, too, does logocentricity (not to speak of legocentricity). And this is not entirely unexpected: if meaning were *not* differentiated prior to language, there would be little point in a system of differences established to signify different meanings. In direct contradiction of Derrida – and pending more convincing arguments than the ones whose feebleness he has concealed beneath his intellectually irresponsible prose – we roundly assert

Il y'a de hors-texte

as the hands with which I wrote and those with which the reader holds this book amply confirm.

We conclude that the not inconsiderable interest of Derrida's works lies in the insights that gave rise to them, his reiteration of the metaphysical hungers that motivated the early Sartre, and before him Husserl and Hegel. But a sympathy for those starting intuitions is quickly extinguished by the antipathy roused by his dubious methods of conducting philosophical discussion and the baseless paradoxes to which he owes his doubtless temporary fame.

Appendix: A Note on Intention

The whole question of the 'through and throughness' of an intention, of the completeness with which our intentions animate our acts, of the extent to which an action realises an intention, is of the greatest interest.

We tend to think of agency and chance as opposites; but there is always an element of chance in agency, even in an act that goes precisely according to plan. I am walking on the beach and I pick up a stone. There can be no doubt that I intend to pick up *a* stone; but the *choice* of this particular stone out of the many thousands that lie to hand is left to chance.

This illustrates the general point that our intentions cannot be utterly specific, with absolute values assigned to all possible variables. The actual moves constituting the action do not uniquely realise the intention; or, to look at it the other way round, the intention cannot legislate over all the features of the action, even if one is not knocked off course in the passage from intention to realisation.

This is a consequence of the fact that, in order to make sense to us, our intentions must be of a general character; from which it follows that there must be unsaturated variables in the original intention. When one intends an action, the intended action is *any* action that corresponds to a certain form. The objects of intentions are, in other words, to a certain degree abstract.

These points become clearer when we consider the idea of an absolutely lucid intention – and an action that knows itself through and through. How do we elucidate our intentions; how do we make our intentions clearer to ourselves, know them at a higher level of self-awareness? Most typically by articulating them to ourselves. But when we verbalise our intentions we are really describing them and evaluating or interpreting them at the same time; indeed we may be altering or even forming them for the first time. Moreover, even if we accept the notion of a pre-formed, pre-verbal intention, there is still the problem that nothing can be totally elucidated linguistically. There is the element of chance in the choice of words and the unexamined forces at work in the selection of descriptors of one's planned actions. A *description* of an intention, in other words, is a plant that, like the intention itself, grows out of a humus of unexamined self. And even if we pretend that the idea of the formulation of a pre-existing intention is unproblematic, there remains the fact that the mesh of descriptors cannot be drawn so tightly as to determine the character of the action uniquely – so that nothing is left to chance.

Actions, then, can never be totally transparent, even (or especially) to the actor. An intention can never absolutely specify a unique action corresponding to it and the intention itself can never be fully elucidated. Chance penetrates to the core of agency not merely because intentions are externally prompted, formed on the spur of the moment, in response to something that is external to oneself, but also because there can be no 'uniquely referring' intentions (cf. there are no 'uniquely referring' expressions). There is a darkness at the heart of intention and there is an inescapable indeterminacy in their relation even to the actions that seem most precisely to realise them.

None of this, however, supports any of the specific post-Saussurean conclusions about the relations between speech and writing, or about the nature of reference, meaning and truth.

7

Statements, Facts and the Correspondence Theory of Truth

The Correspondence Theory of Truth (referred to throughout this chapter as 'the Theory') has assumed many different forms since Aristotle, developing an argument in Plato's *Sophist*, first brought it to the forefront of the debate about the nature of truth. Much of the controversy surrounding the Theory has arisen because its advocates and opponents have had different ideas about what it is that is supposed to correspond to or with what. The uncertainty – sometimes a matter of conscious disagreement but more often one merely of confusion – extends to both ends of the correspondence. Is the correspondence between, say, statements and states of affairs, or between perceptions and things, or between thoughts and things, or what? Various permutations are possible, generating numerous variants of the theory. Almost any X may be said to correspond to almost any Y:

The Correspondence Theory of Truth
X corresponds to Y

X	Y
Perceptions	Objects
Thoughts	Things
Knowledge	Facts
Beliefs	The world
Logos	Res
Propositions	States of affairs
Statements	Reality

When, as has often been the case, it is unclear which variant is being advocated or denied, well-heated but poorly illuminated argument is inevitable. In some versions, the Theory applies to

235

knowledge or perception; in others, it is about *statements*. Even where it is made clear that the version of the Theory under discussion is about the truth of statements – rather than of, say, percepts or beliefs – ambiguity about its scope may remain.

We may usefully divide 'statement' versions of the Theory into stronger forms which purport to give an account of the nature of truth; and weaker forms which claim only to provide a criterion for differentiating true statements from false. In the latter case, the Theory holds that a statement is true if and only if it corresponds to a real (historical or current) state of affairs. (We may have to add 'and this state of affairs is or was the one referred to or meant by the person making the statement' to guard against an accidental correspondence between an insufficiently particularised statement and a reality, other than the particular one that was meant, that happens coincidentally to correspond with it.) This weaker version of the Theory will converge with the stronger version if it is additionally maintained that the essence of truth inheres in this correspondence between statements and reality. In the present discussion, the Theory will be taken to be about the truth of statements rather of knowledge or perception. Although my main task will be to defend this weaker version of the Theory, I shall give reasons for supporting a qualified form of the stronger version towards the end of this chapter.

When the weaker version is stated in its contemporary form – that deriving from Tarski – it is difficult to avoid giving the impression that the Theory is inoffensive to the point of triviality. To use Tarski's example, according to the Theory,

(i) 'Snow is white' is true if and only if snow is white.

Or, to generalise

(ii) 'x' is true if and only if x,

where 'x' is a statement belonging to an object language (in the example given, English) and x is the state of affairs corresponding to it. The entire sentence (i) or (ii) belongs to a meta-language in which the object language to which 'x' belongs can be discussed. If the theory seems non-trivial in the context of Tarski's own paper,[1] it is because he introduces it at least in part to avoid the

Russellian paradoxes that always seem to threaten when one is using statements to talk about statements. This latter does not concern us here but it is interesting to discuss briefly why the weak forms of the Theory often seem trivial.

It is difficult to state the Theory non-trivially because, when we are *talking* or *writing* about truth (and in particular about the truth of statements), both statements and the realities to which they are refer are necessarily presented verbally. We therefore remain on the hither side of language. That is why the formulation

(ii)   '*x*' is true if and only if *x*

seems merely to state, rather unhelpfully, an obvious internal truth about language rather than to cast light on the relations between language and reality. The alternative way of presenting the theory

(iii)   '*x*' is true if and only if ——

where '——' is (rather than merely standing for) a non-verbal act of indicating the state of affairs in question is obviously not possible within the bounds of the printed page.[2] But it is no less impossible outside of the printed page because, as Wittgenstein argued convincingly in *Philosophical Investigations*, one cannot show the referents of words, never mind of sentences, by ostension or some other non-verbal mode of signification such as picturing. One cannot give the equivalent in, say, 'Pointish' of an assertion made in English; though if one *were* able to do so, then the quasi-tautological character of the Theory would disappear.[3]

Despite its apparently truistic nature, the Theory has been singled out for particular attack by post-Saussurean literary theorists. As may be imagined, the grounds of the attack are not often explicitly stated and the Theory is often dismissed in disparaging asides thrown off during the course of muddled, impressionistic idea-skating. Comparatively clear accounts of post-Saussurean opposition to the Theory are given by Eagleton, Belsey and Hawkes.[4] It will be useful to summarise some of the arguments again to indicate the rough direction from which the attack has been mounted.

The general drift is that after Saussure 'we now know' that language is a system composed of arbitrary signs and that this system has its own internal rules for combining the signs. Because of this, statements do not and cannot genuinely refer outside of themselves. 'A language does not construct its formations of words by reference to patterns of "reality", but on the basis of its own internal and self-sufficient rules. . . . Structures are characteristically 'closed' in this way.'[5] Eagleton even suggests that the arbitrariness of the linguistic sign undermines the correspondence theory of *knowledge*: 'for if, as Saussure had argued, the relationship between the sign and the referent was an arbitrary one, how could any "correspondence" theory of knowledge stand?'[6]

Since language is inescapably involved in the construction of ordinary reality, the implications of the arbitrariness of the linguistic sign are, for Belsey, even more far-reaching:

> Signs owe their capacity for signification not to the world but to their difference from each other in the network of signs that is the signifying system. Through linguistic difference 'there is born the world of meaning of a particular language in which the world of things will come to be arranged. . . . It is the world of words which creates the world of things' (Lacan)[7]

There is no correspondence between our knowledge and reality; or, rather, such correspondence as there is is rigged. The Theory, which assumes a correspondence between statements and extra-linguistic reality, is based upon the false premiss of a transparent, referential language and is consequently itself false. 'Il n'y pas de hors-texte.[8]

In Chapter 3 these views were shown to be false and, furthermore, it was emphasised that they could not be legitimated by an appeal to Saussure. A further reason for rejecting the Theory is the incorrect assumption (analogous to that used to undermine realism in fiction and discussed in Chapter 4) that to subscribe to the idea of a correspondence between statements and reality is also to subscribe to the belief that language is a *mirror* of reality. It would be as well to confront this assumption.

Some versions of the Theory do rest upon the mirror analogy. The most famous – or notorious – modern instance is, of course, to be found in the *Tractatus*. In Wittgenstein's theory there was a correspondence between the configuration of a proposition and that of the state of affairs referred to or asserted in it. A proposition was a concatenation of terms each of which corresponded to objects in the real world. The arrangement of objects that constituted the state of affairs was signified by a corresponding arrangement of the corresponding terms. The correspondence of form was not, however, one of spatial organisation. The proposition expressed the corresponding state of affairs by virtue of the convention linking individual terms with individual objects and the *logical* form it shared with the state of affairs. When Wittgenstein found that he could not give meaning to 'logical form', he rightly abandoned the mirror theory but, unfortunately, also repudiated all correspondence theories as well, thus throwing out the baby with the bathwater.

Identity of logical – or indeed any other – form is not only unintelligible but it also solves nothing. This cup is like another cup; but this fact does not make the one cup a sign of or expression of the other. Wittgenstein hoped that the picture theory would explain how propositions had a definite sense and how a new proposition could make sense to someone who, though he was familiar with its constituent terms, had not come across that particular proposition before. The reader could see what the new proposition meant because in some sense it *looked* like what it meant.

Notwithstanding the example of the *Tractatus*, there is no *a priori* reason why commitment to the Theory should entail acceptance of a mirror theory of language. Truth and isomorphism have no privileged relationship to one another. The reverse may, in fact, be the case: truth may *require* non-isomorphism, a distance which makes the embodiment of explicitness possible.

A much more rigorously argued, and consequently more interesting, expression of doubt about the ability of factual statements to refer to objects outside of themselves derives from Strawson and emerged in his famous debate with Austin about the nature of truth.[9] This debate will occupy an important place in the present discussion.

Consider a statement S^R by or in or through which it is asserted that there is a state of affairs R^S – the reality expressed in the statement. According to the Theory, S^R is true if and only if the corresponding R^S does indeed exist or (in the case of statements referring to the past) did exist at the time stated. A common thread running through many of the arguments against this seemingly inoffensive claim comes from the suggestion that the 'correspondence' between S^R and R^S is spurious in so far as S^R and R^S are not genuinely *external* to one another. Strawson thought that the R^S was 'a fact' and, additionally, that facts were not genuine entities on the surface of the globe: a fact is a pseudo-entity somehow internally related to the statements that 'correspond' to it. The implication is that the Theory naïvely overlooks the role that language plays in structuring or even creating the facts it is used to speak of: the role of S^R in the genesis of R^S.

In drawing attention to this, Strawson, perhaps unwittingly, uncovered the non-tautological aspect of the Theory, its positive content, and hence its vulnerability. For the force of the Theory – and that which distinguishes it non-trivially from, say, coherence theories – lies in the unspoken implication that the reality which corresponds to a true statement really is *outside* and *independent* of it – or indeed of any other statement. Or, at the least, there is a core or base of statements whose corresponding realities are not internal to language so that R^S is typically, in some sense, and to some degree, extra-linguistic. It is this that lies at the heart of the Theory and this which has been most forcefully attacked by its opponents.

One way of demonstrating that R^S is *not* internal to S^R, that it does not depend upon the latter for its very existence, would be to show that R^S can be accessed without the mediation of language; that it is available, for example, to sensory perception. In the case of material object particulars picked out by uniquely referring expressions, this seems to present no problem. The word (or token-instance) is produced here (or is sitting here, on the page) and the relevant object is over there. The two are independent of one another. I can gain access to the dog Rover either linguistically, via a referring expression, or directly by sensory perception. In such a case, the referent clearly exists independently of the act of reference. Even though it is picked out from its background by reference, it is already a self-contained whole and could have equally well been picked out by a focusing of sensory attention. (Whether such acts of 'pure reference', even to material object particulars, can ever take place without at least implicit predication or without inclusion in a speech act that performs, for example, assertion, is another matter.)

Things become less clear when we consider general referring expressions. Perception may yield experiences of particular dogs but does not give access to 'dog' or 'animal'. There would appear, therefore, to be no extra-linguistic experience corresponding to 'Dogs are fine animals'. This objection could be overcome by arguing, as many of course have done, that general statements relate to extra-linguistic reality only indirectly, via their particular consequences: they are meaningful only in so far as they have particular instantiation – or imply other statements that do – and can consequently be verified. Extra-linguistic access to the R^S corresponding to the S^R 'Dogs are fine animals' is possible through perception of a particular dog or a series of particular dogs. It may additionally be pointed out that, in many cases, the referring expression, though grammatically general, is implicitly particularised by the linguistic or extra-linguistic context of the statement in which it occurs – permitting, respectively, 'story-relative' identification[10] which depends in part upon what the speaker has already said, and 'body-relative' identification, which mobilises deictic co-ordinates.[11]

This will not satisfy everyone; for the further objection may be raised that when a common (i.e. general) noun is used to secure reference to a particular, the referent of the referring expression differs from any object that could be present to the sense. Referring even to a particular dog as a 'dog' conceptualises it in a way that it is not conceptualised when it is given to unmediated perception.

This objection opens up a whole new can of worms. For it raises the question of whether, in fact, perception is ever entirely innocent of conception; whether, more particularly, sensory perception is ever unmediated by, or uncontaminated with, language. It has been suggested – notably by Geschwind – that it is disconnection of sensory association areas from language centres that accounts for those severe disorders of perception called agnosias.[12] Perception without language is highly deficient; indeed, in the absence of language, sensation cannot give rise to what we would count as fully formed perception. There is, that is to say, no purely extra-linguistic perceptual reality and language is conterminous with all human consciousness above the level of brute, uninterpreted sensation.

A new can of worms indeed. Fortunately, we can close it without damaging the credibility of the case we shall put forward for the Theory. For our aim is not to demonstrate that R^S is perceived in a fashion that is independent of all possible formulations of reality but that R^S is in some sense independent of a particular S^R or group of S^Rs and of the language or group of languages from which S^R originated; that it is not internal to a 'closed' linguistic system. Adherence to the Theory in other words does not require that one should overlook the extent to which language is implicated in the structuring of human reality. Nor does it demand that one should believe that the reality 'out there' is extra-human or extra-social; that it is entirely naturally derived rather than being at least in part historically determined.

The independence of R^S seems undeniable when we reflect how the edges of material object particulars are spatial, not semantic. 'Dog' may be bounded by, and contrasted with, 'cat' and so on at the semantic level; but the individual dog referred to has literal spatial edges. It is *not* a bundle of semantic features. 'Dog' may be a concept bounded by other objects; but the dog on my lap is a patch of space–time, three of whose dimensions are fur-lined.

It may be objected that we have so far dodged the cases that present real problems for the correspondence theorist. We have not yet confronted the many abstract objects that populate the world of statements; and – much more to the point – we have dealt only with the referents of referring expressions and not with the *facts* picked out by *statements*. If we are to defend the Theory, however, we must concern ourselves with the realities that are asserted in factual statements. Now the referents of *statements* seem almost impossible to extricate from language. Whereas it is possible to draw a continuous (fur-)line round a dog one cannot do so around 'The dog is sitting on the mat'. It is not satisfactory to circumvent this difficulty by designating the latter, or its referent, 'a complex object'[13] by analogy with a complex material object made up of several components. For the only available complex object is the compound dog-plus-mat. A line that bounded this object would implicitly encircle much that fell outside of the specific reference of 'Rover is sitting on the mat' – for example, the four paws of the dog (or 'The dog has four paws'). The referent of the statement cannot be transformed into a definable patch of space–time by calling it, say, 'dog-mat'.

It would appear, then, that R^S does not enjoy a bounded, independent existence except in so far as it has been picked out by S^R (or one of its synonyms). It has no continuous non-linguistic edges. If this is true of 'The dog is sitting on the mat', how much more obviously true must it be of 'I am getting on in years' or 'The health of the national economy is in decline'.

Strawson denied that facts are real entities or 'objects on the surface of the globe' and, consequently, since the Theory typically asserts a correspondence between statements and *facts*, repudiated the Theory. Facts seem internal to statements: they are apparently inseparable from the statements in which they are asserted; there is a suspiciously snug fit between them. 'What could fit more perfectly the fact that it is raining than the statement that it is raining. Of course fact and statement fit. They were made for one another.'[14] As Austin points out, this remark gives (and is meant to give) 'the impression of reducing "facts" to an accusative so deeply and hopelessly internal that their status as entities is hopelessly compromised.'[15] The correspondence between logos and res is neither a lucky accident (requiring perhaps divine intervention to explain) nor a happy achievement: it has been rigged. Fact and statement belong to the same realm – the realm of discourse. The fact is not a res but a semi-linguistic entity in disguise, a quasi-res.

Austin's response is not as helpful as one would wish. He points out that, in ordinary conversation, we often refer to entities that are undoubtedly things-in-the-world as 'facts'

> Phenomena, events, situations, states of affairs are commonly supposed to be genuinely-in-the-world, and even Strawson admits events are so. Yet surely of all of these we can say that they *are facts*. The collapse of the Germans is an event and is a fact – was an event and was a fact.[16]

Facts, then, are seemingly out there in the world. That they are *not* inside statements becomes obvious when we consider that the end of a statement does not terminate or eliminate the corresponding fact or that when (to use an example of Strawson's[17]) we tear up a written page we may tear up the statements on it but we do not tear up the facts – even if there are no synonyms or copies of those statements stored elsewhere in the world. The facts remain apparently out there, beyond this or any other page, apparently unharmed.

There seem, then, to be equally good cases for believing that facts are *inside* and that facts are *outside* of language. How shall we adjudicate between them? Or is this unnecessary? Is there, perhaps, some way of reconciling Strawson with Austin, of accommodating the observations both sides have made in support of their respective positions?

Strawson's attack on the extra-linguistic status of facts is highly damaging to the Theory, if the latter is seen to assert a correspondence between statements and *facts*. For, if facts were intra-linguistic and the Theory were about the correspondence between *facts* and statements, the criterion of truth furnished by it would seem at best feeble and at worst implausible: S^R is true when there exists a fact F that itself can exist only by courtesy of S^R. The 'correspondence' would be an internal affair of S^R and R^S would seem, at least in part, to be intra-linguistic, 'marsupialised' within S^R. This enfeebled version of the Theory is in danger of collapsing into a coherence theory in which truth resides in the consistency of statements with one another.

It is fortunate for the correspondence theorist, therefore, that the apparent strength of Strawson's case and much of the dispute between him and Austin originates from a failure to recognise that facts are not the same as S^Rs. Once it is appreciated that Austin is talking about R^Ss and Strawson about *one aspect* of facts, the basis of their disagreement disappears.

We shall try to clarify the nature of facts shortly. For the present, let us again think about the nature of R^S and its relation to S^R. Consider the R^S corresponding to the S^R 'The dog is on the mat'. This R^S is not, as we have already noted, merely a complex of objects. It could be characterised in part as a relationship between two objects. The objects themselves are presupposed in the assertion of that relationship; S^R does not assert or state that they exist. It expresses neither the dog nor the mat but the relationship between them. This relationship has been *brought out* by S^R: although it can be perceived directly, it is only by virtue of S^R (or a synonymous statement) that it emerges fully out of the 'reality mass', R, of perceptual experience.

There is a sense, therefore, in which it is true to say that R^S does not entirely pre-exist S^R; or that it does not exist *as a definable, determinate entity* prior to the S^R that picks it out. Though the related elements – and, indeed, their relationship – pre-exist S^R, the relationship between them acquires separate existence only through S^R. For the relationship does not inhere in either of the objects in question, nor of course in the space between them. It is there to be pre-linguistically perceived but it has to be spoken or written to acquire objective (and even object) status; only when it is embodied in language is it liberated from the nascency of existence in a particular consciousness, freed from the privacy of an individual's view-point and the instability of his attention, to become fully formed and publicly accessible. S^R thus confers upon R^S the objectivity enjoyed by other, self-bounded, parts of R – that is to say, by material object particulars. S^R uproots R^S out of R and remakes it as, say, one thread in a nexus of facts or one atom of a described situation. S^R, in short, does not create R^S but does confer aseity or atomicity or separate existence upon it.

Under this analysis, R^S still remains independent of language inasmuch as it can be accessed non-linguistically. In the case of more general, more complex, more abstract S^Rs, non-linguistic access to the corresponding R^Ss becomes more indirect. Perceptual access is to the consequences, illustrative instances or samples (whichever is appropriate) of R^S and perception is more explicitly verification. Nevertheless, even in the most abstract cases, in so far as S^R is meaningful and true, thus far is R^S extra-linguistic.

This not to imply that we ought to subscribe to an unreformed, or indeed any sort of, verificationism. Meaning, truth and verification remain quite distinct even if they are not totally independent of one another. If an S^R is true, there must be independent access either to the corresponding R^S, or to its components, or to the R^Ss or components of the R^Ss corresponding to the statements implied by S^R.

An R^S, on the present analysis, may have two existence conditions; or, rather, an *existence* condition plus an *emergence* condition permitting it fully explicit, bounded existence. In this respect the referent of a general or abstract term or the R^S corresponding to a factual statement will differ from the referent of the proper name or other expression designating a material object particular. Rover exists and exists explicitly without the help of 'Rover' because he comes furnished with his own (fur-lined) edges. But the smile (on my face), while no less extra-linguistic than Rover, is not so bounded by continuous spatial or spatio-temporal edges and requires the referring expression to separate it from the face whose affective colouring it constitutes. Like the health of the economy or the R^S corresponding to any factual statement, the smile stands in need of an emergence condition to confer separate existence upon it. This condition will be fulfilled by the linguistic expression that is used to refer to it, the statement that asserts that it is the case or that something or other is true of it.

In such cases, R^S requires S^R to bring it out; S^R does not *create* R^S. The latter is not (to use the post-Saussurean term) an *effect* of the former. R^S has an existence condition additional to that of the existence of the appropriate S^R – namely a certain disposition of matter in space and time corresponding to the configuration asserted in S^R. The latter condition is clearly extra-linguistic. R^S remains an independent truth condition of S^R. It is not a puppet owing its existence entirely to S^R.

We are therefore in a position to uphold a non-trivial, non-tautological version of the weaker Theory. It can be stated as follows:

A statement S^R is true if and only if there is a corresponding R^S and false where there is no such R^S.

In a true statement there is a correspondence between a proposed and an actual reality.

So much for S^Rs and R^Ss. But what of facts? Facts are neither statements nor are they purely extra-linguistic realities. If facts *were* identical with statements, no statement could be counter-factual. There would be no call to distinguish a sub-category of 'false statements' or of 'factually true statements'. Nevertheless, facts *do* seem to be inextricably bound up with statements: facts and statements 'fit each other so well' as Strawson said, it is difficult to conceive of a means of gaining access to facts except via the statements through which they are asserted. Are facts, then, intra- or extra-linguistic? Do they belong with S^Rs or R^Ss?

The truth is that they belong entirely with neither: facts are neither entirely inside nor entirely outside of language. A fact is an R^S-picked-out-by-an-S^R. It is the product of the fusion of an S^R and an R^S, of a linguistically encoded meaning and a piece of reality. As such, a fact has two inseparable facets – one corresponding to the S^R and the other to the R^S – standing in relation to one another rather as (to appropriate Saussure's famous metaphor) the recto and verso of a sheet of paper. An S^R without a corresponding R^S is a lie or a mistake or a joke; and an R^S without a corresponding S^R is inchoate or nascent, a percept incompletely crystallised out of the reality mass R.

Those who fail to appreciate the intermediate status of facts are prone to imagine that factual reality must have some kind of sentence-like form and/or to believe that sentences must somehow replicate the structure of the extra-linguistic reality they express. When it is discovered that neither of these is the case, they become suspicious as to whether language can really be open to external reality. Facts, which seem *when discussed* to look like statements, are accused of being intra-linguistic since it is obvious that reality itself does not have a sentential form and statements do not look like the realities they are about. Doubts begin to be expressed about whether or not even factual statements can be true of, or even reach out towards, extra-linguistic reality. Once the intermediate status of facts is understood, however, these doubts are seen to be without foundation.

There are no facts without language and yet facts are not internal to language. So the Theory, in so far as it is concerned with the relationship between statements and extra-linguistic reality, is not about the correspondence between statements and facts[18]

$$S^R : F$$

but between S^Rs and R^Ss. Facts are constituted in this correspondence between S^Rs and R^Ss:

$$\begin{bmatrix} S^R \\ \cdot \cdot \\ R^S \end{bmatrix} = F$$

In order to be 'fair to facts', one must therefore recognise that they are neither wholly intra- nor wholly extra-linguistic but arise out of the *interaction* between language and external reality. And to be fair to the Theory, it must be appreciated that the R^S picked out by an S^R owes its *explicit* existence, but not its existence, to the S^R. It is not helpful, nor is it necessary, to think, as Russell and Moore sometimes did, of facts as a special (and hence problematic) sort of object in the world.

There can, therefore, be a genuine correspondence, rather than a mere internal relation, between statements and reality, *logos* and *rem*. The Theory, which asserts this external relationship between what is said or written and what is the case, is non-trivially true: it affirms the objectivity of facts, that factual truth is not determined solely by what people happen to say. More importantly, it denies that truth is a mere matter of conformity between one assertion or articulated belief and another: truth is a matter of conformity between statements and a world outside of those statements. Contrary to Derrida, we assert that, for at least part of the time 'il y'a de hors-texte'; and *that is the time when language is earning its keep.*

It is necessary to add this last rider to forestall the criticism that the Theory is naïve because it overlooks how most statements do many other things than merely state what they seem to be stating: they imply, persuade, distract attention from what has not been stated, and so on. The Theory alone would be unable to deal with 'Nice and sunny, isn't it?', a true statement given in response to someone complaining that he had just been badly beaten up. Nevertheless, a significant portion of the truth is encoded in factual statements.[19]

A weaker version of the Theory is thus upheld. But what of the stronger version? In accordance with the latter, correspondence between statements and reality is not merely a criterion for classifying statements as being true or false but truth itself. Truth *is* or inheres in the relation between language and the world.

If 'truth' is taken to mean 'factual truth', then it is easy to see how the weaker version of the Theory could pass over into the stronger. But factual truth is only one mode of the truth. A good deal of truth (and falsehood) lies outside of factual statements; indeed outside of statements altogether. If we think of the different relata in the various versions of the Theory mentioned at the beginning of this chapter, then it will be appreciated that there are widely divergent views about the scope of the concept 'truth'. Truth may be seen variously as residing in the relation between: perception and reality; belief and reality; knowledge and reality; thought and reality (adequation of things and the intellect); and so on. It may even be argued that truth resides in reality itself: that either R^s or R is truth. Why, then, choose the relations between *statements* and reality as the privileged repository of truth?

Most importantly, it is obvious that, in the absence of *any* viewpoint or consciousness, there is no truth. Material reality in the absence of consciousness is neither true nor false; it simply is. The claim that it (inexplicitly) embodies truth would have the immediate result of rendering the concept of truth redundant and assimilating the category of truth to that of existence.[20] If a rock on a planet unvisited since the beginning of time embodies truth, then the concept of truth adds nothing to that of existence. In fact, truth is inseparable from explicitness: the rock is not of itself true; truth refers to what has been made explicit about the rock. A single consciousness, however, seems insufficient to establish the concept of truth. For truth is essentially a public matter. The question of truth arises only when there are at least two viewpoints or consciousness. In a postulated solitary consciousness (if such a thing were possible), the truth 'of' or 'about' something would be only implicit, nascent or inchoate. It becomes explicit only where there are two or more consciousnesses in communication – informing, or disagreeing with, one another. Truth emerges when there is a public, when *it* becomes public, and so explicit. One could plausibly suggest that a material reality becomes 'true' or 'the truth' only when it is appealed to (picked out, expressed) to arbitrate between conflicting points of view. And it is in *statements* that that which is true of or about reality becomes most fully explicit because in statements it acquires separate embodiment, a place of its own: truth is most fully developed in true statements. So while truth may not inhere *exclusively* in the correspondence between true statements and reality, it achieves its most complete development towards substantiality there. The development of truth is inseparable from the development of explicitness.

That is why Ramsay's account of truth[21] is so seriously misconceived. According to Ramsay, the concept of truth is empty because to assert '*p* is true' is the same as to assert '*p*'. The 'is true' adds nothing. Truth is a redundant category; '—is true' is an empty predicate. It is not, however, the case that to assert '*p* is true' is the same as to assert '*p*'. There is an important difference between asserting that 'The earth is round' and asserting that '"The earth is round" is true'. Something is made explicit in the second assertion that is not made explicit in the first – namely the truth value of the first. The difference between the assertions may be compared with the difference between '*p*' and '"*p*" is asserted'. To assert that *p* is asserted does not modify *p* but we do not conclude therefrom that the concept of assertion is empty.

Ramsay's argument illustrates an almost perverse determination to disregard the real tendency of the question 'What is truth?'. The question does not imply a search for some object or substance or property which will count as the essence or embodiment of truth. What it really means is: what is the search for truth really aimed at? What, if anything, is there in common between the criteria of truth applicable in different fields of enquiry? What distinguishes truth from falsehood?

But what Ramsay's dismissal of the concept of truth overlooks most importantly is the relationship between explicitness and truth (and falsehood). Most accounts of truth focus upon the distinction between truth and falsehood. (The weak Theory is a good example of this tendency.) Truth, however, cannot be understood entirely in terms of those features or criteria by which it is distinguished from falsehood. Just as a woman is not simply the sum of her differences from a man: she is also composed of that common humanity which woman and man share. Likewise truth is additionally composed of that which truth and falsehood have in common – namely explicitness. Theories and definitions of truth that do not recognise the common basis of both truth and falsehood in explicitness overlook what is essential to it: its basis in and emergence through articulate consciousness.

This is why truth is best seen as *emergent* – beginning with perception (it does, after all, makes sense to speak of true and false perceptions) and developing through judgement and articulation to reach full flower in factual statements. And although there are vital existential truths not unravelled in factual discourse, it seems reasonable to conclude that it is in the correspondence between a statement and extra-linguistic reality that we find truth at its most developed. In this conclusion the weaker form of the Theory converges with the stronger form.

Notes

Notes to the Introduction

1. Hostility to realistic fiction is documented in my book *In Defence of Realism*, first published by Edward Arnold in 1988 and reissued by Ferrington (London, 1994).
2. Michael Boyd, *The Reflexive Novel: Fiction as Critique* (Toronto: Lewisburg Bucknell University Press, 1983) p. 19.
3. Quoted in Jonathan Culler, *Structuralist Poetics* (London: Routledge & Kegan Paul, 1975) p. 193. There is a good deal of doubt whether or not Robbe-Grillet's texts *are* non-referential. See, for example, Robbe-Grillet's own rather pompous prefatory remarks to *In the Labyrinth*, available in English, translated by Christina Brooke-Rose (London: Calder & Boyars, 1967).
4. Terry Eagleton, *Literary Theory* (Oxford: Basil Blackwell, 1983) p. 188. Anyone who reads Eagleton's works would be unlikely to think of him as 'the man with the exploded assurance'; but then he may have very sensibly kept clear of those modern works that, he tells us, 'pulverise order, subvert meaning and explode our assurance'.
5. Frank Lentricchia, *After the New Criticism* (London: Methuen, 1980).
6. Roland Barthes, *The Death of the Author*, available in *Image – Music – Text*, selected and trans. Stephen Heath (London: Fontana, 1977) p. 143.
7. Paul Valéry, *Leonardo, Poe, Mallarmé*, trans. Malcolm Cowley and James Lawler, vol. 8 of *The Collected Works of Paul Valéry* (London: Routledge & Kegan Paul, 1972) p. 304.
8. Alain Robbe-Grillet, *Snapshots and Towards a New Novel*, trans. Barbara Wright (London: Calder & Boyars, 1965) pp. 56–7.
9. Roland Barthes, *Writing Degree Zero*, trans. Annette Lavers and Colin Smith (London: Jonathan Cape, 1967).
10. Tzvetan Todorov, *Grammaire du Decameron* (The Hague: Mouton, 1969) p. 15. This passage is quoted and discussed in Terence Hawkes, *Structuralism and Semiotics* (London: Methuen, 1977).

Notes to Chapter 1: Literature, Language and Reality

1. George Steiner, *After Babel* (Oxford, 1975) p. 123.
2. Robert Alter, *Mimesis and the Motive for Fiction* now collected in *Motives for Fiction* (Harvard University Press, 1984) p. 8.
3. Jacques Lacan, *Ecrits*, selected and trans. Alan Sheridan (London: Tavistock, 1977) p. 65. (Lacan is discussed in Chapter 5.)
4. Jacques Derrida, *Of Grammatology*, trans. Gayatri Chakravorty Spivak (Baltimore: The Johns Hopkins University Press, 1976) p. 158.

5. Frank Lentricchia, *After the New Criticism* (London: Methuen, 1980) p. 188.
6. Ferdinand de Saussure, *Course in General Linguistics*, trans. Wade Baskin (London: Fontana; Glasgow: Collins, 1974) p. 120.
7. See, for example, Roland Barthes, *The Death of the Author*, in *Image – Music – Text*, selected and trans. Stephen Heath (London: Fontana; Glasgow: Collins, 1977) p. 146.
8. Roland Barthes, 'Science versus Literature', *Times Literary Supplement*, 28 September 1967, p. 897.
9. Quoted in Jonathan Culler, *Barthes* (London: Fontana, Modern Masters; Glasgow: Collins, 1983) p. 76.
10. Jonathan Culler, *Structuralist Poetics* (London: Routledge & Kegan Paul, 1975) p. 53.
11. John Searle, review of Culler's *On Deconstruction: The Word Turned Upside Down*, *The New York Review of Books*, vol. 27 (October 1983) pp. 74–9.
12. Geoffrey Hartman, *Saving the Text* (Baltimore: The Johns Hopkins University Press, 1981) pp. 60–1.
13. Although Barthes does admit to being trapped by some of the words he himself made fashionable. In his autobiography, he writes (of himself):

> He is not very good at getting to the heart of things. A word, a figure of thought, a form fastens on him for several years, he repeats it, uses it everywhere . . . but he makes no effort to reflect what he means by such words or such figures . . .: you cannot get to the heart of a refrain; you can only substitute another one for it. And this, after all, is what Fashion does. In other words, he has his internal, personal fashions. (*Roland Barthes*, trans. Richard Howard (New York: Hill & Wang, 1977) p. 127.)

Notes to Chapter 2: Literature as Textual Intercourse

1. Roland Barthes, *The Death of the Author*, in *Image – Music – Text*, selected and trans. Stephen Heath (London: Fontana; Glasgow: Collins, 1977) p. 146.
2. Harold Bloom, *A Map of Misreading* (Oxford University Press, 1975) p. 3.
3. Tzvetan Todorov, quoted in Terence Hawkes, *Structuralism and Semiotics* (London: Methuen, 1977) p. 100.
4. Jonathan Culler, *Barthes* (London: Fontana, Modern Masters; Glasgow: Collins, 1983) p. 81.
5. E. D. Hirsch, Jr, *Validity in Interpretation* (New Haven, Conn.: Yale University Press, 1967) p. 74.

   A yet more exaggerated version of this claim, originating from Pleynet, is quoted by Jonathan Culler in *Structuralist Poetics* (London: Routledge & Kegan Paul, 1975) p. 136:

It is indeed this word (novel, poem) placed on the cover of the book which (by convention) genetically produces, programmes or 'originates' our reading. We have here (with the genre 'novel', 'poem') a *master word* which from the outset reduces the textual encounter, by making it a function of the type of reading already implicit in the law of this word.

6. Jean-Paul Sartre, *What Is Literature?*, trans. Bernard Frechtman (London: Methuen, 1970). See especially ch. I, 'What Is Writing?'.
7. Frank Lentricchia, *After the New Criticism* (London: Methuen, 1980).
8. I. A. Richard, *Principles of Literary Criticism* (London: Routledge & Kegan Paul, 1925). See, for example, p. 267: 'A statement may be used for the sake of the *reference*, true or false, which it causes. This is the *scientific* use of language. But it may also be used for the sake of the effects in emotion and attitude. . . .'
   And poetry was distinguished by being predominantly emotive and hence non-referential, of aesthetic rather than utilitarian value. Richards subsequently regretted the simple-minded way in which his early doctrine was applied and developed more complex schemes of analysis; but it was the early distinction that was influential.
9. From *Ars Poetica*, first published in 1926. This poem, although enjoyable, seems to me to have meaning rather than being, to be more like a statement than a globed fruit, audible and visible rather than mute and palpable.
10. Cleanth Brooks, *The Well Wrought Urn* (New York: Harcourt Brace, 1947).
11. Gerard Graff, *Literature Against Itself: Literary Ideas and Modern Society* (University of Chicago Press, 1979) p. 10.
12. Todorov, quoted in Terence Hawkes, *Structuralism and Semiotics* (London: Methuen, 1977).
13. Michael Boyd, *The Reflexive Novel: Fiction as Critique* (Toronto: Lewisburg Bucknell University Press, 1983); William E. Cain (ed.), *Philosophical Approaches to Literature: New Essays on Nineteenth- and Twentieth-century Texts* (Associated University Presses, 1985).
14. W. M. T. Nowottny, 'Formal Elements in Shakespeare's Sonnets: Sonnets I–VI', *Essays in Criticism*, vol. II (January 1952) pp. 76–84.
15. Roland Barthes, *A Lover's Discourse*, trans. Richard Howard (New York: Hill & Wang, 1978).
16. Harold Bloom, *The Anxiety of Influence: A Theory of Poetry* (Oxford University Press, 1973).
17. Bloom, *A Map of Misreading*, p. 18.
18. Ibid., p. 3.
19. Ibid., chaps 2 and 3.
20. Ibid., p. 19.
21. Ibid., p. 10.
22. It aligns him with Jacques Derrida as one of the great modern heirs of Mr Pickwick. Bloom's recent encomium of Robert Penn Warren in *The New York Review of Books* relates that writer's poetic impulse and choice of themes to the accident by which Warren caused his brother

to lose an eye in childhood. In other words, Bloom seems to have forgotten the irrelevance of extra-poetic influences in a poet's *oeuvre*. It appears that he no longer believes his own unbelievable thesis.

23. Bloom, *A Map of Misreading*, p. 20.
24. Ibid., p. 10.
25. Catherine Belsey, *Critical Practice* (London: Methuen, 1980) p. 45.
26. Michael Riffaterre, 'Intertextual Representation: On Mimesis as Interpretive Discourse', *Critical Inquiry*, vol. 11 (1984) pp. 141–62.
27. See, for example, Frederick Copleston, *Mediaeval Philosophy*, Part II, *Albert the Great to Duns Scotus* (New York: Doubleday, 1962) especially chap. 46.
28. Joseph Weizenbaum's famous ELIZA programme is discussed in his *Computer Powers and Human Reason* (San Francisco: Freeman, 1976).
29. This example is also discussed in R. C. Tallis, 'The Realistic Novel versus the Cinema', *Critical Quarterly*, vol. 27, no. 2 (1985) pp. 57–65.
30. Jonathan Culler, *Structuralist Poetics*, p. 138.
31. Roland Barthes, *S/Z*, trans. Richard Miller (New York: Hill & Wang, 1974) p. 10.
32. Ibid., pp. 20–1.
33. Quoted in Culler, *Structuralist Poetics*, p. 138.
34. Jonathan Culler, *On Deconstruction: Theory and Criticism after Structuralism* (London: Routledge & Kegan Paul, 1983) p. 125.
35. Culler, *Structuralist Poetics*, p. 135.

Notes to Chapter 3: The Illusion of Reference

1. Robert Scholes, 'The Fictional Criticism of the Future', *TriQuarterly*, vol. 34 (Fall 1975).
2. Catherine Belsey, *Critical Practice* (London: Methuen, 1980) p. 46.
3. John B. Carroll (ed.), *Language, Thought and Reality: Selected Writings of Benjamin Lee Whorf* (Cambridge, Mass.: MIT Press, 1956) p. 213.
4. For a marvellously suggestive and wide-ranging exploration of the implications of the idea that 'the universe' is itself an idea, see Paul Valéry's essay 'On Poe's "Eureka"', available in *Leonardo, Poe, Mallarmé*, trans. Malcolm Cowley and James R. Lawler, vol. 8 of *The Collected Works of Paul Valéry* (London: Routledge & Kegan Paul, 1972).
5. See Chapter 7: 'Statements, Facts and the Correspondence Theory of Truth'.
6. See Elizabeth Anscombe, 'The Intentionality of Sensation: a Grammatical Feature', in R. J. Butler (ed.), *Analytical Philosophy*, Second Series (Oxford: Basil Blackwell, 1965).
7. The arguments presented in this section are developed with more technical rigour in Chapter 7: 'Statements, Facts and the Correspondence Theory of Truth'.
8. Geoffrey Leech, *Semantics* (Harmondsworth: Penguin Books, 1974) p. 29.

9. B. Berlin and P. Kay, *Basic Color Terms* (Berkeley, Los Angeles: University of California Press, 1969).

10. Jonathan Culler, *Structuralist Poetics* (London: Routledge & Kegan Paul, 1975) p. 14.

11. Leech, *Semantics*, pp. 31–2.

12. Culler, *Structuralist Poetics*, p. 14.

13. Culler, ibid., p. 14.

14. Ferdinand de Saussure, *Course in General Linguistics*, trans. Wade Baskin (London: Fontana; Glasgow: Collins, 1974) pp. 111–12.

15. See, for example, P. Lieberman, 'On the acoustic basis of the perception of intonation by linguists', *Word*, vol. 21 (1965) pp. 40–54.

16. Jacques Lacan, *Ecrits*, selected and trans. Alan Sheridan (London: Tavistock, 1977) p. 65.

17. Belsey, *Critical Practice*, p. 4.

18. Ibid., p. 46.

19. John Passmore, *Philosophical Reasoning* (London: Duckworth, 1961) ch. 4.

20. Lacan, *Ecrits*, p. 2.

21. Jacqueline Rose, 'The Imaginary', in Colin MacCabe (ed.), *The Talking Cure* (London: Macmillan, 1981) p. 137.

22. Roland Barthes, *The Pleasure of the Text*, trans. Richard Miller (New York: Mill & Wang, 1975) p. 62.

23. Ibid., p. 17.

24. Terry Eagleton, *Literary Theory* (Oxford: Basil Blackwell, 1983) p. 108.

25. Belsey, *Critical Practice*, p. 46.

26. Terence Hawkes, *Structuralism and Semiotics* (London: Methuen, 1977) pp. 16–17.

27. Roland Barthes, *Writing Degree Zero*, trans. Annette Lavers and Colin Smith (London: Jonathan Cape, 1967) p. 68.

28. Ferdinand de Saussure, *Course*, p. 68.

29. Derrida handles the fact that Saussure would be unlikely to accept much of the 'post-Saussurean' theory in a characteristic fashion. He claims that Saussure suppressed or shied away from the consequences of his own discoveries because he was too conservative either to see or to accept their radical implications. See, for example, his essay 'Differance', available in *Speech and Phenomena and Other Essays on Husserl's Theory of Signs*, trans. David B. Allison (Evanston, Ill.: Northwestern University Press, 1973). Derrida's treatment of Saussure – which entitles him to be counted as the greatest and least ashamed of his many misreaders – is discussed in Chapter 6: 'Walking and Differance'.

30. For a lucid account of the arguments and the structuralist and post-structuralist use that has been made of them, Jonathan Culler's *Saussure* (London: Fontana, Modern Masters, 1982) would be hard to better. It is best, however, to consult the 'original' texts as there are few trustworthy commentaries: what Saussure said and what he can be claimed to have implied are often conflated. Of course the 'original' texts are themselves compilations out of lecture notes taken by his students; but there can be little advantage in moving even

further from the 'source' when the *Course* as it stands is so succinct and clear.

31. Belsey, *Critical Practice*, p. 4.
32. Hawkes, *Structuralism and Semiotics*, p. 16.
33. Ibid., pp. 16–17.
34. For an excellent discussion of this distinction see John Lyons's *Semantics* (Cambridge University Press, 1977) vol. I, section 1.2, pp. 5–10.

    Derrida's conflation of the concepts of 'use' and 'mention' is, of course, deliberate. See, for example, the discussion of Austin, expounded in Jonathan Culler, *On Deconstruction* (London: Routledge & Kegan Paul, 1983) pp. 115–20 and especially the footnote on p. 120 where we are told that '*use* is but a special case of *mentioning*'. Culler adds: 'And no matter how wholeheartedly I may wish to "use" certain expressions, I find myself mentioning them: "I love you" is always something of a quotation, as many lovers attest.'
35. Hawkes, *Structuralism and Semiotics*, p. 88.
36. Ibid., p. 84.
37. See Chapter 4.
38. L. Wittgenstein, *Tractatus Logico-Philosophicus*, trans. D. F. Pears and B. F. McGuinness (London: Routledge & Kegan Paul, 1961).
39. See, for example, D. H. Hubel and T. N. Wiesel, 'Ferrier Lecture: Functional Architecture of Macaque Monkey Cortex', *Proceedings of the Royal Society B* vol. 198 (1977) pp. 1–59; or C. G. Philips, S. Zeki and H. B. Barlow, 'Localisation of Function in the Cerebral Cortex: Past, Present and Future', *Brain* vol. 208 (1984) pp. 328–61.
40. This is not offered as an *explanation* of perception!
41. Derridans should note that I am not saying that *langue* and *parole* are, respectively, prior and posterior, or that 'structure' is prior to 'event', but only that the latter cannot be assimilated to the former – as, of course, Saussure was himself at great pains to point out.

    There is an interesting parallel between those who deny the possibility of extra-linguistic reference to reality because they cannot understand how it is done and those who deny that perception gives us access to extra-cerebral reality because they cannot see how the brain could manage it. On this, see Chapter 4.
42. Quoted in Manfred Bierwisch, 'Semantics', in J. Lyons (ed.), *New Horizons in Linguistics* (Harmondsworth: Penguin Books, 1970) p. 171. The concept of the semantic field has limited explanatory power because it is to some extent tautologous as the '*relevant*' elements are inevitably defined in terms of similarity of meaning to the index element.
43. Belsey, *Critical Practice*, p. 46.
44. Roland Barthes, *The Elements of Semiology*, trans. Colin Smith and Annette Lavers (London: Jonathan Cape, 1964) p. 57. If this seems a little unfair, we have to recall how Lévi-Straussian structuralism took many people deep into magic thinking: 'it is the conventions of society which decree what is food and what is not food'. *Only* the conventions of society? Can it be that herein lies the cure for scarcity?

Lévi-Strauss himself of course denied that there was any fundamental difference between magic and rational or scientific thought; the latter was only a rationalisation of the former. (The quotation, incidentally, is from Edmund Leach, *Lévi-Strauss* (London: Fontana, Modern Masters, 1970) p. 32. This is not Leach's own view but it occurs in his largely sympathetic account of its subject.)

45. See Chapter 6: 'Walking and Differance' and Chapter 3, Section 3.
46. The relationship of structuralist thinking – indeed most post-Saussurean theory – to magic thinking is especially clear here.
47. Barthes, *Elements of Semiology*, p. 40.
48. Ibid., pp. 37–8.
49. Ibid., p. 55.
50. Robert Scholes, 'The Fictional Criticism of the Future', *TriQuarterly*, vol. 34 (Fall 1975).
51. Gottlob Frege, 'On Sense and Reference', in *Translations from the Philosophical Writings of Gottlob Frege*, 2nd edn, and trans. P. Geach and M. Black (Oxford and New York: Oxford University Press, 1960).
52. Jacques Derrida, 'The Supplement of Origin', in *Speech and Phenomena* op cit.
53. I owe this way of putting it to Michael Dummett, *Frege: Philosophy of Language* (London: Duckworth, 1973). See especially Chapter 5: 'Sense and Reference'.
54. Cf. Frege (quoted in Dummett, *Frege*, p. 6): 'A word has meaning only in the context of a sentence.'
55. Quoted in Norman Malcolm's *Ludwig Wittgenstein: A Memoir* (Oxford: Basil Blackwell, 1959).
56. Derrida seems to concur with the strange conclusion that Husserl draws from the fact that an expression may be meaningful even though it lacks an existing referent (is 'objectless'). Indeed, he develops it further, asserting that 'what is structurally original about meaning would be the Gegenstandslosigkeit, the absence of any object given to intuition'. And he goes on to claim that

> the absence of intuition . . . is not only tolerated by speech; it is *required* by the general structure of signification when considered in *itself*. It is a radical requisite: the total absence of the subject and object of a statement – the death of the writer and/or the disappearance of the object he was able to describe – does not prevent a text from 'meaning' something. On the contrary, this possibility gives birth to meaning as such, gives it out to be heard and read. (Derrida, *Speech and Phenomena*, pp. 94–5)

(Here, as so often, it is difficult to be sure where Derrida is expounding Husserl's errors and where he is expounding his own. For further discussion on this point see Chapter 6.)

57. The Russellian dream of a language where referring expressions were 'logically proper names' guaranteed to have unique referents – where, in other words, reference to a particular could be automatically secured by combining terms with general meanings alone – remains an impossible dream. Referential terms will always remain logically

opaque because reference is achieved through the cooperation of linguistic (general) meanings and the particular linguistic and extra-linguistic contexts that they have on the occasions of their use.

58. Quoted by Jonathan Culler in *Barthes* (London: Fontana, Modern Masters; Glasgow: Collins, 1983).
59. The rediscovery of the obvious may be a manifestation of the 'Lapsed Structuralism' discussed in Section 4 of this chapter.
60. Hawkes, *Structuralism and Semiotics*, p. 113.
61. Lacan, *Ecrits*, p. 153.
62. Jacques Derrida, *Of Grammatology*, trans. Gayatri Chakravorty Spivak (Baltimore: The Johns Hopkins University Press, 1976) p. 50.
63. John Sturrock, discussing Barthes's *Empire of Signs* in *Structuralism and Since* (Oxford University Press, 1979) p. 77.
64. Eagleton, *Literary Theory*, p. 210.
65. Barthes, *Elements of Semiology*, p. 47.
66. Saussure, *Course*, p. 113.
67. Sturrock, *Structuralism and Since*, p. 6.
68. Roland Barthes, *S/Z*, trans. Richard Miller (New York, Hill & Wang, 1974) p. 40. We might note in passing that Barthes has probably contributed more than any other modern writer – more even than Sartre – to emptying the term 'bourgeois' of meaning.
69. Barthes quoted in Culler, *Structuralist Poetics*, p. 104.
70. The points discussed here are treated more extensively in Chapter 6.
71. Collected in *Speech and Phenomena and Other Essays on Husserl's Theory of Signs*, trans. David B. Allison (Evanston, Ill.: Northwestern University Press, 1973) p. 139.
72. Culler, *On Deconstruction*, p. 188.
73. See Chapter 6, especially Section 6.3.
74. See Chapter 6, especially Sections 6.3 and 6.4.
75. Eagleton, *Literary Theory*, p. 108.
76. Roland Barthes, *Mythologies*, trans. Annette Lavers (London: Jonathan Cape, 1972) p. 113.
77. Barthes, *Elements of Semiology*, p. 11. This is Barthes's conscious inversion of Saussure's suggestion that linguistics would become part of a greater, more broad-based, science of signs.
78. Barthes, *Mythologies*, pp. 111–17.
79. Hawkes, *Structuralism and Semiotics*, p. 113.
80. Emile Benveniste, *Problems in General Linguistics*, trans. Mary Elizabeth Meek, Miami Linguistics series No. 8 (Coral Gable, Flor.: University of Miami Press, 1971).
81. Quoted in Hawkes, *Structuralism and Semiotics*, p. 100.
82. Quoted in ibid., p. 96.

Notes to Chapter 4: Reference Restored

1. The myth gains a good deal of support from the use of that unfortunate ambiguous word 'mimesis'. It is often stated that realism aims at mimesis, where mimesis is understood to mean at

least metonymic *replication* of reality. The 'mimetic fallacy' is, however, a fallacy *about* realism, not the fallacy *of* realism.

2. 'Philosophy and the Form of Fiction', in R. Scholes (ed.), *Fiction and the Figures of Life* (New York: Alfred A. Knopf, 1970) p. 12.

3. Quoted – without protest – by Jonathan Culler in *Structuralist Poetics* (London: Routledge & Kegan Paul, 1975) p. 109.

4. The phenomenon of 'lapsed structuralism' has been discussed in Section 3.4.

5. Saussurean linguistic theory incorporates a modified conceptualism. The signified is a concept. The latter does not, however, pre-exist language as a psychological entity. A word is not a pre-existing sound associated with a pre-existing object; on the contrary, one does not start 'from the terms and construct the system by adding them together'; rather, 'it is from the interdependent whole that one must start and through analysis obtain its elements' (Saussure, *Course*, p. 113). Their co-presence in the linguistic *system*, their mutual pressure, stabilises the concepts and gives them more definite edges. They are consequently 'objective concepts' in the sense to be discussed below (see also Section 3.1).

6. Ludwig Wittgenstein, *Philosophical Investigations*, trans. G. E. M. Anscombe (Oxford: Basil Blackwell, 1953) p. 32.

7. Several philosophers (notably Russell) tried (unsuccessfully) to give reference to certain logical connectives, correlating 'or', for example, with a feeling of hesitation. Such psychologising of function terms would require identifying a mood or other psychological state to correspond to each of the grammatical features of a language – an artificial and implausible exercise.

8. Traditionally, proper names are said to have reference but no sense; but the situation, as John Searle and other have shown, is not as simple as this: see, for example, John Searle, *Speech Acts* (Cambridge University Press, 1969) section 7.2, 'Proper names'.

9. So that talk of equivalent logical multiplicity between a state of affairs and the proposition that describes it (in the style of early Wittgenstein) could seem to make sense.

10. See John Lyons, *Semantics* (Cambridge University Press, 1977) vol. I, ch. 4.

11. Ibid., pp. 96–9, 109–14.

12. Ibid., p. 111.

13. '*A picture* held us captive. And we could not get outside it, for it lay in our language and language seemed to repeat it to us inexorably' (L. Wittgenstein, *Philosophical Investigations*, p. 115).

14. Edmund Gosse, quoted in Damien Grant, *Realism* (London: Methuen, 1970) p. 15.

15. See the epigraph to Chapter 3.

16. Robert Scholes, *The Fabulators* (New York: Oxford University Press, 1967).

17. Raymond Tallis, 'The Realistic Novel versus the Cinema', *Critical Quarterly*, vol. 27, no. 2 (1985) pp. 57–65.

18. The interested reader is referred to John Lyon's lucid, subtle and

comprehensive review of deixis in *Semantics*, vol. II, pp. 636–724. His definition of deixis: 'a function of personal and demonstrative pronouns, of tense and a variety of other grammatical and lexical features which relate utterances to the spatio-temporal coordinates of the act of utterance' would be difficult to better.

19. P. F. Strawson, *Individuals: An Essay in Descriptive Metaphysics* (London: Methuen, 1959). See especially pp. 18, 23, 24.
20. A truthful realistic fiction should be not only consistent (allowing, of course, for diametrically opposed viewpoints of the characters within the fiction) and plausible but also *representative*, so that the novel is a metonym for a larger reality than that which it describes. The metonymic claim of fiction is more problematic and will be dealt with in another work.
21. Where reference ends and description begins is not easy to establish, except in grammatical terms, when 'reference' captures that which falls under the subject and 'description' encompasses the predicates applied to the subject. This over-simple account does not accommodate the fact that reference may be achieved through description, a referring expression being a 'definite description'. A theory of reference, as Russell found, tends to pass into a theory of description.
22. Roland Barthes, *The Death of the Author*, in *Image – Music – Text*, selected and trans. Stephen Heath (London: Fontana, 1977) p. 142.
23. Terence Hawkes, *Structuralism and Semiotics* (London: Methuen, 1977) p. 156. The passage from which this phrase is taken (quoted a little further on in my text) is of great interest to the pathologist of modern literary theory.

Notes to Chapter 5: The Mirror Stage

1. Jacques Lacan, *Ecrits*, selected and trans. Alan Sheridan (London: Tavistock, 1977). The translations are Sheridan's.
2. Catherine Belsey, *Critical Practice* (London: Methuen, 1980).
3. Terry Eagleton, *Literary Theory*, (Oxford: Basil Blackwell, 1983).
4. Colin MacCabe (ed.), *The Talking Cure* (London: Macmillan, 1981).
5. Ellie Ragland-Sullivan, 'The Magnetism between Reader and Text: Prolegomena to a Lacanian Poetics', *Poetics* (December 1984) pp. 381–406.
6. Anika Lemaire, *Jacques Lacan*, trans. David Macey (London: Routledge & Kegan Paul, 1977).
7. Jacqueline Rose, in MacCabe, *The Talking Cure*, p. 137.
8. Ibid., p. 136.
9. Ibid.
10. Lemaire, *Jacques Lacan*, p. 81.
11. Malcolm Bowie 'Jacques Lacan' in J. Sturrock (ed.), *Structuralism and Since* (Oxford University Press, 1979).
12. Lacan, 'Les formations de l'inconscient', *Bulletin de Psychologie* (1956–7); quoted in Lemaire, *Jacques Lacan*, p. 83.

13. Ibid.
14. Lemaire, *Jacques Lacan*, p. 86.
15. MacCabe, *The Talking Cure*, pp. 194–6.
16. This is discussed in more detail in Section 5.3(b).
17. Lacan, quoted in MacCabe, *The Talking Cure*, p. 149.
18. Sturrock, *Structuralism and Since*, p. 133.
19. Lemaire, *Jacques Lacan*, p. 180.
20. Eagleton, *Literary Theory*, p. 108.
21. Lacan is, of course, wrong about chimpanzees. They are also fascinated by their mirror images. A recent book on Lacan (Bice Benvenuto and Roger Kennedy, *The Works of Jacques Lacan* (London: Free Association Books, 1986)) quotes Köhler's account of the behaviour of chimpanzees presented with a mirror. They

> concentrated all their interest on the image; this interest did not decrease . . . but remained so strong that the playing with the reflecting surfaces became one of the most popular and permanent of their 'fashions' (W. Köhler *The Mentality of Apes*, trans. E. Winter (Harmondsworth: Penguin, 1957); quoted in Benvenuto and Kennedy, p. 53)

Curiously, Benvenuto and Kennedy find this passage from Köhler *illustrative* of Lacan's point about the mirror stage, rather than contradicting it. They do add this, however:

> It might be that the chimpanzee does not recognise what he sees as his own image, unlike the child, and this is what distinguishes the human as subject from the animal who merely remains fascinated by reflections.   (p. 53)

But this is, of course, mere conjecture.
22. Including, of course, the Nobel Prize winning work of Hubel and Wiesel and the elegant studies of Colin Blakemore.
23. Lemaire, *Jacques Lacan*, p. 81.
24. MacCabe, *The Talking Cure*, p. 193.
25. For a full philosophical discussion of the mysterious process by which one identifies oneself – in a mirror and elsewhere – see P. F. Strawson, *Individuals* (London: Methuen, 1959). The world picture he deduces from self-identification is precisely the opposite of Lacan's 'the world of words creates the world of things' – as are the rigour and honesty with which he conducts his argument. See especially chs 1.6 and 3.
26. Rose, in MacCabe, *The Talking Cure*, p. 138.
27. Ibid., p. 137.
28. Ibid., p. 160.
29. MacCabe, ibid., p. 193.
30. R. Jacobson, *Shifters, Verbal Categories and the Russian Verb* (Cambridge, Mass.: Harvard University Press, 1957).
31. This possibility is considered by Benvenuto and Kennedy in *The Works of Jacques Lacan*:

Of course, an infant may never actually see a real mirror image
reflecting himself. In this case he may not have an image of himself
which is distinct from the mother's gaze.   (p. 54)

Curiously, this is not regarded as a stumbling block for the theory.
They merely go on to say that:

Lacan's mirror stage refers to a particular moment of recognition
and jubilation, when the infant is moving away from the simple
reflection of the mother's gaze.

Whether this is meant to imply that the mirror stage is in truth a
metaphor, or that one can have a mirror stage without mirrors, is
unclear.

32. Eagleton, *Literary Theory*, p. 108.
33. Sturrock, *Structuralism and Since*, p. 145.
34. Ibid., p. 149.
35. Ibid., p. 146.
36. Ibid., p. 150.
37. Lemaire, *Jacques Lacan*, p. 249.
38. Ibid., pp. 247–248.
39. Charles Larmore, in MacCabe, *The Talking Cure*, p. 120.
40. Lemaire, *Jacques Lacan*, p. 88.
41. Sturrock, *Structuralism and Since*, p. 160.
42. Ibid., p. 144.
43. Ibid., p. 131.
44. Larmore, in MacCabe, *The Talking Cure*, p. 126.
45. Summarised in Lemaire, *Jacques Lacan*, p. 177.
46. Margaret Boden, *Piaget* (London: Fontana, 1977) p. 96.
47. Ibid., p. 97.
48. It is interesting to compare the genetic epistemology of Piaget and
    Lacan. Scientifically and stylistically, they are, of course, worlds
    apart. But their approaches differ in other significant respects. The
    Lacanian infant seems insufficiently cognitive: the world is the
    internal accusative of its desires; it encounters not objects but 'the
    Other'. The Piagetian infant on the other hand seems excessively
    'cognitive', operating with no motivation other than a rather abstract
    curiosity that is divorced from immediate need.
49. Sturrock, *Structuralism and Since*, p. 150.

Notes to Chapter 6: Walking and Differance

1. This is the figure given by Claire Russell and W. M. S. Russell,
   'Language and Animal Signs', in Noel Minnis (ed.), *Linguistics at
   Large* (London: Paladin, 1973).
2. Jacques Derrida, *De la Grammatologie* (Paris: Minuit, 1967). In most

places in this chapter, I have used the translation by Gayatri Chakravorty Spivak (*Of Grammatology*, Baltimore: the Johns Hopkins University Press, 1976).

3. Jacques Derrida, 'Speech and Phenomena: Introduction to the Problem of Signs in Husserl's Phenomenology'; this essay is available in English translation in *Speech and Phenomena and Other Essays On Husserl's Theory of Signs*, trans. David B. Allison (Evanston, Ill: Northwestern University Press, 1973).

4. Barbara Johnson, *The Critical Difference: Essays in the Contemporary Rhetoric of Reading* (Baltimore: the Johns Hopkins University Press, 1980) p. 9.

5. Ferdinand de Saussure, *Course in General Linguistics*, trans. Wade Baskin (London: Fontana; Glasgow: Collins, 1974) pp. 23–4.

6. Cf. Martin Esslin, *Antonin Artaud* (London: Fontana, Modern Masters, 1976) p. 70: 'I must smash language in order to touch life.'

7. Christopher Norris, *Deconstruction: Theory and Practice* (London: Methuen, 1982) p. 31.

8. Exodus 31:18.

9. Norris, *Deconstruction*, p. 28.

10. One would not expect Derrida to be diffident or embarrassed about summarising the world. Others – Sartre, Lévi-Strauss, Foucault – were already at it when he began his career as a *maître à penser*. As has already been remarked, Parisian *maîtres à penser* are born omniscient. How, otherwise, could they have arrived at a position to talk about 'discourse' (all that has been said and written), 'the bourgeoisie' (many millions of people of many different nations), and so on?

11. Norris, *Deconstruction*, p. 29.

12. Jonathan Culler, *On Deconstruction: Theory and Criticism after Structuralism* (London: Routledge & Kegan Paul, 1983) p. 102.

13. Ibid., p. 107.

14. For a discussion of the polemic methods of post-Saussurean writers and their commentators, see Chapter 1, Section 2. The reader may also like to compare Derrida's style with Lacan's, discussed in Chapter 5, Section 3.

15. J. L. Austin, *How to Do Things with Words* (Oxford University Press, 1963).

16. Derrida, quoted in Culler, *On Deconstruction*, p. 127.

17. 'And no matter how wholeheartedly I may wish to "use" certain expressions, I find myself mentioning them: "I love you" is always something of a quotation as many lovers have attested' (Culler, ibid., p. 120). There is no absolute or sharp distinction between use and mention; rather as is the case with 'value' and 'reference', it is a question of degrees, of positions on a spectrum extending from one pole to another. Even farting may be a kind of citation, though usually it is not and in a cholera epidemic its sincerity may be confidently assumed.

18. Derrida, quoted in Culler, *On Deconstruction*, p. 126.

19. Norris, *Deconstruction*, p. 110.

20. The reader will note Derrida's characteristically careless use of Saussure's terms in this and subsequent quotations. By 'signifier' he probably means 'sign'.
21. See *Form and Meaning* – collected in *Margins of Philosophy*, trans. Alan Bass (Brighton: Harvester Press, 1982) p. 162.
22. Culler, *On Deconstruction*, p. 272.
23. Ibid.
24. For an account of the ways in which misreading has been defended, see Culler, ibid., pp. 272–9.
25. Ibid., p. 188.
26. Ibid., p. 123.
27. J. L. Austin, *Sense and Sensibilia* (Oxford University Press, 1962) p. 2.
28. Culler, *On Deconstruction*, p. 104.
29. Not content with rendering the concept of writing totally opaque, Derrida does the same for the that of 'the book'. In *OG*, he speaks of 'the death of the civilisation of the book which manifests itself particularly through a convulsive proliferation of libraries' (p. 8). A strategic redefinition of the term 'book' – as that upon which any durable sign has been inscribed – would permit one to conclude that books antedate writing 'in the graphic sense'. For, as everyone knows, stones, sand and the bark of trees (all forms of arche-paper) were around long before the invention of writing.
30. 'Positions', quoted in Culler, *On Deconstruction*, p. 99.
31. Marges, quoted in Culler, ibid., p. 127.
32. Ibid.
33. Benjamin Libet, 'Unconscious Cerebral Initiative and the Role of Conscious Will in Voluntary Action', *The Behavioural and Brain Sciences*, in press.
34. George Herbert Mead, *Mind, Self and Society* (University of Chicago Press, 1934).
35. The exchange between Searle and Derrida is examined in detail in section 2.2 of Culler, *On Deconstruction*, pp. 110–34.
36. Jean-Paul Sartre, *Being and Nothingness*, trans. Hazel Barnes (London: Methuen, 1957).
37. P. D. Ouspensky, *In Search of the Miraculous* (London: Routledge & Kegan Paul, 1950) pp. 117–18, 121.
38. We desire that which we see others desire as Spinoza argued in his *Ethics*.
39. J. B. Leishmann in his introduction to his translation of *The Duino Elegies* (London: The Hogarth Press, 1967).
40. Rainer Maria Rilke, 'The Second Elegy', *The Duino Elegies*, ibid., p. 228.
41. Sartre, *Being and Nothingness*, p. 615.

Notes to Chapter 7: Statements, Facts and the Correspondence Theory of Truth

1. See 'The Semantic Conception of Truth and the Foundations of Semantics', in *Philosophy and Phenomenological Research*, vol. 4 (1944) pp. 341–76.
2. That is what is so odd about G. E. Moore's 'Proof of an External World' (*Proceedings of the British Academy*, 1939):

   > I can prove now that two human hands exist. How? By holding up the two hands and saying, as I make a certain gesture with the right hand 'Here is one hand', and adding, as I make a certain gesture with the left hand 'and here is the other'

   Clearly this is not a proof at all. If it is anything, it is a report of a series of acts that Moore carried out imagining that it might be a proof; or a recipe for carrying out a proof. In either case, it does not appear on the printed page.
3. On this theme, see Roland Barthes's discussion of isologous systems in *Elements of Semiology*, trans. Annette Lavers and Colin Smith (London: Jonathan Cape, 1967) pp. 43–4.
4. Comparatively clear accounts of post-Saussurean opposition to the Theory are to be found in: Terry Eagleton, *Literary Theory* (Oxford: Basil Blackwell, 1983); Catherine Belsey, *Critical Practice* (London: Methuen, 1980); and Terence Hawkes, *Structuralism and Semiotics* (London: Methuen, 1977).
5. Hawkes, *Structuralism and Semiotics*, p. 16.
6. Eagleton, *Literary Theory*, p. 108.
7. Belsey, *Critical Practice*, p. 136.
8. Jacques Derrida, *Of Grammatology*, trans. Gayatri Chakravorty Spivak (Baltimore: the Johns Hopkins University Press, 1976) p. 158.
9. J. L. Austin and P. F. Strawson, 'Truth', *Proc. Aristotelian Society, Supplementary Volume* (1950) pp. 111ff.
10. A term borrowed from P. F. Strawson, *Individuals* (London: Methuen, 1959) p. 18.
11. See, for example, the illuminating discussion in John Lyons, *Semantics* (Cambridge University Press, 1977) vol. 2, pp. 636–724. These points are also touched on in Chapter 4.
12. Norman Geschwind, 'The Development of the Brain and the Evolution of Language', in *Monograph Series on Language and Linguistics*, Georgetown University, Washington DC, vol. 17 (1964) pp. 155–69.
13. So that a sentence becomes (as in Locke, Frege's later works and Wittgenstein's *Tractatus*) a complex proper name.
14. P. F. Strawson quoted in J. L. Austin, *Unfair to Facts*, p. 160. This paper is most readily available in *Philosophical Papers*, J. O. Urmson and G. J. Warnock (eds).
15. Austin, ibid., p. 169.
16. Austin, ibid., p. 156.

17. P. F. Strawson, Editor's Introduction to *Philosophical Logic* (Oxford University Press, 1967) p. 15.
18. That is why Austin's paper is ultimately unsatisfactory as a defence of the Theory. Although the version of the Theory he supported in his earlier paper tried to avoid using 'facts' and 'corresponds', he makes it obvious that he considers that if there is anything that corresponds to statements it is facts.
19. We could define a statement as D. W. Hamlyn does, as 'a form of language that is true or false'. *The Theory of Knowledge* (London: Macmillan, 1970).
20. For a more detailed treatment of these points, see R. C. Tallis, 'As If There Could Be Such Things As True Stories', *Cambridge Quarterly*, xv (1986) no. 2, pp. 95–107.
21. F. P. Ramsay, *The Foundation of Mathematics* (London: Routledge & Kegan Paul, 1931) pp. 142–3.

Index